KU-626-701

PARENTS AND CHILDREN

The Law of Parental Responsibility

AUSTRALIA AND NEW ZEALAND
The Law Book Company Ltd.,
Sydney: Melbourne: Perth

CANADA AND U.S.A.
The Carswell Company Ltd.
Agincourt, Ontario

INDIA
N.M. Tripathi Private Ltd.
Bombay
and
Eastern Law House Private Ltd.
Calcutta and Delhi
M.P.P. House
Bangalore

ISRAEL
Steimatzky's Agency Ltd.
Jerusalem: Tel-Aviv: Haifa

MALAYSIA: SINGAPORE: BRUNEI
Malayan Law Journal (Pte.) Ltd.
Singapore and Kuala Lumpur

PAKISTAN
Pakistan Law House
Karachi

PARENTS AND CHILDREN

The Law of Parental Responsibility

THIRD EDITION

Brenda M. Hoggett, M.A.

Law Commissioner, Barrister,
Professor of Law, University of Manchester

LIVERPOOL
UNIVERSITY
LIBRARY

LONDON
SWEET & MAXWELL
1987

First Edition   *1977*
Second Edition   *1981*
Third Edition   *1987*

Published in 1987 by
Sweet & Maxwell Ltd. of
11, New Fetter Lane, London
Computerset by Promenade Graphics Ltd., Cheltenham
Printed by Thomson Litho Ltd.,
East Kilbride, Scotland

British Library Cataloguing in Publication Data

Hoggett, Brenda M.
   The law of parents and children.——3rd ed.
   1. Child care——Law and legislation——
England
   I. Title
   344.204'32795   KD3305

   ISBN 0–421–36050–X

All rights reserved. No part of this publication
may be reproduced or transmitted, in any form or
by any means, electronic, mechanical, photocopying,
recording or otherwise, or stored in any retrieval
system of any nature, without the written permission
of the copyright holder and the publisher, application
for which shall be made to the publisher.

©
Brenda M. Hoggett
1987

Preface

This book is about the legal relationship between parents and their children and what can go wrong with it. It was first written for social workers and others who are professionally concerned with the care and upbringing of children, but it has also found friends among lawyers and law students, and I hope that it will continue to do so.

A good deal has changed since the previous edition in 1981, particularly in the fields of criminal justice and child care law. Any law book is out of date in some respects almost before it is published, but I have tried to state the law as it is on May 18, 1987; I have also anticipated the coming into force of the Adoption Act 1976 (which is at last scheduled for January 1, 1988) and the Family Law Reform Act 1987. Some minor amendments to supervision orders in criminal proceedings were contained in Schedule 6 to the Criminal Justice Bill, which fell with the dissolution of Parliament, but are indicated alongside the present law in the text.

A great many more changes may eventually take place as a result of the Government's review of child care law and the Law Commission's review of the private law relating to the upbringing of children. I have included as many of their proposals as I can. Both reviews aim to simplify an area of law which is already large and complicated, every day. New and more challenging issues, some of which could scarcely have been predicted a few years ago, are arising all the time; what, for example, should be the legal status of a child born as a result of a surrogacy arrangement, under which the egg of one woman was fertilized by the sperm of a man to whom she was not married at the time, the resulting embryo being frozen and stored for some years before implantation in another woman with the agreement of the man to whom she was married, but with the intention that the child should then be transferred to the donors who had subsequently married one another? We can be sure that, no matter how much some areas are simplified, child law will go on engaging our attention for a long time to come.

Another thing which has not changed over the years is my gratitude to the many people who, in different ways, have helped me to write this book. They are too numerous to mention or to acknowledge in a text without foonotes. I have also gained a great deal in

understanding from my colleagues at the Law Commission and elsewhere in public service. Above all, however, thanks are due to
Jonathan Whybrow, who in addition to his duties as a Research
Assistant at the Commission, has helped me in the preparation of
this new edition. As before, I am grateful to everyone: but it is no
one's fault but my own if I have got anything wrong.

May 1987   Brenda Hoggett

Contents

TABLE OF CASES

References are given to the most accessible reports of cases referred to in text. Abbreviations used:

TABLE OF STATUTES

TABLE OF STATUTORY INSTRUMENTS

Introduction

Most people would probably still define a "normal" family unit as a husband and wife and the children of their marriage. Even if moral and religious restrictions on sexual relationships between adults are much weaker, this unit is still thought to provide the ideal upbringing for children. All children have physical needs which must at first be supplied by someone else if they are to survive at all, and it is scarcely surprising that society looks first to the natural mother to supply those needs and to the natural father to protect and support both mother and child while she is doing so. Equally it is now recognised that all children have complex emotional and psychological needs, which are probably best supplied if they are brought up throughout their childhood by a couple who are warmly and deeply committed both to one another and to their children. Marriage is thus assumed to be the best means of achieving both these ends. Society has indeed become much more interested in the welfare of children, principally but not entirely for humanitarian reasons. Stable, happy children will grow up into stable, happy adults, ready to reproduce the "normal" family unit, and it is thought that the stability and continuity of society itself depend upon the stability of its smallest unit, the family. These assumptions may all be challenged by those who think them devices for perpetuating social structures and sexual stereotypes of which they disapprove, but few would deny that this is indeed the "normal" family at present promoted by both society and the law.

Moreover, most of the legal problems confronting the child care practitioner arise either because of some crisis in, or because of some departure from, such a "normal" upbringing. Thus any event which necessitates the separation of a child from one or both of his parents, or even some lesser degree of official intervention in the family, is clearly a crisis of great importance both to social work and to the law. Part II of this book will therefore be devoted to the legal controls which operate when four of the most common of these crises happen to a child—when his parents have for some reason to arrange for someone else to look after him, when his parents' own relationship is breaking up, when he himself is getting into trouble with the law, or when his parents are treating him badly. However, the actual crisis is rarely the end of the story, for as a result the child's upbringing is bound to depart from the norm; there are also some departures arising from events which are not in themselves legal crises, as where the parents are unmarried or one or both have died; in either case, people or authorities other than the child's own parents may acquire an interest in his future and conflicts can easily arise. Many, but by no means all, of these can be resolved in accordance with what is best for the child, but the subject is so complex that it seems simplest to divide it according to the relationship between the adult or agency involved and the child, whatever the circumstances in which that relationship may have arisen. Thus Part III will be devoted to the claims and responsibilities of unmarried parents, of guardians over orphaned children, of step-parents, of local authorities over the children in their care, and of relatives and other foster-parents caring for other people's children. The final chapter will be devoted to the most final step of all, adoption.

Obviously, several of these people or agencies may be involved in the future of one unfortunate child who has already suffered the crisis of separation. It may be necessary to consult several chapters in order to see the complete picture in any individual case, but each should present a relatively clear-cut factual situation to which the law's response can be described and evaluated. Before doing so, however, it seems logical to ask what the law has to say about the relationship of parent and child within the family, and in particular to see what the powers and responsibilities of a parent may be.

Part I
The "Normal" Family

1 Parental Rights and Duties

It is much easier to define a "normal" family—a husband and wife and the children of their marriage—than it is to define the powers and responsibilities of the people in it. Although modern statutes often mention parental rights, powers or duties, the law does not provide us with a neat little list of them. There is only a patchwork of legislation and decided cases on particular points. In any event, legal relationships between parents, children and others with an interest in the child can never be quite like those between adults. A legal right assumes that someone else has a corresponding duty to respect it, and that the courts will enforce that duty if the right-holder asks. Nowadays the courts will refuse to force anyone, whether the other parent, an outsider, or even the child himself, to respect the parent's rights unless this is in the child's best interests. Similarly, however, who has the right to enforce parental duties? Their whole object is to provide for the upbringing of someone who is not only too young to bring himself up but also too young to force others to do it for him. Parental responsibilities therefore depend largely upon the ability of other people or the authorities to oblige the parents to adopt acceptable standards of child care. Often the only way in which they can do this is through the partial or even total removal of the parents' rights. Finally, what of the child's rights? Both parents' and outsiders' responsibilities exist to secure things to which the child is thought to have a right but the child will usually have to accept what others think good for him. Children may have greater claims to the care and protection of others than have adults, but only as they grow older will they acquire the freedom of choice which adults enjoy. Increasing attention is now being paid to balancing their right to develop to maturity through learning to make their own decisions against the need to protect them against the consequences of those which turn out to be wrong.

1. *The Law's Development*

Parental rights and duties therefore involve a complicated tripartite relationship between parents, children and outsiders and an equally complicated relationship between private law, which governs legal relations between individuals, and public law, which governs legal relations between individuals and state authorities.

(i) Private Law

Early private law had little interest in how children were brought up. It was designed mainly to serve the dynastic needs of the landed classes and so concentrated on the identification of reliable heirs through the concept of legitimacy and the preservation of their property through guardianship and the control of marriage. The husband obviously enjoyed a great deal of practical power over both his wife and their youthful progeny, and the courts eventually recognised this to the extent of translating it into "rights" which they would enforce against the wife, the child and the outside world in almost every case. They recognised that fathers had concomitant obligations, but they were baffled by the problem of enforcing them: the child was too young to do so, the mother was regarded as one person with her husband and thus unable to challenge him, and the outside agencies which might have been given the right to interfere simply did not exist.

A few limits were recognised. The child would come of age at 21 and gain his freedom. Habeas corpus would not be issued to help a father regain possession of an unwilling child once the child had reached the "age of discretion," apparently 14 for boys and 16 for girls. The law of tort (actionable wrong-doing) always recognised the child as a person, provided that a "next friend" would sue on his behalf, so that a child might sue for excessive punishment. The father never became entitled to his child's property, and although he might have management powers the child could sue him for misusing them. The Court of Chancery, exercising the Crown's powers of guardianship over wards of court, would usually take the father's side, but on occasions it might refuse to do so because he had behaved so badly as to forfeit his rights.

However, in most cases the courts would enforce the father's wishes about the upbringing, education and religion of his legitimate minor children, even if this involved removing an eight-month-old baby from his mother. Moreover, he could rule his family from the grave, by appointing a guardian who, though rather more subject to the courts' control, would take precedence over the mother. The father's rights were inalienable and could never be voluntarily surrendered. Illegitimate children, on the other hand, being born outside the recognised family unit, were irrelevant to the scheme of things and belonged to no-one.

Private law came to recognise the interests of children alongside its recognition of the value of mothering. At first, the courts would only grant a mother's claim, even to access, if the father had forfeited his rights. Then, from 1839 until 1886, her rights to apply to the courts for access and even custody were gradually extended, and in 1886 she was given guardianship rights after the father's death. In 1925, courts were expressly told to ignore the question of whether the father's rights were technically superior to those of the mother (or even vice versa), and their rights to act as and appoint guardians after death were made equal. Meanwhile, the courts were also acquiring powers to intervene in the marriage itself, through divorce, separation and maintenance claims. In these, they were permitted to make custody and other orders concerning the children of the marriage.

At first these developments only applied where there was a parental dispute or a death. Until then, the father remained sole natural guardian of his legitimate children. The mother could only challenge him by splitting up the family or by asking the court to take over the child's guardianship by making him a ward of court. Respectable married women were understandably annoyed that their legal powers over their own children were less than those of the widow, the divorced or separated wife, or the unmarried mother. Thus the Guardianship Act 1973 now provides: "In relation to the custody or upbringing of a minor, and in relation to the administration of any property belonging to or held in trust for a minor or the application of income of any such property, a mother shall have the same rights and authority as the law allows to a father, and the rights and authority of mother and father shall be equal and be exercisable by either without the other" (s.1(1)). If the parents disagree, either may apply to the court for its direction (s.1(3)). This does not apply between unmarried parents, where the mother has sole rights and authority unless and until the father is granted some (s.1(7); Children Act 1975, s.85(7)).

Having acquired all these powers to intervene, the courts required a principle upon which to adjudicate parental disputes. At first, they remained more sympathetic to the father's wishes, not only because of his common law rights but also because Victorian judges believed that he was usually the best judge of what was best for his child. However, they did develop the principle that the child's welfare could *override* his wishes, and in 1886, they were told to put the child's welfare *first*, before the conduct of the parties and the wishes of them both. Then in 1925 the matter was put beyond doubt in what is now section 1 of the Guardianship of Minors Act 1971 and the most important principle in child law today:

"Where in any proceedings before any court . . . (a) the legal custody or upbringing of a minor; or (b) the administration of any property belonging to or held on trust for a minor, or the application of the income thereof, is in question, the court, in deciding that question, shall regard the welfare of the minor as the first and paramount consideration, and shall not take into consideration whether from any other point of view the claim of the father, in respect of such custody, upbringing, administration or application is superior to that of the mother, or the claim of the mother is superior to that of the father."

In other words, the child's welfare is now "the first consideration because it is of first importance and the paramount consideration because it rules on or determines the course to be followed" (Lord MacDermott in *J.* v. *C.* [1970] A.C. 668). Moreover, in *J.* v. *C.* the House of Lords decided that that principle did not only apply to disputes between parents with equal rights. It applies whenever a child's custody or upbringing is in issue in private litigation, whether between the parents, or between parents and child, or between parents and "strangers," such as relatives, friends or foster parents. Such "strangers" have fewer ways than parents have of bringing a case before the courts, but once there the child's welfare is paramount.

(ii) Public Law

The private law's notions of parental rights had little relevance for families without property, where attempts to enforce parental responsibility were more prominent. The state intervened first through the criminal law, which tried to punish concealment, abandonment and neglect. The object was often to prevent the children becoming a burden to the rest of us, as much as to protect the children themselves. This was certainly the case with the poor law procedures for obliging "liable relatives" to maintain their children. Once the poor law was forced to take over, it could interfere quite substantially with the parents' so-called "rights."

The modern statutory powers and responsibilities of local authorities are more concerned with the protection of the children and their "rights." These responsibilities have developed piecemeal from several sources. They include the control of private arrangements made by parents for others to look after their children; the making and monitoring of adoption placements; the provision of day care or full substitute care for some children whose parents cannot provide it themselves; and the compulsory supervision or care of children whom the courts have found to be delinquent, troublesome, or at risk of harm in their own homes. Local education authorities are responsible for securing that children are properly educated and for controlling the employment of school-age children.

Compulsory intervention is possible through several different procedures with different grounds. They cannot usually be invoked simply because the "first and paramount consideration" of the child's welfare might require it. It is in the interests of children, as well as their parents, that some limits are set to the state's powers to impose what it thinks best. But these powers are the main means by which parental duties can be enforced and parental rights curtailed or removed; and if a public authority finds that its statutory powers are inadequate to protect the child's interests properly, it may invoke the "first and paramount consideration" by making the child a ward of court.

2. *Parental Powers and Duties Today*

Children are assigned to their parents at birth and thereafter the parents may direct much of their children's lives. But they are always bounded by the laws of tort and crime; the courts will not necessarily respect their wishes; and there are many ways of depriving them of one, some or all of their powers. In some cases, the law will respect their child's wishes rather than theirs. What follows is an attempt to explain how these features operate on particular aspects of a child's life. By "child" is meant someone below the age of majority, which is now 18 (Family Law Reform Act 1969, s.1); by "parent" is meant both mother and father if they are (or have been) married to one another, but only the mother if they are (or were) not.

(i) Name

Parents may choose the surname by which their child is known. It is customary but not obligatory to choose the husband's name. It used to be said that this was a feature of his natural guardianship (*Re T. (orse H.) (an infant)* [1963] Ch. 238) and it is certainly not one of those rights which are taken away if the mother is granted custody (*Y. v. Y. (child: surname)* [1973] Fam. 147). But it may now be a matter of "upbringing" over which they have equal powers from the beginning. Any disputes between them will therefore be decided according to what is best for the child. These are most likely to arise after the parents have been divorced and the mother has remarried, but the courts' views on what is best have not been entirely consistent (see further in Chapter 8). It is unlikely that either local authorities having a child in compulsory care or third party custodians may change the child's name, but of course an adoptive parent may do so automatically.

(ii) Care and Possession

Parents have the right to care for their children, either personally or by arrangement with others. They may decide how a child's physical needs, for food, clothing, shelter and hygiene, are to be met. They may decide the "place and manner in which his time is spent," (Children Act 1975, s. 86) although there are practical limitations as the child grows older. They also have a duty to do these things: they will be criminally liable if they abandon their child or neglect to supply him with the basic necessities of life until he is 16 (see further in Chapter 5); and they may be held liable in damages to their child if they cause him harm by failing to take the care of him that a reasonable parent would take. Fathers may be sued for injuries caused before the child was born, but mothers may only be sued for injuries caused by careless driving during pregnancy and not, for example, for drug-taking or refusing medical treatment (Congenital Disabilities (Civil Liability) Act 1975). The father does not have a right to the possession of his unborn child which will enable him to prevent the mother having a lawful abortion (*Paton* v. *British Pregnancy Advisory Service Trustees* [1979] Q.B. 276; and see *C.* v. *S.* [1987] 2 W.L.R. 1108).

As well as the crimes of kidnapping, child-stealing, and abducting girls under 16, which protect children as much as their parents, it is an offence for a non-parent to remove or keep a child under 16 from the "lawful control" of the person entitled to it, if done without lawful authority or reasonable excuse (Child Abduction Act 1984, s.2). However, parents no longer have the right to sue outsiders for damages for enticing away or harbouring their children. They may resort to self-help, but if they have to turn to legal procedures, the courts will only support them if it is in the child's interests to do so.

The child himself may also have a voice. The parent's right of physical restraint was traditionally limited until the child reached the "age of discretion." Lord Denning has described the parent's right to custody as a "dwindling right which the court will hesitate to enforce against the wishes of the child, the older he is. It starts with a right of control and ends with little more than advice." (*Hewer* v. *Bryant* [1970] 1 Q.B. 357). The House of Lords took the same view in *Gillick* v. *West Norfolk and Wisbech Area Health Authority* [1986] A.C. 112. Although the courts may have greater powers than parents, they will seldom make custody orders against the wishes of a child of 16, and will pay some attention to the views of younger children.

Most children, therefore, may leave home at 16; some may be allowed to do so below that age if it is in their best interests, but all remain subject to the courts' powers of control until 17 (in care proceedings) or 18 (in wardship and other private law proceedings).

Parents cannot usually delegate the care of their children to other people without official control, although it is the other people rather than the parents who are controlled (see Chapter 2). Parents can never surrender their right and duty to care by mere agreement (Children Act 1975, s.85(2)), but they can agree between themselves about how it shall be exercised during a period of separation (Guardianship Act 1973, s.1(2)). They may be deprived of it, either temporarily or permanently, by a wide variety of procedures in public and private law which will be described in later chapters. But although it may occasionally be possible to prevent a mother taking her baby home from hospital, it is never possible to remove parental rights before a child is born.

(iii) Discipline

Parents may prescribe standards of behaviour for their children and try to secure obedience to them. In some respects, they have a duty to do so, for the law may intervene if a child of 10 or more commits criminal offences (and for which the parents may be ordered to pay the fines, see Chapter 4) or any child under 17 becomes so troublesome that care proceedings are taken. This right and duty is backed up by the parents' right to administer "lawful chastisement," which gives them a defence to both civil and criminal liability for assault or ill-treatment. The punishment must conform to certain standards and it is no defence that the parent comes from a different country or culture in which harsher punishments are acceptable (*R. v. Derriviere* (1969) 53 Cr.App.R. 637). It must be both moderate and reasonable. This means that it must be imposed for a good reason, that is because the parent genuinely believes that the child has broken a fair and reasonable rule; it must be in proportion to the child's "offence"; it must take into account the child's age, understanding, and physique; and it must not be imposed for an ulterior motive, such as the "gratification of passion or of rage" (*R. v. Hopley* (1860) 175 E.R. 1027) or perverted sexuality. In short, it must conform to a model of just punishment: but this should probably be distinguished from the equally lawful physical restraint which is needed to save a very young or handicapped child from danger and to teach him to save himself.

Parents who delegate the care or education of their children to others may also delegate this right, but they should make this clear and they may also impose limitations. State schools have statutory power to discipline their pupils, within the limits laid down by the local education authority and the Education (No. 2) Act 1986, section 47 of which prohibits corporal punishment. Similarly, community homes and voluntary children's homes are governed by their own regulations (see Chapter 9). The risks of abuse are certainly no less in institutions than they are in private homes.

(iv) Medical Treatment

Parents may give their consent to medical or dental treatment of their child, but this is because that treatment would otherwise be an invasion of the rights of the *child*, rather than because it would be an invasion of the parents' rights. This means that a child who is old enough to understand a treatment proposal may give his own consent to it, at least if it is designed for his own benefit and not for other purposes. By statute, the consent of a 16-year-old is as good as if he were 18 (Family Law Reform Act 1969, s.8(1)), and a 16-year-old may be informally admitted for psychiatric treatment without reference to his parents (Mental Health Act 1983, s.131(2)). The 1969 Act does not affect the validity of any other consent (s.8(3)), so that a younger child who is capable of understanding what is proposed may also give an effective consent (*Gillick* v. *West Norfolk and Wisbech Area Health Authority* [1986] A.C. 112).

This must mean that the consent of a capable older child can override his parents' objections to the treatment. It may also mean that the objections of such a child (for example of a 14-year-old girl who does not want an abortion) can override the parents' consent. Parents do usually have the right to decide on behalf of children who are too young to decide for themselves. What if the parents are opposed to the treatment? They will be criminally liable for failing to provide a child under 16 with adequate medical aid; conscientious objection will be no defence, provided that risk to the child was foreseen (see Chapter 5). But this will not help the child. In an emergency or where the parents have abandoned the child, doctors may proceed without either his or his parents' consent (*Gillick*). Similarly, they may carry out an examination, for example in cases of suspected child abuse. After all, in these cases legal action by the child is extremely unlikely to be taken, let alone to succeed, and there is no action which the parents can take at all, at least after the event.

The parents can also be deprived of the right to decide, whether for or against any particular proposal, by making the child a ward of court. Thus in *Re D. (a minor) (wardship: sterilisation)* [1976] Fam.

185, an educational psychologist wished to challenge the decision of
the mother and a paediatrician that an 11-year-old girl should be
sterilised. She suffered from a rare congenital handicap which might
affect her capacities as a mother and was fast approaching puberty.
The judge held that this was a proper use of the wardship procedure,
even though no other criticism could be made of the mother's fitness
or the quality of care she lavished upon the child. The judge also
decided that the operation was *not* in the child's best interests. It
would deprive her of the chance of a normal adult life when it was
still not known how severely her handicap would affect her, while
she would suffer no immediate harm if it were not performed. In *Re
B. (a minor) (Wardship: sterilisation)* [1987] 2 W.L.R. 1213, the House
of Lords allowed a severely handicapped 17-year-old girl to be sterilised, but Lord Templeman thought it so drastic that it could only
lawfully be done with the leave of a High Court judge in wardship.
Hence there may be limits to the parental power to decide on behalf
of incapable children.

Another way of challenging parental decisions might be to bring
care proceedings on the ground of harm to the child's health or
proper development (see Chapter 5). This is cheaper and more convenient than wardship, but not necessarily quicker. It is also needlessly intrusive, because it transfers all parental powers and duties to
the local authority. Yet it does not allow the authority to change the
child's religion, which may be the source of the problem.

If parents delegate care to others, they can also delegate this right,
and if a child is received into local authority care they will usually be
asked to do so. The community homes and boarding-out regulations
(see Chapter 9) certainly assume that authorities may arrange
routine treatment, but at least in voluntary care parents should be
consulted on major steps. They no longer have a statutory duty to
co-operate with the school medical services, but the normal principles apply.

(v) Travel

Parents may decide whether their children can be taken out of the
country, on holiday or permanently. The Crown requires the consent of a parent before issuing a passport to a child under 16. It may
also be necessary to prevent the child's removal, even by a parent
who has a right to his custody. A father may plan to "kidnap" the
children to prevent their mother getting custody; or a mother who
has custody may plan to emigrate and deprive the father of all contact. Divorce court custody orders usually provide that the child
must not be taken out of England and Wales without the permission

of the court or the other parent, and it is possible to apply for such an order before the case comes to be heard. Similar prohibitions may be imposed where custody orders are made in other sorts of case (see Chapter 3). The immediate effect of making an application for a child to become a ward of the High Court is that the child may not leave the court's jurisdiction without its permission. Above all, in addition to the abduction offences mentioned earlier, it is now an offence even for a parent to take a child out of the United Kingdom without the consent of the other parent or the court (unless he believes that the other has or would have consented, or has tried but failed to contact him, or—if there is no custody order—the other has unreasonably refused to consent). This applies to others with custody as it applies to parents (Child Abduction Act 1984, s.1). The police at ports and airports may therefore be alerted to stop these offences occurring.

(vi) Access

If parents have delegated the care of their child to someone else, they will usually have the right to visit or remove him when they wish. Whenever a parent is deprived of his child in family litigation (see Chapter 3), the court will usually grant him reasonable access unless there are strong reasons against it. But the governing criterion is what is best for the child, and the courts are fond of describing access as a right of the child rather than a right of his parents. It is one aspect of the law's growing respect for the right of the child to preserve his links with both sides of his family. The same policy applies to children in local authority care, but the law's help is at present more limited (see Chapter 9).

(vii) Education

This again is a right and duty of both parent and child. Parents may decide how their child will be educated, but if he is of compulsory school age, they also have a duty to cause him to receive efficient full time education suitable to his age, ability and aptitude, either by going to school or in other ways (Education Act 1944, s.36). The local education authority can require the parent to convince them that this is being done; and if unconvinced can make a school attendance order requiring him to register the child at a particular school (s.37), although under the Education Act 1980, the L.E.A. first have to give a notice which may enable the parent to find a preferable school which is prepared to have the child (s.10). If the parent disobeys the order, he will be guilty of a criminal offence unless he can convince the court that the child is being properly educated elsewhere (1944 Act, s.40). Parents also commit an offence if a registered pupil does not attend school regularly, whether this is their own or the pupil's fault (ss.39 and 40), for example where he is excluded for arriving late or breaking the rules. The only excuses allowed are days set aside for religious observance, or if the L.E.A. does not arrange transport for children not in walking distance, or where the child is sick, has leave of absence, or is prevented by some "unavoidable cause." This last must affect the child and not the parents: older girls cannot be kept at home to look after the family when the mother is ill or out at work or has deserted them (*Jenkins* v. *Howells* [1949] 2 K.B. 218).

Instead of or as well as prosecuting the parents, the L.E.A. may bring care proceedings on the basis that the child is not being properly educated (see Chapter 5). As admission to care is rarely the most appropriate solution for truants or others who are having problems at school, it is proposed to replace this with proceedings leading only to supervision of the child or his parents (R.C.C.L., 1985; D.H.S.S., 1987). Where educational problems are a symptom of wider difficulties within the family, however, care proceedings would still be possible.

In return, the L.E.A. must provide sufficient and suitable schools for all the children in its area (1944 Act, s.8). It must also have regard to the general principle that, so far as efficient education and use of public money allow, children are to be educated in accordance with their parents' wishes (s.76). This does not give a parent a right to force the authority to provide or pay for what he wants (*Watt* v. *Kesteven County Council* [1955] 1 Q.B. 408). Instead, under the Education Act 1980, parents have to be given an opportunity of expressing a choice, together with a certain amount of information which may help them to make it. The L.E.A. must respect that choice, unless it prejudices efficient education or use of resources, or the parents choose a selective school for which their child is not qualified. Parents also have a right of appeal against their child's allocation to (or refusal by) a particular school, to an appeal committee which consists of members of the authority and others. The L.E.A. is bound by the committee's decision, but no criteria have been laid down for it to apply (ss.6 to 8).

Where a child is assessed by the L.E.A. as having "special educational needs," he should generally be educated in an ordinary school (Education Act 1981, s.2); but the L.E.A. may decide to make a special "statement" of his needs and of the provision to be made for them (s.7). The parents can appeal against this special provision (s.8), but the appeal committee's decision is not binding on the L.E.A.; however, the parents could then appeal to the Secretary of State; unlike other parents, they can also appeal to him against the school named in a school attendance order (ss.15 and 16), but they cannot challenge the L.E.A.'s decision by making the child a ward of court (*Re D (a minor)*, *The Times*, May 30, 1987).

Thus parents no longer have the right to choose *not* to educate their child. The choices available to them will depend upon what they can afford to pay or what the L.E.A. is prepared to offer. If they are fighting for the best school available at public expense, their case will be decided by the local appeal committee. If they are fighting for the right to educate their child at home or in some other way, their case will be decided by the local magistrates. If their child has been found to be in "special educational need" their case may be decided by the Secretary of State. If they are fighting between themselves, the court will be governed by what is best for the child; but just like everyone else, it will be limited by what they can afford to pay or the L.E.A. is prepared to offer. It is all very well to say that mother and father now have equal rights to decide, for example, whether their daughter shall stay on at school after 16. If the mother has no money, and the L.E.A. is not prepared to help, there is little a court can do to oblige the father to go on maintaining her. On the other hand, it is unlikely these days that a court would force a 16-year-old to stay on at school if she did not want to do so.

(viii) Religion

Parents may decide whether to bring their child up in a particular religious faith, but they have no duty to do so. The authorities can only intervene if the parents' choice of religion does some positive harm to the child, so as to bring them within the grounds for care proceedings or prosecution; sincere religious belief is then no defence. But the authorities are usually under some obligation to respect the religion of a child who comes under their care, and this will normally have been determined by his parents. This is reflected in both the community homes and boarding-out regulations and in the choice of a "relative or friend" to whom a child may be discharged from voluntary care (see Chapter 9). Even if an authority has parental rights, it has no right to cause the child to be brought up in a religion other than the one in which he would otherwise have been brought up. A parent can no longer impose a religious condition upon her agreement to adoption, but an adoption agency must so far as possible respect her wishes when choosing a placement for the child. Where the parents are in dispute between themselves, the welfare principle will apply: this usually means that the court will not disturb a religious faith which the child has already acquired (see Chapter 3). Thus the law respects the child's right to

practise his own religion rather than the parents' right to pass their
own on to him.

(ix) Finance and Property

The obligations of day-to-day care will obviously involve a parent,
or anyone else, in expense, which may be compensated to a greater
or lesser extent by state benefits (such as child benefit, family
income supplement or guardian's allowance). With one exception,
however, only natural parents can be *ordered* to make financial provision for their children, whether to the other parent, or to compensate the state or a local authority for its expenditure on the child, or
to the child himself. A child who has reached 18 may himself apply
for support during his education or for some other special reason,
but only if his parents divorce (*Downing* v. *Downing* (*Downing intervening*) [1976] Fam. 288) or separate; a child of 16 may ask for a previous order to be revived (see Family Law Reform Act 1987, s.14;
Guardianship of Minors Act 1971, new ss.11D and 12C(5)). The
exception is a spouse who has treated a child as a member of the
marital family: he may be ordered to provide for that child if the
marriage breaks up or someone else is appointed custodian or after
his death.

Parents have no claim to property or money which belongs to
their child, but they do have power to administer both his assets and
his income, and the duty to do so honestly and carefully. This *is*
among the powers acquired by local authorities over children in
compulsory care (except, at present, for those committed in family
proceedings), but it is not included in an order for "legal custody"
(Children Act 1975, s.86). If the parents are in dispute between
themselves, the court will be guided by the welfare principle. It is
most unlikely that the courts would assist a parent who wanted to
interfere with an older child's disposition of his own earnings (*Hewer*
v. *Bryant* [1970] 1 Q.B. 357), although they might support a reasonable charge for accommodation.

It is sometimes suggested that "parental rights" over a child's
property include their right to succeed to his estate if he dies without
leaving a will or a spouse or children with a prior claim. But it cannot be so. Parental rights and duties refer to the various matters
which are connected with the control of the child and his affairs
before he reaches 18 (see Children Act 1975, ss.85(1) and 107(1)).
This is quite different from the various rights which may arise
because two people are *related* to one another in a particular way. For
example, where parents are not married to one another only the
mother has the "parental rights and duties" automatically, but the

father still has the right of intestate succession; again, adoption law
provides for the transfer of "parental rights and duties," but also
finds it necessary to provide for the effect of adoption upon the
child's relationships for other purposes, including succession.

(x) Appointment of Guardians

Parents have the right to appoint a guardian to step into their
shoes in the event of their own death (see Chapter 7). This is a right
which they do not lose as a result of a custody order, or even, it
seems, the transfer of parental rights to a local authority.

(xi) Marriage

Marriages by persons under 16 are void. If the child is 16 but
under 18, and not a widow or widower, marriage law requires that
his parents give their consent. But as the law says little about how
the parties' age or parental consent should be proved, allows some
marriages at very short notice, and sometimes overlooks the use of
false names, it is by no means impossible to get married without consent; the marriage is still quite valid, although there may be criminal
penalties. Nor is the law at all clear about whose consent is required
(Marriage Act 1949, s.3 and Sched. 2). If the parents are (or were)
married to one another, the consent of both is required; where either
or both is dead, the consent of any guardian appointed by the
deceased is required as well as that of any surviving parent; where
the parents are divorced, or separated by court order or agreement,
or one has deserted the other, only the parent to whom custody has
been granted by the order or agreement, or who has been deserted,
must consent. If both parents have been deprived of custody by a
court order, only the person to whom custody has been granted must
consent. If a local authority has parental rights, it is not clear
whether only the authority, or only the parents, or perhaps all three,
must consent. There are numerous other gaps in the list, for example
where there is a custody order but no separation order between the
parents. The obvious intention was that whoever has parental rights
over the child's person should have this right as well. In practice, the
child's marriage will bring whatever parental control remains over
the age of 16 to an end.

The registrar's department may dispense with the consent of a
parent who is absent, inaccessible or incapable, and even if the
required consents are not forthcoming, the couple can apply to the
High Court, county court or magistrates' court for permission to
marry. As almost all applications are made in the magistrates'
courts, it is not known on what principles they operate. Thus the

parents' rights are by no means as strong as might be expected. Their only other course is to make the child a ward of court, which immediately prohibits the child from marrying without the court's permission. It is contempt of court to disobey; but the court might hesitate to make matters worse by sending one of them to prison.

(xii) Adoption

Parents have the right to decide whether their child may be adopted (see Chapter 11). This right is not lost unless and until the child is adopted or freed for adoption. Their agreement may sometimes be dispensed with, but the child's welfare is not the "first and paramount consideration" in this, the most final step of all.

3. *Do Parents have Rights?*

In view of all this, is there any such thing as parental "rights"? As against the child, the parents have the powers which are necessary to carry out their obligations of bringing the child up, but even these give way as the child becomes old enough to make his own decisions. As against one another, they have equal status and so any dispute must be decided in accordance with the child's best interests. As against outsiders, they have a prior claim and important procedural rights if their status is challenged; but although some procedures have specific grounds based upon harm to the child or the parents' shortcomings, others are governed simply by what is best for the child. In substance, therefore it is difficult to say that parents have "rights," although they undoubtedly have responsibilities and these give rise to a prior claim and, in everyday life, a considerable amount of power and authority.

Part II
Childhood Crises

2 Substitute Care

A parent may want or need someone else to look after his child for a great many different reasons and there are many different ways in which he may seek to arrange it. The purpose of this chapter is to examine the legal controls over the making of such arrangements: occasionally, parental delegation of care may lead to a challenge to the parent-child relationship itself, but this will be discussed in later chapters. Here we shall look first at those arrangements over which there are no controls; then at the provision of day care, by child-minders, private nurseries, and local authorities; and finally at full-time substitute care provided by private foster parents, voluntary organisations and local authorities.

There are always potential dangers in the separation of a child from his parents, whether this is voluntary or involuntary, although these will depend very largely on the reason for the separation and the quality of the substitute care provided. If the authorities attempt to impose too rigorous standards upon child-minders and foster parents, it will reduce the supply. If this reduces the supply while demand remains high, it will increase the risk that parents will turn to even less satisfactory illegal arrangements, which are extremely difficult to police.

This is one reason why local authorities have such extensive responsibilities to provide child care services themselves. These are extremely expensive and their consumers can rarely be expected to pay a realistic price. Hence they must be limited to priority or "deserving" groups. Local authorities also have a responsibility to reduce the need for families to seek substitute care at all. They must "make available such advice, guidance and assistance as may promote the welfare of children by diminishing the need to receive children into or keep them in care or to bring them before a juvenile court" (Child Care Act 1980, s.1(1)). This may be done through voluntary organisations or individuals (s.1(2)), and may include help in kind, or in exceptional circumstances, in cash. As unsatisfactory home conditions and homelessness have been quite common reasons for children to come into care, this allows authorities to provide grants or loans for furniture, fuel supply, hire-purchase, rent or mortgage arrears, or to guarantee a mortgage so that, for example, a mother may keep the home after her marriage has broken up. This raises difficult problems of demarcation between the responsibilities of social services and supplementary benefits and of the proper use of administrative discretion. The object is to provide an additional and exceptional resource in the pursuit of social work strategy rather than for the more general relief of poverty.

Historically, the law relating to child care services has developed quite separately from the law relating to the health and welfare services for children who are handicapped or disabled. All are now provided by local authority social services departments and a major recommendation of the Review of Child Care Law (R.C.C.L., 1985) was that the two systems should be brought together. It is now proposed to give local authorities a broad "umbrella" power to provide all sorts of services—at home, at day centres, with child-minders, or long or short term residential facilities—to promote the care and upbringing of children and to help prevent the breakdown of family relationships which might eventually lead to compulsory care (D.H.S.S., 1987).

1. *Care at Home, by Relatives or by Guardians*

Parents often provide substitute care for their children, whether because they are working, or ill, or having another baby or simply going out. Some child care experts have given the impression that it may be damaging for any young child to be deprived of the almost continuous care of his mother, at least until the age of about three (see discussion in *Kellmer Pringle*, 1974). Others have pointed to the lack of evidence that this is so (*Rutter*, 1971, 1984; *Morgan*, 1975), provided that the substitute care is good and reasonably stable; and children may be almost as attached to places as to people.

At all events, many parents prefer to provide care in their own homes if at all possible. It is certainly the conventional middle class solution. Whether for that reason, or because the risks to the child are indeed much less, or because we recognise that there are limits to official interference in family life, this is the one form of care over which there are no direct legal controls whatever. Whether it is for a day, a night, a week or many months, and whether it is provided by a relative, a friend, an au-pair girl or a trained nanny, there is no requirement for notification, registration or supervision. Few would suggest that there should be. The only control operates after the event, either through prosecution for neglect, abandonment or exposure to the risk of unnecessary suffering or injury to health, or through procedures to remove the child because of ill-treatment or neglect (see Chapter 5). Neither lays down precise standards about when, at what age and for how long, children may be left alone, or about the age and qualifications of the people with whom they should be left.

Although legal controls normally begin to operate once a child is cared for outside his own home, there are two exceptions. If a child is looked after in the home of an adult relative, neither the controls on private fostering (Foster Children Act 1980, s.2(2)(*a*)) nor those on private child-minding (Nurseries and Child-Minders Regulation Act 1948, s.4(2)) apply. "Relative" here means a grandparent, brother, sister, uncle or aunt, including those related by marriage or adoption, and those of full or half blood, and, if the parents are or were not married to one another, his father and any person who would be a relative if they had been (1980 Act, s.22; 1948 Act, s.13(2)). This exemption does not apply if the child is in the care of a local authority or voluntary organisation and has been boarded-out with the relative. If the child has become eligible for public care and the family wish to claim the benefit of a boarding-out allowance, official scrutiny and control are thought justified.

The other exception is where the child is cared for in the home of a guardian who has been legally appointed to take over the rights and responsibilities of a parent who has died (see Chapter 7; 1980 Act, s.2(2)(*a*); 1948 Act, s.4(2)). A legal guardian is exempt even if he is unrelated to the child. Thus parents have an almost unfettered right to choose someone to take over completely after their death, yet if they arrange for a non-relative to assume temporary care during their lives, statutory controls will often operate. Traditionally the rich have appointed guardians and the poor have turned to private fostering and child-minding. But can the exemption of unrelated guardians any longer be justified (*Law Commission*, 1985)?

2. *Day Care*

To many, day care outside the home will seem the next best alternative. If the care is properly suited to the child's needs and he can retain and build a good relationship with his parents, there is little risk of harm. Indeed, it may be a valuable way of relieving stress in the home, or redressing material or social disadvantage. However, because demand always seems to exceed supply and usually relates to pre-school children, and also because the parents can rarely afford high fees, there is a considerable risk that the people or places which agree to take children in will neither appreciate their needs nor be able to cater for them properly. The law therefore attempts to impose minimum standards upon private facilities through registration and inspection. The details are currently under review (D.H.S.S., 1985 and 1987), but the machinery will remain much the same.

(i) Child-minders

A good child-minder may provide the warmth, continuity and domestic environment most suited to a very young child. She also provides much the cheapest service, not only because there are no capital costs, but also because of her low status in the child care hierarchy. But the private, unsubsidised minder can only charge what the market will bear, and her inadequacies are particularly difficult to detect and prevent (*Jackson and Jackson*, 1979).

Local authorities must keep registers of people in their area who *for reward* (in cash or in kind) receive children *under five* into their homes to be looked after for the day (or for part or parts of the day if it amounts to more than two hours), or for any longer period of not more than six days (Nurseries and Child-Minders Regulation Act 1948, s.1(1)(*b*)). The register may be very useful in publicising minders and offering some choice to parents, but its main purpose is to achieve minimum standards.

Applicants for registration must state whether they, or anyone employed in looking after the children, or any person of 16 or more living in the home, suffer from any disqualification equivalent to those against private fostering (Health Services and Public Health Act 1968, s.60(7); for the disqualifications, see below). Registration *must* be granted and a certificate issued (1948 Act, ss.1(2) and (3)), unless the applicant, or anyone looking after the children, is unfit to do so; or the premises are unsuitable, because of their condition or equipment, or for any reason connected with their situation, construction or size, or because of the other people there (s.1(4)). The authority may impose conditions limiting the number of children the minder may take, bearing in mind how many other children may be in the home at various times of the day (s.2(2)); covering the number and qualifications of staff, the safety and maintenance of the premises and equipment, the arrangements for feeding and the children's diet, and the keeping of records (1968 Act, s.60(9)); finally, it may require precautions to be taken against infectious illnesses (1948 Act, s.2(3)). The D.H.S.S. suggests guidelines on space and facilities, and a maximum of three children (including any of her own below school age) for a minder who does not employ help (*Ministry of Health*, 1968). Conditions may be revoked or varied at any time and it is an offence not to comply with them (s.4(2)).

The local authority is not obliged to offer supervision and guidance, but a social worker may enter a registered minder's home at any reasonable time and inspect it, the children and her records (s.7(1)). It is an offence to obstruct him (s.7(4)). If he suspects breach of the conditions, he may get an entry warrant from a magistrate (s.7(2)). The authority may cancel registration if the conditions are not complied with or if circumstances exist which would justify a refusal to register in the first place (s.5). There is a right of appeal to a magistrates' court against the refusal or cancellation of registration and against any conditions imposed (s.6).

It is an offence to receive a child in the circumstances in which registration applies (s.1(1)(*b*)), unless the minder is either registered, or a relative, or her home is already open to entry and inspection because she is an official or a private foster parent (ss.4(2) and 9(2)). It is planned to remove the exemption for foster parents and also to take power to include nannies or au pairs who are paid to look after children other than their employer's (D.H.S.S., 1987). Although registration is of the person and not of the place, if the minder moves house she is not regarded as registered to receive children in her new home until she notifies the local authority (s.4(3)). If illegal minding is suspected, an entry warrant may again be obtained (s.7(2)). It is not an offence in itself for the parent to place a child with an unregistered minder, but he could be guilty of aiding and abetting the minder's offence, or even, in an extreme case, of neglect.

Nevertheless, illegal minding is known to be common. In 1976, some 900,000 mothers of pre-school children were at work, some 200,000 for more than 30 hours a week; but there were only about 61,200 nursery places available, and 34,000 minders registered to care for a maximum of 83,000 children. Even allowing for the tiny proportion of mothers who can afford help in the home, and the much greater number who rely on relatives, there is a large gap which must be being met by illegal minding (*Central Policy Review Staff*, 1978); and these figures take no account of parents who need to arrange day care for other reasons than their work. Registration is largely unenforceable, as the "victims" are too young to complain and their hard-pressed parents do not want to, and social workers cannot make regular house-to-house checks. Many social workers would prefer to see more incentives to registration, in the shape of training, advice, equipment and even cash subsidies (*Terry*, 1979), and this is the direction in which many local authorities are moving.

(ii) Private Nurseries and Playgroups

Nurseries are usually regarded as more satisfactory than child-minders. It is not always preferable to have very young children cared for with many others in an institutional setting but places are much easier to control than are people operating in private homes. Local authorities must also keep registers of premises, other than those used wholly or mainly as private dwellings, where children (at present up to the age of 16 and whether or not for reward) are received for the same periods as under the child-minding provisions (1948 Act, s.1(1)(a)). Application for registration is made by the person planning to receive the children, but the offence of illegal receiving is committed by the occupier of the premises (s.4(1)). The other provisions relating to refusal of registration (s.1(3)), certificates (s.3), cancellation of registration (s.5), conditions (s.2(1), (3), and (4)), entry and inspection (s.7(1) and (2)), and appeals (s.6) are virtually identical. Premises which are provided or assisted by local social services or education authorities, or are controlled in other ways, are exempt (s.8, and Foster Children Act 1980, s.2).

It is now planned to introduce a single register of responsible persons, to replace the separate registers of minders and nurseries, and to limit registration to facilities for the under-fives. Some of the present exemptions may be removed and group schemes covered if they last for up to 27 days. The object is to control the general standards of day care and short term holiday facilities for young children, while providing more individual supervision for children who are fostered for longer periods (D.H.S.S., 1987).

(iii) Local Authority Responsibilities

One solution to the problem of illegal and sub-standard services is to provide far more local authority services. Social services authorities have power to make arrangements for the care of children under five who are not at school and to make reasonable charges according to the parents' means (National Health Service Act 1977, Sched. 8, para. 1). This allows them to provide day nurseries, employ their own day foster parents or child-minders, or provide support for self-employed minders. They also have extensive powers to provide facilities for mentally or physically handicapped children and adults (1977 Act, Sched. 8, para. 2; National Assistance Act 1948, ss.21 and 29; Chronically Sick and Disabled Persons Act 1970, s.2; see also Disabled Persons (Services, Consultation and Representation) Act 1986). Local education authorities may provide nursery schools or places, but these are for much shorter periods and without charge. Lack of co-ordination and the emphasis on costly institutional places for the few have both been criticised (*Central Policy Review Staff*, 1978). But even if scarcity of resources prompts a change to more cost-effective services, public facilities will still be confined to clear priority groups—the lone parent or the potentially damaging home. Ordinary married mothers who go out to work are not usually among them.

3. *Full Time Care*

There are the same sort of options for full time care as there are for day care, and their control presents the authorities with the same sort of problems; but these are even greater, as the risks to the child are also greater.

(i) **Private Fostering**

Some parents' reasons for requiring substitute care will not bring them within the priority groups for whom the local authority service is available, a prime example being Commonwealth couples who have come here to study. There are others, and middle class unmarried mothers may be an example, who for good or bad reasons would prefer to make their own arrangements. Here again, demand exceeds supply and appears to be largely confined to the under-fives. The risks are obvious and severe. Indeed, the horrors of the Victorian baby-farming cases led quite early to the imposition of controls, but these now compare unfavourably with the protection available to children in public care. They are based, not on general registration, but on letting the local authority know of the individual placement, so that it may supervise and remove the child if necessary, or even prohibit it in advance. The law is contained in the Foster Children Act 1980, but a few changes are now planned (D.H.S.S., 1987).

(a) *Definition of "foster child"*

The Act protects children under 16 (and those placed before that age whose fostering continues after it, s.18) whose care and maintenance are undertaken by someone who is not a relative, guardian or custodian (s.1). There is no need for any "reward," so that children whose parents never arranged to pay, or, as seems quite common, fail to pay the sums agreed, are included. The Act excludes all children who are fostered for no more than six days (s.2(3)(b)) and those who are fostered for not more than 27 days by a person who is not a regular foster parent (s.2(3)(a)); a regular foster parent is one who during the past year has had one or more children to whom she was neither related nor a guardian for a total of three months or for three separate periods each of more than six days. This is all very confusing and it is now planned to limit these controls to all fostering which lasts for more than 27 days (D.H.S.S., 1987).

The Act also excludes children who are being looked after in a place where a parent, adult relative or guardian is living (s.2(2)(*a*)) and children who are thought adequately protected by other means. These are: children in the care of local authorities and voluntary organisations (s.2(1)); children in voluntary children's homes (s.2(2)(*b*)), in hospitals, nursing homes (s.2(2)(*d*)), or homes for the mentally disordered (s.2(5)), or in any home or institution provided by a public or local authority (s.2(2)(*e*)); children who are in the care of any person in compliance with a supervision order under the Children and Young Persons Act 1969 (s.2(4)), or who are subject to compulsory powers under the Mental Health Act 1983 (s.2(5)); and children who have been placed for adoption by an adoption agency or who are "protected" under the adoption legislation (s.2(6)). Children in boarding schools where they are receiving full time education are usually excluded (s.2(2)(*c*)); but if they stay there for more than two weeks during the school holidays, the local authority must be notified and can exercise its usual powers apart from imposing conditions or prohibiting the placement (s.17). Children in private children's homes, however, are at present covered by this legislation.

(b) *Advertising*

It is an offence to advertise that a person will undertake or arrange private fostering, unless the advertisement discloses that person's name and address (ss.15 and 16(1)(*g*)). There is also power to make regulations as to who may advertise such services, or prohibiting parents from advertising for foster parents for their children, but no such regulations have been made.

(c) *Notification*

At present, the duty of notifying the local authority lies with the foster parent. She must give notice between four and two weeks before the placement, unless the child was received in an emergency or became a "foster child" while already in her care, in which case she must notify within 48 hours after the event (s.5(2)). The Children and Young Persons Act 1969 exempted foster parents who had already notified one child and had not ceased to foster since then, on the dubious ground that regular supervision would make notification of each new arrival unnecessary. Under the 1980 Act, this exemption will eventually be removed. The foster parent must also notify a change of address, within the same time limits as a new arrival (s.5(4)), or the death of any foster child, within 48 hours of the event (s.6(1)). Under the 1969 Act, foster parents are only required to notify giving up fostering in general. Under the 1980 Act, it will eventually be necessary to notify each departure within 48 hours, unless the child is expected to return within 27 days (s.6(2) and (3)), in which case notice will be necessary if the plan changes. The Act will also break new ground by requiring the *parent* to notify private fostering arrangements (s.4), but this has not yet been done. Failure to notify is an offence (s.16(1)(*a*)), but there is every reason to believe that many placements never come to the notice of the authorities at all. As with child-minding, there is no positive incentive to comply with requirement which could have unwelcome results for both the parents and the foster parent. But a dual obligation might make it a little more likely.

(d) *Regulation of placements*

The authority may prohibit a foster parent from taking a particular child, or having any child in her particular home, or having any child anywhere in the authority's area, if it thinks that the premises or the foster parent are not suitable, or that it would be detrimental to the particular child to be kept by that person in those premises (s.10).

Some people are disqualified from taking foster children at all unless the authority gives specific consent. These are: people who have had children removed from their care under this legislation, the Children and Young Persons Acts, or the adoption legislation; people who have been refused or had cancelled registration for themselves or their premises under the Nurseries and Child-Minders Regulation Act 1948; people who have been deprived of parental rights by a local authority resolution; and people who have been convicted of any of the offences listed in Schedule 1 of the Children and Young Persons Act 1933, even if they were discharged or placed on probation (s.7(1)). No one else can take a foster child if there is such a person living or employed on the premises (s.7(2)). But the list does not include people who have applied unsuccessfully to become local authority foster parents.

The authority can also impose conditions upon foster parents, as to the number, age and sex of any foster children, the accommodation and equipment provided, medical arrangements, the number, qualifications and experience of anyone employed in looking after the children, record-keeping, fire precautions, and the giving of particulars about the person in charge or about the children themselves (s.9(1)).

A "person aggrieved" (who may be a foster parent or employee, or possibly even a parent or the child himself) can appeal to a juvenile court against a prohibition or condition (s.11); but it is an offence to contravene them or to take a child when disqualified (s.16(1)(*d*) and (*c*)). All this is a far cry from the careful selection procedures for local authority foster parents. Parents have the freedom to place their children with almost anyone they like, but the reality of supply and demand gives them very little choice, and many placements are made with people whom the local authority would consider unsuitable (*Holman*, 1973). Nor is there any social worker to take care over the actual transfer of the child; some are simply "dumped" without prior warning after a casual arrangement between the adults.

(e) *Supervision*

The local authority has a duty to satisfy itself as to the well-being of every foster child in its area, whether or not it has been specifically notified of his existence. The duty to supervise is however extremely vague, for the authority is only required to arrange visits "from time to time" and to give advice as to the "care and maintenance" of the children (s.3(1) and (3)). This is backed up by the power of the visiting social worker to enter and inspect any premises in the area where foster children are to be or are being kept (s.8); and to seek a magistrate's warrant to enter the premises by force if need be, if there is reasonable cause to believe that a foster child is being kept there and entry has been or seems likely to be refused or the occupier is absent (s.13(1)). Any refusal to allow visiting of a foster child or inspection of the premises is automatically reasonable ground for suspecting that the child may be neglected or ill-treated, or the victim of offences, so that a warrant for a policeman to enter and remove the child may be obtained (see Chapter 5).

Refusal to allow visiting may be adequately covered, but a more serious problem is the vague and limited nature of the visiting required. Although most of the children are under five, and the foster parents have not been carefully chosen, visits are in practice much less frequent than they are to children boarded-out by the authority itself (*Holman*, 1973). The 1980 Act will eventually permit regulations to lay down when or how often children should be visited (s.5(2)), but this has not yet been done. There is no power to insist on regular medical examination. More important, the purpose of the visit is to check up on the "well-being" of the children and to offer advice about their "care and maintenance," yet nowadays inadequate physical care does not seem to be a major problem. The real difficulty is that these foster parents are having to cope with all the problems of the fostering relationship, but without professional selection, preparation or support. That relationship is in practice less secure than that of a local authority foster parent and child, for although there may be less risk of a social worker deciding to change the placement, there is more risk that the parent will remove the child suddenly and without warning. Yet the foster parents will receive little, if any, advice about this aspect of their role as temporary substitutes for the child's own family. Many will wish to behave exactly as if the child were their own. Thus Holman (1973), identified "role uncertainty" as a major and potentially harmful characteristic of private fostering. These children may therefore receive less protection than those in public care, although they are in general a more vulnerable group.

(f) *Removal*

The local authority does have power to bring about the removal of the child, not only by the usual procedures (see Chapter 5), but also by applying to a full juvenile court for a place of safety order under section 12 of the 1980 Act. The court must be satisfied that a foster child is or is about to be kept by a person who is unfit to have him, or is disqualified or prohibited from having him, or in any premises or environment likely to be detrimental to him. If there is imminent danger to the child's health, the visiting social worker may make an emergency application to a single magistrate. The court or magistrate may authorise the removal of the child (and, if the foster parent has defied a specific prohibition, all her foster children), for a specified period of up to 28 days. If he needs to be detained longer, the authority must bring him before a juvenile court, which may then either release him or make an interim order under the Children and Young Persons Act 1969 (Children and Young Persons Act 1963, s.23). The usual hope, however, is to be able to restore him to his own family, and so the authority must, if practicable, inform his parent, guardian or someone acting as such. Alternatively, the child may be received into local authority care, even though the normal grounds for doing so do not exist (1980 Act, s.12(5)).

Thus it is more difficult to remove children from an unsatisfactory private foster home than it is to change an official placement (see Chapter 9). If local authority places are in short supply, a social worker may hesitate to suggest removal of a child who will then have to go into care, particularly as it is likely that he would not have been eligible in the first place.

(g) *Parental rights*

The parents themselves do not surrender any of their parental rights and duties by fostering the child (Children Act 1975, s.85(2)), whatever they may have agreed with the foster parents. They may therefore come and take him back at any time. The ways in which a particularly determined and resourceful foster parent might try to prevent this are discussed in Chapter 10.

(ii) Voluntary Organisations and other Children's Homes

Most voluntary organisations caring for children were set up to provide a service similar to that now provided by local authorities. Their legal position is remarkably similar. There is obviously no statutory duty to take certain sorts of children, but the organisation will have its own criteria based on the terms of its foundation. A child is legally in the care of a voluntary organisation if the organisation has "actual custody" of him, or, having had actual custody, has transferred it to someone who does not have legal custody (Children Act 1975, s.88). The organisation will choose the most appropriate form of care from amongst those available to it. Most will live in the organisation's own homes, which may be either voluntary homes, or assisted or controlled community homes; some will be boarded-out with foster parents, under the same rules as those for local authority fostering (see Chapter 9).

Equally, the organisation acquires no rights in the child simply because the parents have placed him in its care. It is under the same duty as a local authority to regard the child's long term welfare as the first consideration and to consider the child's wishes (Child Care Act 1980, s.64A); it has the same power as a local authority to insist upon a "breathing space" of 28 days before returning a child who has been in its care for six months (s.63); it is also possible for a local authority to pass a resolution transferring to a voluntary organisation the parental rights and duties over a child in the organisation's care, on the same grounds, and with much the same procedure and effects, as for children in local authority care (ss.64 to 67). It is now planned to abolish the resolution procedure for both groups (D.H.S.S., 1987).

Voluntary homes are registered and controlled by D.H.S.S. (1980 Act, ss.56 to 62 and 70), although local authorities also have a duty to visit the children there (s.68) and provide after-care for those who leave after school-leaving age (s.69). There is provision for private children's homes to be registered by local authorities under the Children's Homes Act 1982; this is not yet in force, although the individual children may be covered by the private fostering legislation. It is now planned to have a comprehensive registration scheme for all homes (D.H.S.S., 1987).

(iii) Local Authority Care

By 1948, local authorities had two types of responsibility to care for children. One was to act as a "fit person" to look after children whom the courts had removed from home because they were delinquent, troublesome or being neglected or ill-treated. The other was the responsibility of the former poor law authorities to care for orphaned, abandoned and destitute children. When it was recommended that they should set up specialist children's departments in order to discharge these responsibilities properly (spectacular failures in public care are not a new phenomenon) (*Curtis*, 1946), the opportunity was taken to expand the second area and to oblige them to provide a service for a great many children whose parents were, for any reason, either temporarily or permanently unable to care for them themselves.

The service established in 1948 is legally distinct from the same authorities' powers to provide accommodation and other services for mentally and physically handicapped or disordered children (under the National Health Service Act 1977, Sched. 8, para. 2 or the National Assistance Act 1948, ss.21 and 29). These children are not usually received into care under the Child Care Act 1980 and so do not have the benefit of the protection it provides (all of which is discussed in Chapter 9).

There would be two main benefits in bringing them all under one umbrella. The children would all receive the same attention, through the regulations about visiting them, reviewing their care and planning for their future. Equally, their families would all be expected to be involved in and consulted about the care provided for their children. The service was always intended to be voluntary, but was not sharply enough distinguished from the authorities' compulsory powers, perhaps because the source of the need was seen to be the parents' problems rather than the child's. It could be a major advance to see them all as families who, for whatever reason, need some help with looking after their own children (R.C.C.L., 1985; D.H.S.S., 1987).

3 Marriage Breakdown

Many suspect that marriage breakdown has increased as dramatically as the divorce rate, which more than doubled between 1970 and 1976. Part of the rise may be explained by legal and procedural changes, which have enabled a higher proportion of already broken marriages to be dissolved. But this cannot be the whole explanation, for the underlying trend was established before the law was changed. The law may have contributed to a climate of opinion in which divorce is a more acceptable solution to an unhappy marriage, but there are many other factors which are at least as significant. Among these are smaller, consciously planned families, which release women earlier from their demands; improvements in the social and economic status of women, which have liberated them from traditional restraint and their husbands from traditional responsibility; and above all, a far higher expectation of personal fulfilment and happiness from marriage, which sees no need for the traditional moral justifications for release from its commitment. A higher rate of marriage breakdown might even reflect a more positive attitude than there was in the days when marriage was the only respectable career for a woman (*Fletcher*, 1973; *Mortlock*, 1972).

There must still be concern about the effects upon the increasing numbers of children involved (*Wallerstein and Kelly*, 1980). Prolonged one-parent status often brings financial stringency, housing problems and downward social mobility, and these all tend to be worse where the marriage was broken by divorce rather than death (*Finer*, 1974; *Ferri*, 1976). A significant link has been found between marriage breakdown and delinquency, emotional disturbance and poorer educational achievement in the children (*Rutter*, 1971; *Ferri*, 1976). It is not known, however, how far these may be attributed to economic disadvantages, or to social stigma, or to parental bitterness and disharmony, rather than to the separation itself. The outcome may be rather different now that divorce is more widespread and possibly more amicable. It is known that those children who are able to maintain satisfactory links with both parents after the break do much better than those who cannot (*Richards and Dyson*, 1982; *Maidment*, 1984a; Richards 1986).

If the parents separate, some decision must be reached about the children. Custody *disputes* are remarkably rare (*Maidment*, 1976; *Eekelaar and Clive*, 1977), but the courts are usually involved in monitoring the arrangements in some way. The various legal procedures available to parents who break up will first be listed, followed by an account of the orders which may be made about the children involved, and finally by some discussion of the principles upon which the courts seem to operate in disputed cases.

1. *Procedures on Marriage Breakdown*

(i) Divorce

This is by far the most common procedure; it dissolves the marriage, leaves each party free to remarry and gives the courts wide powers to deal with "ancillary" financial questions and the children's future. The sole ground for divorce is that the marriage has irretrievably broken down and this can only be established by proving one or more of five facts: that one party has committed adultery and the other finds it intolerable to live with him; that one has behaved in such a way that it is not reasonable to expect the other to live with him; that one has deserted the other for at least two years; that they have lived apart for at least two years and both agree to a divorce; and that they have lived apart for at least five years, irrespective of the wishes or behaviour of the other spouse, although if that spouse can prove that the divorce would cause her grave hardship she may be able to resist a decree (Matrimonial Causes Act 1973, ss.1, 2 and 5). Around 66 per cent. of the 144,000 divorces granted in 1984 were based upon the first two facts and around 70 per cent. were granted to wives. Only 500 were defended to a hearing. From 1986, virtually all divorces will be heard in county courts.

(ii) Other Matrimonial Causes

These are also heard in county courts and should not be confused with matrimonial proceedings in magistrates' courts. A decree of nullity brings to an end a marriage which suffered from some fundamental defect, such as an inability to consummate it (1973 Act, ss.11 to 16). A decree of judicial separation merely relieves the parties of their duty to live together while leaving the marriage intact; one of the five facts necessary for divorce must be proved, but irretrievable breakdown is not needed (ss.17 and 18). A spouse who does not want or cannot yet obtain any decree, may apply to the divorce court on the ground that the other is not maintaining her or the children properly (s.27), but this is rarely done.

(iii) Matrimonial Proceedings in Magistrates' Courts

More commonly, a spouse may seek financial provision in a magistrates' court, on the ground that the other has failed to maintain her or the children properly, or has behaved in such a way that she cannot be expected to live with him, or has deserted her (Domestic Proceedings and Magistrates' Courts Act 1978, s.1); she may also ask the court to approve financial arrangements which they have agreed (s.6) or to confirm by order the level of payment which has been made voluntarily for the past three months (s.7). The court then has extensive powers to deal with the children's future. Magistrates also have powers to protect both a spouse and the children from domestic violence (ss.16 to 18), but there is no ancillary power to make orders about the children's custody.

(iv) Guardianship of Minors Act Proceedings

Parents who do not wish to seek remedies for themselves may still wish to litigate about their children. While they are living together, they may refer disputes about the children's upbringing to a court under section 1(3) of the Guardianship Act 1973; otherwise they may apply for custody or access under section 9 of the Guardianship of Minors Act 1971. These applications may be made either to the local magistrates' or county court or to the High Court.

(v) Wardship

An alternative method of resolving the children's future is to make them wards of court. The power of the High Court to assume the guardianship of children who are in need of its protection stems from the ancient notion that the King was the father of his people. It has never been defined or curtailed by statute. It may be invoked by parents who are seeking to enforce their wishes against a recalcitrant child or who are battling between themselves over custody or upbringing; but where the parents have already begun proceedings in another court, the High Court will not usually allow them to use wardship as a "second bite at the cherry," unless there are things which it can do and the lower court cannot.

The immediate effect of any application is that the child becomes a ward of court automatically and thereafter no important step may be taken without the court's consent; parents find it particularly useful where "kidnapping" is feared; but other specific orders may be obtained very quickly if needed. The court may always "deward" a child and this will happen automatically after 21 days unless steps have been taken to arrange a hearing date. The object of this rule was to prevent children becoming or remaining wards of court by accident rather than to speed up what can be a very slow process. It is slow because it is so careful; all interested parties will usually be represented by lawyers; the Official Solicitor may be asked to represent the child separately; evidence in the form of affidavits will be exchanged before the hearing; and although judges may quickly be found in an emergency, the Family Division of the High Court is not large and it can take months to arrange a full hearing; but decisions other than to ward or deward can now be taken in a county court.

Wardship may also be used by friends, relatives, foster-parents or other interested people who may have no other way of bringing their claims or fears for a child before a court (see further in Chapter 10); or by local authorities who feel unable to protect the child adequately under their statutory powers (see Chapters 5 and 9). The traditional preoccupation with the marriage and property of orphans and heiresses has now been overtaken by quite different concerns.

(vi) Injunctions

Parents may ask the High Court for an injunction to protect their own or their children's interests; divorce courts also have power to grant injunctions to protect either spouse or children pending or even after the hearing of a divorce or other matrimonial cause; and all county courts have power to grant injunctions protecting a spouse, or a person who is living with the other as a spouse, or a child living with that spouse, from molestation and dealing with the short-term occupation of the matrimonial home (Domestic Violence and Matrimonial Proceedings Act 1976). These orders can protect the health and safety of children where their parents are in conflict, but custody and maintenance have to be dealt with under other legislation.

(vii) Informal Separation

There is nothing to prevent a husband and wife separating without ever going to court and there is reason to believe that, at least before divorce became so much more widespread, many couples did so. Some may make a separation or maintenance agreement. Provided that the normal rules on making contracts are observed, these are legally enforceable, but the courts have wide powers to alter financial arrangements contained in any written agreement and it is not possible for a spouse to contract out of the right to apply to the courts. Hence it is now more usual to ask the court to make an order by consent. Similarly, while separation agreements may provide for who is to exercise parental responsibilities (Guardianship Act 1973, s.1(2)), the court may always decline to enforce this if it is not in the child's best interests.

2. *The Orders Available*

In proceedings (i) to (v) the courts have similar, but not identical, powers to consider and make orders about the children's future.

(i) The Duty to Consider the Children's Future

In guardianship and wardship proceedings, which are essentially about the children, it should be impossible to overlook their interests. Divorce and matrimonial cases are essentially about the parties' marriage and in a large proportion there will be no dispute about the children at all. But marriage breakdown can have such serious consequences for them that the law imposes a positive duty upon courts to consider their welfare, whatever their parents may have decided.

Before making a decree of judicial separation, or making absolute a decree of nullity or divorce, the court must discover all the relevant "children of the family" (1973 Act, s.41). A "child of the family" is not only a natural or adopted child of the marriage, but also any *other* child who has been treated by both parties as a child of their family, apart from one officially boarded-out by a local authority or voluntary organisation (s.52(1)). The obvious example is a step-child, including a wife's extra-marital child whom the husband thinks is his own, but privately fostered children or orphans being cared for by relatives are also covered. The essential criterion is that the child was regarded and treated by both as a member of their common household, so that it is as much his home as anyone else's which is breaking up. For the purpose of this section, the relevant children of the family are those under 16, those under 18 who are still being educated or trained (even if, like apprentices, they also have a job), and any others of whatever age whom the judge orders to be included because there are special circumstances, such as handicap.

The court must then examine the proposals for the future of all these children, which must be set out in a separate document accompanying the petition and discussed in a personal interview with the judge (even though the divorce itself now usually goes through without a hearing). The judge must then be able to declare that the

arrangements made are satisfactory, or the best that can be devised
in the circumstances, or that it is impracticable for the parties to
make any (perhaps, for example, because the local authority has
parental rights). Occasionally, the court may decide that there are
special circumstances making a decree desirable even though such a
declaration cannot yet be made, but if so the parties must undertake
to bring the future of the children before the court within a specified
time. In most cases, however, if the court will not make a declaration
the parties do not get their decree.

This sounds excellent, but there are obvious problems. The judge
is being asked to perform a "welfare" rather than an adjudicatory
function and it is a matter of chance whether he will be any good at
it. If he is troubled by any matter, he may call for a welfare officer's
report, but judges vary considerably both in the matters which
trouble them and in their readiness to ask for reports (*Hall*, 1968;
Davis, MacLeod and Murch, 1983; *Dodds*, 1983); examples are where
the petitioner has not seen the children for some time and thus cannot tell the judge much about them, or where very young children
are with their father, or where there are obvious stress factors such
as handicap, health or housing problems. But the judge has little
time to find out where the real problems lie. Even if he is unhappy
with what is proposed, he can only oblige the parents to think again.
He cannot force an unwilling parent to take the child and the
alternative of committal to care will usually be much worse than
leaving things as they are. Once the decree has gone through, the
only means of ensuring that the agreed arrangements are kept is to
make a supervision order, which would be quite impracticable in
every case. In any event, it is no longer so obvious why the courts
should be expected to impose their preferred solutions or single out
these children for special attention (*Maidment*, 1984b; *Law Commission*, 1986).

There is no such procedure in matrimonial proceedings in magistrates' courts, but the case must not be disposed of without considering what order, if any, to make about any children of the family
(1978 Act, s.8(1)).

(ii) Custody Orders

A court hearing divorce, nullity or judicial separation proceedings
may make such order as it sees fit for the "custody and education" of
any child of the family under 18, whether or not it also grants the
decree; alternatively, it may direct that proceedings be taken to
make the child a ward of court, but this is rare (1973 Act, s.42(1)). A
divorce court which is asked only for financial provision may also

make a custody order, but only if and for so long as it makes a financial order (s.42(2)). Magistrates who are asked for financial provision may make orders for the "legal custody" of any child of the family under 18, whether or not they make an order for a spouse (1978 Act, s.8(2)). Orders for "legal custody" are the main object of proceedings under section 9 of the 1971 Act. Custody orders are not made over wards of court, but care and control will be delegated to whoever is best suited to have it.

The courts have power to grant custody to someone other than the warring spouses or parents. In divorce courts, third parties such as grandparents or step-parents may "intervene" in the proceedings in order to ask for it. In magistrates' matrimonial and Guardianship of Minors Act proceedings, courts who wish to grant legal custody to third parties should treat the case as if the third party had applied, and been qualified to apply, for custodianship under the Children Act 1975.

A custody order may be made while a child is in care (*M.* v. *Humberside County Council* [1979] Fam. 114), but normally this will simply determine who is to have the child should the care order be discharged or who may discharge the child from voluntary care. However, it has also been held that a divorce court has power to make a custody order which will *override* the care order and thus result in the child's immediate discharge from care (*E.* v. *E. and Cheshire County Council* (No. 2) (1979) 1 F.L.R. 73). It is now proposed that juvenile courts hearing applications to make or discharge care orders should be able to allocate custody between parents or spouses (and sometimes to others instead) (D.H.S.S., 1987).

In the Children Act 1975, "legal custody" is defined as "so much of the parental rights and duties as relate to the person of the child (including the place and manner in which his time is spent)" (s.86). It thus includes the *right* to "actual custody," which is defined as "actual possession of his person" (s.87(1)), and presumably such accompanying rights as medical treatment and discipline, but no rights over his property. "Custody" in the divorce courts has no statutory definition and presumably includes control over property. But the Court of Appeal has said that it does not give the custodial parent a pre-emptive right to take decisions about education or other "major matters" (*Dipper* v. *Dipper* [1981] Fam. 31). As we saw in Chapter 1, the right to consent to the child's marriage normally goes with custody, but the right to change his surname does not, and all courts have power to forbid the custodial parent to take the child out of the country without consent. The parents' rights to appoint guardians and decide whether the child should be adopted are not affected. Unlike adoption, a custody order may always be revoked or

varied at a later date and has no effect upon the wider aspects of
family relationships, such as inheritance. In matrimonial cases, an
order will only affect the rights of a parent who is not a party to the
marriage in question if he has been given an opportunity of taking
part (and in the divorce courts even then only if one of the parties to
the marriage is a parent).

(iii) Joint and Split Custody

Divorce courts have power to split up the bundle of rights and
responsibilities in any way they see fit. They may wish to consolidate
a new family, for example by awarding joint custody to the mother
and her new husband; or more commonly they may wish to encourage the parents to continue to share responsibility for their children's upbringing. The usual way of doing this is to grant them joint
custody, while giving care and control to one, although as between
married parents only an order for care and control is needed, as both
have equal rights already. Where the parents are both interested
and concerned, and able to co-operate about their children, joint
custody orders are not only permitted (*Jussa* v. *Jussa* [1972] 1 W.L.R.
881) but increasingly favoured by some courts as well as parents
(*Priest and Whybrow*, 1986). The parent without care and control then
has a voice in strategic decisions, such as religion, education or
major medical treatment, but should not interfere in day-to-day
matters. Orders for dividing or sharing day-to-day responsibilities
are not so favoured (*Riley* v. *Riley* [1986] 2 F.L.R. 429) although
many mothers might prefer more help with everyday life and less
interference with strategic decisions which they then have to put into
effect.

A less satisfactory solution is to grant custody to one parent and
care and control to the other; this was originally devised so that the
"guilty" wife could look after her young children while their father
retained overall control. Nowadays, it is thought wrong to deprive
her of an equal voice in decision-making unless the circumstances
are quite exceptional (*Dipper* v. *Dipper* [1981] Fam. 31; *Williamson* v.
Williamson [1986] 2 F.L.R. 146; in *Jane* v. *Jane* (1983) 4 F.L.R. 712,
this was done because she might refuse consent to medical treatment). In magistrates' matrimonial and Guardianship of Minors
Act cases, the courts have no power to grant joint legal custody or to
separate legal custody from the actual care of the child; but they
may order that the person granted legal custody shares specified
rights or duties, which could include all except actual custody, with
the person who has been deprived of it (1978 Act, s.8(4); 1971 Act,
s.11A(1)).

(iv) Access

From the point of view of the concerned parent who has lost day-to-day care of his child, retaining some part of custody is obviously better than only having access, for this is nothing more than the right to see the child for a reasonable time at reasonable intervals. There is always room for disagreement about what is reasonable: it will depend upon the facilities available, the distances involved, the age, character and inclinations of the children, and the qualities of the parent and any new partner. Staying with the parent for a weekend or holiday is likely to be reasonable if he is caring and careful, has suitable accommodation, and the children are willing to go. If the parties cannot agree, either may apply to the court for access to be defined, although it is always hoped that they will come to sensible arrangements. The court can also impose conditions, for example, that the children meet him on neutral ground or in the presence of an unprejudiced friend or relative. A supervision order may be a way of helping the parents to reach agreement, but the supervisor should not normally be asked to decide upon or supervise the access itself (*Practice Direction* [1980] 1 W.L.R. 334).

It is sometimes argued that the children's interests would be better served by a clean break from the distressing associations of the past. The break might also remove a damaging source of worry for the custodial parent, who should perhaps be left to decide for herself what will be best (*Goldstein, Freud and Solnit*, 1973). Others feel that a complete severance of ties may do serious harm to the child and his later sense of identity and personal worth, particularly if he is of the same sex as and grows up closely resembling the absent parent who, he has always been told, treated his mother so badly. Children who have lost a parent on divorce continue to grieve for them for a long time afterwards (*Wallerstein and Kelly*, 1980).

The courts support the second view, for they have described access as a right of the child rather than a right of the parent (*M.* v. *M.* (*child: access*) [1973] 2 All E.R. 81. They are also aware that a parent who is allowed some contact with his child may be more likely to respect his financial obligations towards them, although in theory one is not a *quid pro quo* for the other. Access is thus a claim of parenthood which the courts tend to respect unless there is a very clear indication to the contrary and despite the distress it may cause to custodial parent or child. But many parents find access so difficult (or are so uninterested) that they cease to exercise it within a remarkably short time (*Maidment*, 1975, *cf. Murch*, 1980). The courts are also reluctant to interfere in the custodial parent's reasonable way of life, even if she moves abroad (*Poel* v. *Poel* [1970] 1 W.L.R. 1469;

Barnes v. *Tyrrell* (1981) 3 F.L.R. 240, *Chamberlain* v. *De La Mare* (1982) 4 F.L.R. 474), so that access becomes well-nigh impossible.

Divorce courts can grant access to anyone whom they think the child will benefit from seeing. Other courts may grant access to grandparents when making custody orders in magistrates' matrimonial or Guardianship of Minors Act proceedings (1978 Act, s.14; 1971 Act, s.14A), or after the death of the parent through whom the grandparent claims relationship (s.14A(2)). In matrimonial cases, magistrates are expressly prohibited from granting access if the child is in local authority care for any reason (s.8(2)(b)); in general, this should now be dealt with under the procedure in the Child Care Act 1980 (see Chapter 9).

(v) Supervision Orders

Supervision was originally devised as a method of following up the approved arrangements in divorce cases. Orders may now be made by any court which grants custody of a child to any person, or in divorce or wardship cases where it simply decides who is to have care of the child (1973 Act, s.44; 1978 Act, s.9; Guardianship Act 1973, s.2(2)(a); and for wards of court, Family Law Reform Act 1969, s.7(4)).

In theory, there should be "exceptional circumstances" making it desirable that the child should be under the supervision of some independent person, but practice varies considerably. Orders usually result from a welfare officer's report (*Eekelaar and Clive*, 1977). Whereas these are often obtained in cases of disputed custody, only a divorce court, in the course of investigating the proposed arrangements, is likely to call for one in an undisputed case. Officers also vary in their readiness to recommend supervision (*James and Wilson*, 1984). Surprisingly, perhaps, some courts with particularly high rates of joint custody also have high rates of supervision orders (*Priest and Whybrow*, 1986). The objects of supervision are now much broader than originally envisaged (*Law Commission*, 1987a). The purpose may be to provide support for the children or the custodial parent after the trauma of divorce; or to protect the children where the court or the other parent has a nagging doubt about the wisdom of the custody decision; or it may be hoped that the supervisor will help the parents to co-operate with one another, for example over access. It would certainly help supervisors if the court were to make it plain what the purpose was (*Booth*, 1985) and also consulted them first (*Law Commission*, 1987a).

The supervisor may be either the court welfare officer (in the High Court or divorce courts) or a probation officer (in magistrates' or county courts) or the local social services authority. Social services may be thought more appropriate where the object is child protection, and probation where the problem is short term adjustment to divorce. The various Acts do not prescribe duties for the supervisor, who can decide for himself what is necessary. More unfortunately neither do they give him any specific powers to carry it out. He cannot insist on seeing the parents, the child, or the home or on being informed of changes of address. But if the order were to have the same requirements as an order made in care proceedings, should it also have the same grounds (*Law Commission*, 1987a)? In divorce courts the supervisor may ask for directions about the exercise of his powers; he may also ask the court to make, or vary the existing, custody, access or financial arrangements, or to commit the child to care instead. In magistrates' matrimonial and Guardianship of Minors cases, he may only ask the court to vary or discharge the supervision order itself, but under the 1978 Act the court may then vary custody or commit to care.

Unless a time limit is fixed, the order lasts as long as the custody order to which it is limited, but can be varied or discharged on the application of the supervisor or any party. A fixed but extendable time limit could be helpful (*Booth*, 1985; *Law Commission*, 1987a), as dead or unimplemented orders seem to be a real problem.

(vi) Committal to Care

In all these proceedings, the court may find that there are exceptional circumstances making it impracticable or undesirable to entrust the child to any of the possible candidates. If he is under 17, the court can instead commit him to the care of the local authority (1973 Act, s.43; 1978 Act, s.10; Guardianship Act 1973 s.2(2)(*b*), and for wards of court, Family Law Reform Act 1969, s.7(2)). These orders are a growing phenomenon in wardship but only a tiny proportion of those made in divorce and other family proceedings (*Priest and Whybrow*, 1986; *Law Commission*, 1987). Some local authorities find it convenient to intervene in divorce to seek committal, rather than bring care or wardship proceedings. The authority must always be given an opportunity of "making representations" before an order is made.

The order lasts until the child is 18, unless it is earlier discharged on the application either of the local authority or of any party to the original proceedings. Contributions to the child's maintenance in care are ordered by the court, rather than the usual system, until the child is old enough to contribute himself. In divorce or wardship cases, the court may give directions to the local authority about the exercise of its caring functions; this includes a power to direct access (*Re Y. (a minor) (child in care: access)* [1976] Fam. 125) or to suggest whether attempts should be made to restore the child to his parents (*Turney* v. *Turney and Devon County Council* (1981) 4 F.L.R. 199). The relationship between local authority, parents and child is discussed in Chapter 9.

(vii) Money and Property

The most comprehensive financial powers are enjoyed by divorce courts, for they are usually regulating the total break-up of the family. They may order either party to make periodical payments, sometimes with security, or to provide lump sums for the other party or for the children (1973 Act, ss.23 and 24). These may be ordered even though the divorce, nullity or judicial separation proceedings are unsuccessful (s.23(2)). If a decree is granted, however, the court also has power to order the transfer or settlement of any property owned by either spouse to or for the benefit of the other spouse or the children (s.24).

The court must give first consideration to the welfare of the children of the family while they are under 18 (s.25(1)). It must also take into account the relative financial needs and resources of both spouses and the children, the standard of living enjoyed by the family before the breakdown, and any physical or mental disability of either spouse or the children. For the spouses, it must consider their ages, the duration of the marriage, the contribution made by each to the welfare of the family (including looking after the home and caring for the family), and the potential loss of benefits such as pensions (s.25(2)), but must also explore the possibilities of a "clean break" bringing their mutual financial obligations to an end (s.25A). For the children, it must consider their actual or expected education and training; in ordering a spouse to make provision for a child of the family who is not his own, the court must consider whether, and if so to what extent, on what basis, and for how long, he assumed any financial responsibility for the child, whether he did so knowing the child was not his; and the liability of anyone else to maintain the child (s.25(3)). The way in which the spouses have behaved towards one another will be irrelevant unless the behaviour of one was so much worse than that of the other that it would be inequitable to disregard it.

In practice one of the most important considerations is the need to preserve a home for the children. Capital provision is not granted to the children themselves; the courts assume that children cannot expect more from their parents than support during their childhood and education, even if the family is very rich (*Lilford (Lord)* v. *Glyn* [1978] 1 W.L.R. 78). They can, however, expect a home while they are growing up. One possibility is to re-settle the matrimonial home so that it cannot be sold without the agreement of both parties until the children have finished their education (*Allen* v. *Allen* [1974] 1 W.L.R. 1171); another is to transfer it to the custodial parent outright, perhaps in return for a lump sum or a reduction in periodical payments which would otherwise be ordered (*Hanlon* v. *Hanlon* [1978] 1 W.L.R. 592). Thus the decision on custody may well dictate what is to happen to the home. In *L.* v. *L.* (1980) 2 F.L.R. 48, the husband had looked after a little girl (now aged three), with the help of an aunt while he was at work, for several months after his wife left to live with another man. When her new relationship broke up, the wife applied for custody and was successful; the court also ordered that the husband should leave the matrimonial home, a council house, so that mother and daughter could live there together.

Having to look after young children also affects whether the parent (usually the wife) can be expected to go out to work and thus whether she may have a claim to periodical payments. In suitable cases, her income may be brought up to one-third of their total joint incomes and periodical payments ordered for the children as well. In most cases private support rights are totally inadequate to provide for the needs of broken families, partly because orders are difficult to enforce and partly because there is simply not enough money to maintain two households. There is no automatic allowance which an unsupported lone parent may claim from the state, apart from a small increase in child benefit for one child, and many rely on means-tested supplementary benefit or, if working for more than 24 hours a week, on family income supplement. In both, the assessment of means takes fully into account any maintenance paid for either parent or child, which therefore benefits not them, but the state. If it is paid through a magistrates' court, it may be diverted straight to the D.H.S.S., so that the mother may receive her regular benefit in full, irrespective of how much the father has paid into court.

The courts are not supposed to take supplementary benefit into account as a resource available to the wife and children, for otherwise the father could often throw the whole burden on to the state. But neither should they usually reduce his income below what he would receive for himself and his new family were he on supplementary benefit himself, for this would simply impoverish them both (*Barnes* v. *Barnes* [1972] 1 W.L.R. 1381; *Allen* v. *Allen* [1986] 2 F.L.R. 265). The courts recognise that the difference between what he can afford and what she and the children need may have to be made up by the state. They will never do this where he can afford a sum which will keep them above supplementary benefit level altogether, but if he cannot, their question becomes not "how much do they need?" but "how much should he keep?" The courts may, however, be less generous to the father than the D.H.S.S. would be when making an agreement with a "liable relative" (*Shallow* v. *Shallow* [1979] Fam. 1). The D.H.S.S. may let him keep as much as a quarter of his net income on top of what would be his own supplementary benefit requirements. The courts may sometimes make an order which is intended to preserve the principle that his first duty is to the children of his first family, even if this will leave his new family at or slightly below supplementary benefit level (*Tovey* v. *Tovey* (1978) 8 Fam. Law 80) (see *Hayes*, 1979).

In matrimonial cases, magistrates may order periodical payments and a lump sum of up to £500 for a spouse if she is successful and for the children in any event. Under the Guardianship of Minors Act (as amended by the Family Law Reform Act 1987) the High Court and county courts may order unlimited lump sum and property adjustments as well as periodical payments for the children, but magistrates may only order periodical payments and lump sums of up to £500 (s.11B). The Family Law Reform Act 1969 (s.6) authorises only periodical payments for a ward of court.

Orders cannot be made for children who have reached 18, unless they are, will be, or would be if maintenance were ordered, still undergoing education or training (even if combined with a job) or there are other special circumstances. Such a child may apply himself if there are divorce proceedings (*Downing* v. *Downing* (*Downing intervening*) [1976] Fam. 288) or his parents are separated; a child of 16 may ask for a previous order to be revived (1971 Act, ss.11D and 12C(5)). Orders made for younger children will normally end at 17, unless the court decides to specify a later date at the outset or the order is subsequently varied; but they cannot be extended beyond 18 unless the same conditions are fulfilled. Maintenance for wards of court, however, may continue beyond 18 whenever the court thinks fit, but must end at 21. A former ward of 18 and under 21 may himself apply.

3. *The Criteria for Awarding Custody*

"Where in any proceedings before any court . . . the legal custody or upbringing of a minor . . . is in question, the court, in deciding that question, shall regard the welfare of the minor as the first and paramount consideration . . . " (Guardianship of Minors Act 1971, s.1).

What factors do the courts take into account when considering the welfare of children?

(i) Assessing the Child's Welfare

The courts are always saying that each custody case is an exercise of their discretion in its own individual circumstances and that there are no "rules" or even "principles" as to what is best. The appeal court will only interfere with the decision of the court which heard the evidence and saw the people involved if it was "plainly wrong" (*G.* v. *G. (minors: custody appeal)* [1985] 1 W.L.R. 647). It is however possible to describe the sort of matters which the courts are likely to take into account.

(a) Most obvious is the child's physical welfare. This was the courts' major preoccupation in earlier days and even now that other factors loom larger, its mundane importance should not be overlooked. Is either party likely to neglect or ill-treat the child? How suitable is the accommodation offered? How well can each parent supply the child's basic needs for food, clothing, hygiene? How will a working parent cope with school holidays, late afternoons, or a pre-school child? It is not a question of which family is the better-off, for the courts may well find it easier to believe that a woman can provide better physical care, especially for a young child, than can a man (*e.g. Re K. (minors) (children: care and control)* [1977] Fam. 179; *cf. B.* v. *B. (custody of children)* [1985] F.L.R. 166). Full-time care, even on supplementary benefit, may be preferred to part-time care from a working parent. But where there is a substantial disparity in material standards between otherwise equally suitable homes, the courts may not be able to ignore it. However, in the matter of physical care, as in so many things, the mother usually enjoys a built-in advantage.

(b) The courts realised long ago that children had more than physical needs, but at first this tended to be reflected in concern for their "moral" welfare. The parents' behaviour towards one another is no longer of much significance in itself (*Re K.* again; see p. 50 below), but its effects upon the children can be crucial. The courts realise that adultery does not make a woman a bad mother, but there could be adverse effects if she were a prostitute or a homosexual or the children had previously been brought up on the strictest moral principles. Similarly, a criminal or violent history or homosexuality in the father may be taken into account. The courts will also consider the religious upbringing offered. Although they do not prefer one religion above another they may prefer some religious or moral guidance to none at all, and may prefer the (perhaps stricter) values of one parent to those of the other (*May* v. *May* [1986] 1

F.L.R. 325). There are some religious sects which they recognise may do positive harm to the children, particularly if they have only recently been espoused by one of the parents (*Re B. and G. (Minors) (Custody)* [1985] F.L.R. 493). Apart from those rare cases, where a child has already acquired a settled religious faith they will be reluctant to disturb it.

(c) Recently, these considerations have been supplemented and even over-shadowed by concern for the child's emotional well-being. The characters and mental health of the parents will obviously be important. At best, the court should make a close investigation of the quality of the relationships surrounding the child, and of the strength of his attachments, not only with his natural parents but also with the people offered as parent substitutes (*e.g. Stephenson* v. *Stephenson* [1985] F.L.R. 1140). This consideration has at least led the courts to abandon the old practice of deciding cases entirely on affidavit evidence; now all the adults involved should be seen as witnesses and an attempt made to assess their characters and qualities as parents. In practice, however, the court may be tempted to rely on rather stereotyped ideas of a child's emotional needs. Here again the mother can enjoy a built-in advantage, for the courts tend to assume that the natural mother is best for a young child (*Re W. (a minor) (custody)* (1982) 4 F.L.R. 492; *cf. B.* v. *B.* and *Stephenson* v. *Stephenson* above). On the other hand, it is sometimes assumed that older boys need a father's firm hand and guidance (*e.g. May* v. *May* above).

(d) A vital factor is the need to cause as little disruption as possible to the child's already disrupted life. The court may conclude that the parent best suited to supply the child's needs is the one who is not at present looking after him. Where the parents have not been separated for long, the court may not be deterred from ordering a transfer (*Allington* v. *Allington* [1985] F.L.R. 586). It would not be right if the one who happened to retain the children at the separation enjoyed too great an advantage. The court may also be able to order that the parent granted custody returns to the matrimonial home. The problem becomes acute when the parents have been separated for some time. Gone are the days when the court could contemplate with equanimity the transfer of a child aged seven from the only home she had ever known (*Re Thain* [1926] Ch. 676). Nowadays they are well aware of the child's need for stability and continuity, not only in relationships with parents, but also in physical surroundings, school, friends, and above all, brothers and sisters (*Re C. (a minor) (custody of child)* (1980) 2 F.L.R. 163; *B.* v. *B.* above). Thus the courts frequently urge that custody disputes should be tried as quickly as possible and need not wait for the solution of other issues between the parents (*Jones* v. *Jones* [1974] 1 W.L.R. 1471). There are however no rules requiring cases to be heard according to a particular timetable and views differ about whether this would be practicable (*Booth*, 1985; *Law Commission*, 1987). The speed of litigation depends largely on the parties, who do not normally include the child. The whole adult world tends to forget that a child's sense of time is entirely different from its own and what may seem a short time to parents and court may have been an age for the child (*Goldstein, Freud and Solnit*, 1973). A reading of the reported decisions of the Court of Appeal suggests that the courts are sometimes prepared to disturb a long-standing and quite satisfactory status quo, particularly if the children have been with their father (*Maidment*, 1981), yet the empirical evidence suggests that transfer of the child from one parent to another as a result of a court order is rare; it is far more likely to result from the parents' own arrangements (*Eekelaar and Clive*, 1977). Those arrangements are also the main reason why the mother ends up looking after the child, whether under a sole or a joint custody order, in around 90 per cent. of cases (see *Priest and Whybrow*, 1986).

(ii) The Child's Own Views

The High Court or divorce court may order that the child be separately represented, perhaps by the Official Solicitor, but this is rarely done. Apart from the welfare officer's report, his interests will have to emerge from the competing claims of his parents, and it is a mistake to assume that adults who are themselves under emotional strain will necessarily present all the relevant material to the court or even be aware of it. Their lawyers' first duty is to the adult client, although many will urge parents to consider carefully the children's welfare when tendering advice. The rarity of disputes may result partly from legal advice as to the prospects of success (particularly for fathers) and partly from the parents' own appreciation of the damage which a dispute could do. But how can the child's own views become known? It will rarely be in his interests to call him as a witness, but in the High Court and county courts the judge may interview him in private (although he cannot be given an assurance that any confidences will be respected, *Elder* v. *Elder* [1986] 1 F.L.R. 610). Magistrates cannot even do this and will have to rely on the welfare officer's report. A court will rarely, if ever, make an order which is contrary to the wishes of a child of 16. Below that age, it will take them into account, the more so the older the child, and if the child is adamant it may have little other option (*M.* v. *M.*, (*minor : custody appeal*) [1987] 1 W.L.R. 404); but it will also bear in mind that he may be influenced by the spite of one parent or the bribery of another (*Re S. (infants)* [1977] 1 W.L.R. 396; *Re D.W.* (1983) 14 Fam.Law 17). There is also a view that, although the child's feelings for his parents may be very important, he should not be made to feel responsible for choosing between them (*Adams* v. *Adams* [1984] F.L.R. 768).

(iii) Welfare Officers' Reports

All courts have power to call for an independent report on all matters relevant to the child's welfare. In the High Court and divorce courts this is provided by the welfare officer, who (except at the Royal Courts of Justice in London, where there are full-time welfare officers) is in fact the principal probation officer for the area (Matrimonial Causes Rules 1977, r. 95). In magistrates' matrimonial cases (1978 Act, s.12(3) to (9)) and under the Guardianship of Minors Act (Guardianship Act 1973, s.6) the report may be provided either by a probation officer or by an officer of the local authority. Reports may be called for by a single magistrate before the full hearing.

These reports are not confidential to the court. They do not have to be read aloud, but a copy must be given to each of the parties and if they wish to challenge anything, the officer must be called to give evidence. However, he cannot be made to, and should not, reveal anything which he learned in the course of trying to reconcile a marital dispute between the parties, unless they both agree. Reconciliation was the original reason for the involvement of probation officers in matrimonial cases. Nowadays, there is more emphasis on conciliation, working with the parties to improve communication between them, to help them to come to terms with the separation, and to co-operate rather than to fight about its practical consequences, including the future of their children (*Parkinson*, 1986). But while a report-writer may adopt a conciliatory approach, the courts have emphasised that the two functions should be kept quite separate (*Re H. (conciliation: welfare reports)* [1986] 1 F.L.R. 476; *Scott* v. *Scott* [1986] 2 F.L.R. 320).

If the court does call for a report, it will be looking for straightforward information about the family and each of the homes offered, but also for an assessment of the quality and stability of relationships within them and with the child and the quality of care which they may offer. It is therefore highly desirable that the same officer should visit each home, although if they are far apart this may not be possible. The court will also want to know how the child is getting on at school, something of his own character and relationships, and what he feels about the situation. If a definite recommendation is made, it carries a great deal of weight, so much so that the court should always give reasons for rejecting it (*Stephenson* v. *Stephenson* above; *Re T.* (1980) 1 F.L.R. 59).

Thus a great deal of responsibility is placed upon the authors of these reports, and it is important that they should differentiate quite clearly between matters of which the officer has first hand knowledge and matters which are merely hearsay, and also between statements of fact and expressions of opinion (*Thompson* v. *Thompson* (1975) [1986] 1 F.L.R. 212). A parent who wishes to challenge unverified statements is placed in an unjustifiable dilemma, for he may have to choose between antagonising the court and allowing a false picture to emerge. Neither will assist the child.

(iv) Expert Evidence

The courts' attitude to expert evidence is said to be entirely different. They cannot call for independent medical reports and so the evidence will be presented on behalf of one or both of the parties. Thus, otherwise healthy children should not be taken to paediatricians or psychiatrists by one party without the other party's consent (*Re S. (infants)* [1967] 1 W.L.R. 396); in wardship and matrimonial cases the court's leave is required for any psychiatric examination (*Practice Direction* [1985] 1 W.L.R. 1289). If medical evidence is offered, the courts affect to treat it with great caution. If the child is suffering from some physical or mental disorder, his doctor's evidence will obviously have an important bearing on who is best suited to care for him, "but if one has the case of a happy and normal infant in no need of medical care . . . who is taken to a psychiatrist or other medical practitioner for the sole purpose of calling the practitioner to give quite general evidence on the dangers of taking this, that or the other course . . . [this] may be valuable if accepted but . . . only as an element to support the general knowledge and experience of the judge in infancy matters . . . " (*J.* v. *C.* [1970] A.C. 668).

This attitude is understandable. The courts do not wish to abandon their discretion to doctors, who do rely heavily on retrospective studies of self-selected groups in offering this evidence. But it is a little unfair. The judges might not have learned to respect the value of mothering or the dangers of disruption had it not been for medical evidence and they ought not to run the risk of ignoring further developments in child psychology now. The difficulty is that the science is not sufficiently developed for any one view to command authority, but the courts may be tempted to accord it that (see *Mnookin*, 1975; *King*, 1981).

(v) Other Considerations

The other consideration which is sometimes urged by the parents is their own conduct towards one another. The way in which they have behaved towards their children is obviously a vital factor in judging the children's welfare and sometimes their behaviour towards one another may be relevant to their suitability as parents, particularly in the case of violence. The parties however often want the law to take their "innocence" or the other person's "guilt" into account for its own sake. It is only natural for a caring father whose wife has left him for another man to resent her claim to the children.

The law used to agree with him. As late as 1962, the Court of Appeal declined to give the care of two little girls aged four and six to their mother, although they clearly thought that she could look after them better, because the "claims of justice" could not be overlooked and she had wantonly destroyed the home to go and live near her "paramour" (*Re L. (infants)* [1962] 1 W.L.R. 886). This suggested that the claims of justice might be balanced against the welfare of the children, and even that such a wife should not be given all that she wanted, because then she would have no inducement to return. Both ideas have since been firmly rejected by the Court of Appeal (*Re K (minors) (children: care and control)* [1977] Fam. 179; *S. (B.D.)* v. *S. (D.J.) (children: care and control)* [1977] Fam. 109).

Re K. is a good general illustration. It concerned a boy of five and a girl of two. Their father was an Anglican clergyman; their mother had been a teacher of religion; but the marriage was not happy and the mother fell in love with another man. She eventually decided to set up home with this man, although they would not be able to marry for many years. She did not wish to leave without the children and so applied for their custody before going. The father strongly opposed this, arguing that the children would suffer harm by being brought up by their mother and a man living together in blatant defiance of all that their father believed in, but also that as the "unimpeachable" parent his wishes were entitled to consideration.

Nevertheless, the court held that the children should go with their mother. No modern judge could easily contemplate removing a two-year-old girl from a good mother who intended to live with a man whom the children knew well and liked, or separating the children from one another. The harm which they might suffer from knowing of their mother's immorality would happen whether they stayed or went, for they were bound to see a lot of her and to ask why they were not together. There was no such thing as an "unimpeachable" parent and his wishes could not be taken into account against the welfare of the children. Where the welfare considerations are more evenly balanced, however, a mother who had left her children for some time with a father who has learned to cope, or whose life-style appealed less to the court (*e.g. May* v. *May*, above) might well fail.

(vi) Commentary

In *Re K.*, the court relied upon the explanation given of the words of section 1 of the Guardianship of Minors Act by Lord MacDermott in *J.* v. *C.* [1970] A.C. 668:

" . . . they must mean more than that the child's welfare is to be treated as the top item in a list of items relevant to the matter in question. I think they connote a process whereby, when all the relevant facts, relationships, claims and wishes of parents, risks, choices and other circumstances are taken into account and weighed, the course to be followed will be that which is most in the interests of the child's welfare as that term has now to be understood. That is the first consideration because it is of first importance and the paramount consideration because it rules on or determines the course to be followed."

In effect, therefore, the child's welfare is now the sole consideration. Would it not be desirable for the law to say so, and even expressly to rule out matters such as the parents' marital behaviour?

Would it also be desirable to give both the courts and welfare officers more help in deciding what was relevant to the child's welfare? The Court of Appeal has frequently stressed that each case must be decided on its own merits and that there are no guiding rules or principles. In finance and property cases, the divorce courts have a list of relevant factors to consider, and many other countries (such as Australia and the Canadian Provinces) provide similar "checklists" of factors in custody cases. The Law Commission (1986) has recently suggested one which might be adopted here: it covers the child's existing attachments and the consequences of disrupting them, and the capacity and disposition of each party to cater for the child's physical, educational, social and other needs in the future.

Such a list might reduce the risks of inconsistency and subjectivity in deciding disputed cases. But these are a relatively small proportion. Much more important is helping the whole family to adjust its relationships for the future. There is now a great deal of evidence about the difficulties of maintaining contact after a divorce (see *Maidment*, 1976 and 1984a; *Murch*, 1980). One response to this is the joint custody order, which symbolises the continued relationship of both parents with the child and may encourage the one with whom the child is not living to keep in touch. However, joint legal custody is not the same as shared physical custody, in which the couple continue to share the day-to-day care between them, as happens in some parts of the U.S.A. Is joint legal custody a recipe for interference and control over the custodial parent without providing her with any concrete help in her difficult task? But is shared physical custody a recipe for even more disputes and disagreements, while depriving the child of the secure home base he needs? It is extremely difficult to devise a system which can give the child a secure home base, with a parent who can feel confident of her ability to bring him up, while maintaining and reinforcing his relationship and links with the other side of his family (see generally *Richards and Dyson*, 1982; *Maidment*, 1984; *Law Commission*, 1986). Perhaps one motto for the courts could be that where the family have made their own arrangements they should leave well enough alone.

4 Juvenile Offenders

When an adult is thought to have behaved in a way which the law defines as criminal, the process is relatively straight-forward. He will usually be prosecuted. He will be brought before a magistrates' court, which will either try him or, if the offence is serious, commit him to be tried by a judge and, if he pleads not guilty, a jury in the Crown Court. The case will be heard in open court, before press and public, and if he pleads or is found guilty he will be sentenced. The sentence is designed to protect society by removing, reforming or deterring him, and by deterring others, but it is also a punishment intended to reflect the extent of society's disapproval of his conduct. As such it will usually be related in gravity and length to the gravity of the offence, on a so-called "tariff." This sounds and is punitive, but it also serves to limit the sentences of those who have committed relatively minor offences, even if they are virtually certain to do it again when released. However, the tariff goes up as the offender's previous convictions go up, climbing a sort of "ladder." On the other hand, the tariff sentence may be reduced if there are mitigating factors suggesting that a more lenient course would do more good for the offender and thus for society. In a few cases, notably of mental disorder, the court may make an order which is intended entirely to do good rather than to punish. But the price which the offender must pay is that those who are doing him good must be allowed as long as they need to complete the cure. The tariff no longer applies.

If the alleged offender is a juvenile, his treatment by the criminal process may have more in common with the treatment of the mentally disordered than with the normal adult offender. The normal adult is presumed to know the law, to know what he was doing, and to have chosen freely to do it. He may properly suffer his just desserts, provided always that his guilt has been admitted, or proved beyond reasonable doubt in a trial which bristles with procedural and evidential safeguards. These safeguards are not designed solely or even mainly for the benefit of the individual accused. They are there to reassure the rest of us that no-one is unjustly punished. If *we* keep to the rules, nothing can be done to *us*.

If the offender is a juvenile, it is harder to ascribe his offences to free will and much easier to put them down to the normal naughtiness of growing up or to poor family and environmental influences. It seems foolish to invoke the majesty of the law to deal with the first, while the second might merit not punishment but a sympathetic attempt to mend matters before it is too late. This approach justifies a more flexible attitude to whether a juvenile should be taken to court at all. Once he is there, it may encourage the court to concentrate more on providing the help which he seems to need, and less on the reason for his being before the court. The "help" can, however, involve long term removal from home or similarly serious interventions.

Our present law is an uneasy and highly controversial compromise between the "justice" and "welfare" models (*Parsloe*, 1978; *cf. Priestley, Fears and Fuller*, 1977; *Taylor, Lacey and Bracken*, 1979; *Morris, Giller, Szwed and Geach*, 1980). First, the criminal law refuses to regard the very young as responsible at all, and may be reluctant to accept the responsibility of others, but there are other ways of getting troublesome juveniles to court. Secondly, there is much more flexibility in the decision to take court action against those whom the law does hold responsible. Thirdly, juveniles are usually brought before a court whose constitution and procedure have been designed with them in mind. Last, the orders which may be made are quite different from the sentences which may be imposed upon adults and the criterion for choosing between them is also different. By "juvenile" is meant a "child" under 14 or a "young person" under 17 but unless it is necessary to distinguish between them "child" will be used for both. The dividing line of 14 or 15 is, however, becoming more and more important for juvenile offenders.

1. *The Criminal Responsibility of Juveniles*

Should children be expected to learn and obey the same rules as the rest of us? By and large, the criminal law is the same for children as it is for adults. There are only a few crimes which cannot be committed below a certain age: for example, boys under 14 cannot be found guilty of rape. But it is conclusively presumed that no child under 10 can be guilty of any crime (Children and Young Persons Act 1933, s.50). They cannot be prosecuted or brought before the court in care proceedings based on the condition that they have committed an offence.

A child of 10 and under 14 can be found guilty of crime, but in theory it is presumed that he is incapable of it (*doli incapax*) until the prosecution proves otherwise. To rebut this, in addition to proving the offence, the prosecution must show that the child knew it was seriously wrong (*J.M.* v. *Runeckles* (1984) 79 Cr.App.R. 255). It is not enough for a boy of nearly 12 to see the consequences of his acts and know that they amounted to childish mischief (*H.* (*a minor*) v. *Chief Constable of South Wales, The Times,* July 5, 1986). It may sometimes be enough to show that the child was of normal intelligence for his age (*J.B.H. and J.H.* (*minors*) v. *O'Connell* [1981] Crim.L.R. 632), but it is not necessary.

Were this presumption strictly applied, it might lead to the acquittal of many children, particularly those whose mental age is far lower than their chronological age or who have received little moral guidance from home. But these are just the children for whom a "welfare" minded court might consider that some intervention was essential. The same is true of the general principle of criminal responsibility known as *mens rea* or guilty mind. Most crimes require not only the commission of a prohibited act, but also a particular state of mind in doing it. This could easily be lost sight of in a general desire to do something about a child who is obviously a problem, who may well not be represented by a lawyer, and who is likely to think that merely doing the deed is enough and therefore to admit his guilt. In any case, whether or not he is criminally responsible, a child of any age may be brought before the same court in care proceedings, which have much the same structure and much the same result, because he is beyond his parents' control, or in moral danger, or not going to school. The court is not then burdened by the concepts of criminal responsibility, or the stricter standards of proof. The child may find it hard to understand the difference between care proceedings and punishment, particularly for truancy. Some countries solve this problem by giving the same "due process" safeguards to "unmanageable" children as they do to offenders. In this country, it is proposed to draw a sharper distinction between punishment and protecting the child from harm, by abolishing these so-called "status offences" as a separate category in care proceedings (R.C.C.L., 1985; D.H.S.S., 1987).

2. *Taking Juveniles to Court*

(i) The Aims of the Children and Young Persons Act 1969

The philosophy behind the 1969 Act (*Home Office,* 1965 and 1968) was that each case should be looked at in the light of the needs of the individual. If these could be met in other ways, then prosecution was to be avoided. Indeed, for children under 14, it was to be prohibited altogether, except for homicide (s.4); and for young persons, it was to be limited to particular types of case and where nothing else would do (s.5(1) to (7)). However, an alternative was to be provided, not only for those cases where prosecution was prohibited or restricted, but to allow a less punitive form of proceeding in any case. This was care proceedings, where the applicant had not only to show that the child had committed an offence but also that a court order was needed to give him the care or control which he required (s.1(2)). In theory, care proceedings do not involve the stigma of prosecution and the only orders available are designed to help and not to punish. However, these changes were attacked from the beginning for being unfair to children who committed identical offences, perhaps together, but who came from different backgrounds. The restrictions on prosecutions were never brought into force, so that the more cumbersome alternative of care proceedings has scarcely ever been used. It is now proposed to abolish it (R.C.C.L., 1985; D.H.S.S., 1987). The reasons are practical, but the welfare philosophy on which it was based has fallen foul of radical thought on both the left and the right.

(ii) The Decision to Prosecute

Thus the authorities retain their unfettered discretion on whether to prosecute. Nevertheless, it is accepted that juvenile offenders require a different approach from adults and the Home Office (1985a) has given guidance to the police in an attempt to get more consistency from force to force.

One possibility is undoubtedly to do nothing. Another is for the police officer to deliver an unofficial "ticking off" on the spot. Either may be thought right if there is serious doubt about whether the child is responsible, or the offence is very trivial, or if the family is known or can be contacted quickly and is willing and able to take any necessary action itself. The incident is not formally recorded and a damaging over-reaction to "normal" naughtiness is avoided. But the police have always to bear in mind that if certain children, particularly those from "good" homes (which is still so often thought associated with social class), appear to be escaping official action altogether, others may feel a grave sense of injustice.

A common alternative is the official caution. This is a formal warning, delivered by a senior uniformed policeman, to the effect that although the matter will be taken no further on this occasion it would be advisable not to do it again. It is recorded against the child and the Home Office suggests that it should be made known as part of his antecedents if he later appears in court. The experience may deter many a child from again incurring official displeasure, and its immediacy and form may make it more effective as well as less damaging than a court appearance. Cautioning has steadily increased; in 1984, it was used for 79 per cent. of children found guilty or cautioned and 50 per cent. of young persons (*Home Office*, 1986a).

On the other hand, cautioning does give the child a "record" of sorts and there is a risk that official cautions have increased, not only at the expense of court appearances, but also at the expense of informal on-the-spot warnings. Perhaps worse, the police should obviously not use a caution unless the child and his parents have admitted his guilt. The child, therefore, is faced with a choice between admitting it and being "let off" with a caution, or denying it and being taken to court. However scrupulous the police, there are few children who would not take the former. The same problem arises with all official methods of "diverting" children out of court, whether by informal supervision or other voluntary steps. Hence the police should have enough evidence to launch a prosecution before they decide to caution instead.

Court action may be thought right for many reasons. It appears to be almost automatic for traffic offences, however trivial, on the curious ground that these are not "real" crime. If the child does not admit his guilt, the police may be reluctant to let the matter go even if a court appearance would not otherwise be indicated. If the offence was committed in the company of others, the police may wish to treat them all alike to avoid allegations of bias. This may mean that if someone of 17 or over is involved, the child may not escape prosecution as the adult will not, but discrimination between them may often be justified by the circumstances of the offence. The views of any victim of the offence may also be considered, for if the child is prosecuted, the court may order either the child or his parents to pay compensation. Most important of all are the seriousness of the offence and of the child's past record of offending. While minor and first offenders should normally be cautioned to keep them out of the system as long as possible, and serious or persistent offenders prosecuted, in the middle much will depend on the offender's character and family circumstances.

The police are therefore advised to make more extensive enquiries and to consult other agencies before embarking on prosecution. Many have specialist juvenile liaison machinery for the purpose. The Crown Prosecution Service is also instructed to regard prosecution as a last resort and to check that these guide-lines have been followed before continuing a prosecution begun by the police. Once proceedings are begun, the local authority (1969 Act, ss.5(8) and (9) and 2(3)) and, if the child is 13 or over, the probation service (s.34(2)) must be notified.

(iii) Procedure before Trial

Some children may simply be summonsed to appear in court, but if a child is arrested (with or without a warrant), he may be detained for inquiries like any other offender, under the Police and Criminal Evidence Act 1984 (the maximum without charge is 36 hours, extendable by magistrates for up to 96 hours). Whenever a juvenile is in police detention, his parent or guardian, or the local authority if he is in care for any reason, or failing these anyone else who has assumed responsibility for him, should be found and told as soon as possible; and his supervisor under the 1969 Act should also be told (1933 Act, s.34(2)–(11)).

A detained juvenile should not be interviewed or asked to make a statement without an "appropriate adult" (once again, his parent or guardian, or the care authority, or a social worker, or some other responsible adult who is independent of the police), unless delay would involve immediate risk of harm to people or serious harm to property (1984 Act, s.66; Code of Practice, C13). A non-parent is obviously preferable if the parent may himself be involved in the offence. The adult's role is active: to advise the child, observe the fairness of the interview, and to help the police and child communicate with one another. The police are warned that the child's information may be "unreliable, misleading or self-incriminating" and to check it if they can. The child has all the same rights as anyone else under the Act (for example, to consult a solicitor or phone a friend) as well. Children should not be interviewed at school unless the Head agrees and the circumstances are exceptional and they should only be arrested there if it is unavoidable.

Detained juveniles should not be put in police cells unless there is nowhere else where they can be properly supervised (Code of Practice, C8). Generally, while juveniles are detained in police stations, or being taken to and from court, or waiting in court, arrangements must be made to prevent their associating with any adult defendant apart from a relative or one jointly charged with the same offence. Girls must be under the care of a woman (1933 Act, s.31).

Once a child is charged, he must normally be given bail, although unlike an adult he may be detained "in his own interests" (1984 Act, s.38(1)). If detained, this must be in the care of a local authority unless this is impracticable (s.38(6)). He must normally be brought to court next day (s.46). He then has a right to bail (Bail Act 1976), unless there are good reasons for thinking that he would not appear, or would commit an offence or obstruct the course of justice while on bail, or he requires to be detained for his own protection or welfare.

If he is refused bail, he must be remanded to the care of the local authority (1969 Act, s.23(1)), unless the court is able to certify that he is too "unruly" and send him to a remand centre or prison instead (s.23(2)). Girls under 17 and boys under 15 cannot be declared unruly at all. A boy of 15 or 16 must either be charged with a very serious offence (punishable in an adult with 14 or more years in prison) or with an offence of violence; or have been previously found guilty of an offence of violence; or be a persistent absconder from or serious disrupter of a community home. The court must have a written report (but this is not conclusive; *R.* v. *Leicester City Juvenile Court, ex p. C.* (1984) 149 J.P. 409) from the local authority that there is no suitable accommodation for him in a community home, unless on the first remand in the first two cases, there has not been time to obtain one (Certificates of Unruly Character (Conditions) Order 1977). The local authority to whose care a child is committed on remand may later apply for him to be declared unruly, subject to the same conditions (s.23(3)). Whether remanded to care or prison, a child has the usual right to apply to a Crown Court judge for bail, and if he was unrepresented on the first remand, he must be granted legal aid (subject to means) on the second (Legal Aid Act 1974, s.29).

3. *Juvenile Courts*

(i) Jurisdiction

A juvenile who is prosecuted must normally be tried in a juvenile court, rather than an ordinary magistrates' court or the Crown Court, even if the offence is a serious one for which an adult would choose to be tried by jury. A young person's right to choose jury trial was abolished in 1969. There are, however, some exceptions to the rule that juveniles must be tried in the court which was specifically designed for them.

(a) All "homicide" charges must be tried in the Crown Court; these include murder, manslaughter and other unlawful killings, but not attempts.

(b) Young persons who are charged with very serious offences may be sent for trial in the Crown Court if the magistrates think that it ought to be possible to order them to be detained for a long fixed period (Magistrates' Courts Act 1980, s.24); children under 14 cannot be sent to the Crown Court for this reason, but if they are there for some other reason, the detention order could be made.

(c) Juveniles who are charged jointly with "adults" of 17 or more must first appear in the ordinary magistrates' court (1933 Act, s.46(1)). If the charge is serious, the court may, but need not, commit the juvenile for trial with the adult in the Crown Court; and if so, the juvenile may also be committed for charges which are connected with it (Magistrates' Courts Act 1980, s.24). If the juvenile has pleaded not guilty, while the adult has pleaded guilty or been discharged or been committed for trial in the Crown Court, the magistrates' court could send the juvenile for trial in the juvenile court (Magistrates' Courts Act 1980, s.29). Otherwise, both will remain in the ordinary magistrates' court. Lastly, a juvenile *may* also, but need not, be tried there on charges which are not joint, but are in some way connected with an offence with which an adult is charged (1933 Act, s.46(1) and 1963 Act, s.18).

(d) If a juvenile appears in the adult court by mistake, the magistrates may if they wish go on and decide the result (1933 Act, s.46(1) and note s.46 (1A) where juveniles plead guilty to motoring offences by post).

However, if a juvenile is tried in an adult court for any reason, he must normally be sent to the juvenile court to be dealt with, unless the magistrates decide merely to order a discharge, or fine, or parental recognisances, or driving penalties, or in the Crown Court the charge is homicide or the court thinks it undesirable to send him to the juvenile court (1933 Act, s.56(1) and 1969 Act, s.7(8)). Incidentally, a juvenile court may continue if a person reaches 17 after proceedings have begun (1963 Act, s.29), but he may also elect jury trial and be given an adult sentence if he reaches that age before the decision is taken (*R.* v. *Islington North Juvenile Court, ex p. Daley* [1983] 1 A.C. 347).

(ii) Constitution

Special courts for the trial of juvenile offenders were first set up in 1908. The object was and is to provide a tribunal which is separate from the adult courts with all their undesirable associations and better suited to the children's needs. However, all suggestions for a radical departure from the ordinary court process have been rejected and juvenile courts remain in effect specially constituted magistrates' courts.

The aim of keeping juveniles apart from adult courts is probably best realised in very large towns, where the pressure of business is sufficient to justify a specially designed court in a different building, or in much smaller places, where it is possible to hold juvenile courts on different days albeit in the same building. The only legal requirement however is that a juvenile court must not be held in the same *room* in which an adult court has sat or will sit within an hour of the juvenile hearing (1933 Act, s.47(2)). The authorities must also make arrangements to prevent children waiting at court from associating with adult defendants unless they are relatives or jointly charged with the juvenile (1933 Act, s.31).

The magistrates must have been selected to serve on the juvenile panel. In London the panel is chosen by the Lord Chancellor, but in the provinces by the local magistrates themselves. No qualifications are laid down but members must be under 65 (Juvenile Courts (Constitution) Rules, 1954). The Home Office suggests that they should be between 30 and 40, and certainly not over 50, when first appointed. They should have practical experience of dealing with young people, through teaching, youth organisations, welfare or similar work, and "a real appreciation of the surroundings and way of life of the children who are likely to come before the courts." But no formal commitment to a "welfare" rather than a retributive theory of juvenile justice is required and courts vary considerably in style and approach.

Magistrates are expected to undergo some training, usually in short evening or weekend courses. With the exception of a few full-time salaried stipendiary magistrates, who are trained lawyers with considerable practical experience but who usually do not sit in juvenile courts, they are part-time unpaid laymen. They are advised on the law by their clerk, but while the Clerk to the Justices must be a lawyer, the assistant sitting in court may be unqualified. Lay magistrates must sit in twos or threes to try cases, and in juvenile courts there should be one of each sex. Stipendiaries may sit alone, but only if delay is "inexpedient."

Children's panels in Scotland are also composed of laymen, but they are specially recruited and trained with a particular emphasis on the welfare philosophy upon which the whole Scottish system is based.

(iii) Trial Procedure

The procedure is basically the same as that of an ordinary magistrates' court, with some modifications. This is thought more suitable for children than the procedure of the Crown Court, because it is quicker, simpler and less formal. These are indeed advantages if the child admits the offence, but summary trial does have drawbacks if a child denies his guilt on a serious charge. The prosecution evidence does not have to be written down and given to him or his legal advisers in advance, as it is when someone is committed for trial in the Crown Court. The prosecution may be required to produce at least a summary of its evidence in some cases (Magistates' Courts (Advance Information) Rules 1985), but the defence task is still more difficult. Again, the magistrates combine the roles of judge and jury. They decide on guilt as well as on disposal, on any legal points as well as on disputed facts, and on the admissibility of evidence. These issues are kept strictly separate in the Crown Court, and with the best will and advice in the world lay magistrates can find this hard to do.

Most criticisms of juvenile courts, however, tend in the opposite direction. They are after all still courts and conduct themselves in much the same way as do adult tribunals. Outlawing such terms are "conviction" and "sentence" (1933 Act, s.59) is mere window dressing. The major modifications relate to the privacy of the hearing and the publicity which may later be given to it. The law tries to diminish the trauma and stigma to the child while preserving the equally important principle of open justice. The only people who may be present are those directly concerned in the case, and representatives of the media (1933 Act s.47(2)). Either or both of the child's parents may be required to attend at any stage, and must be so required if the court thinks it desirable, unless this would be unreasonable (s.34). The general public are not admitted. Nevertheless an alarming number of people can take part, and the child and his parents may be confronted with a bewildering row of tables, accommodating at least two magistrates, their clerk (who does most of the talking and is thought by many children to be in charge), the probation officer, the local authority's juvenile court liaison officer, a prosecutor and sundry police officers or ushers. Press reports or other publicity given to juvenile hearings must not disclose anything tending to identify the child himself (1933 Act, s.49), but the court or Home Secretary may make an exception in order to avoid injustice to "a" child or young person. Examples may be where another child's reputation may be cleared by publishing the actual offender's name, or where the child is acquitted and publication may be necessary to clear his own name. Children appearing in other courts do not have the same protection, but the court always has power to prohibit identifying publicity (s.39). It usually either does so or relies on the restraint of the press itself.

The actual hearing follows the same pattern as in other courts, and this is often confusing to a child or his parents, who are given only limited help by the rules (Magistrates' Courts (Children and Young Persons) Rules 1970, Pt. I). The court has to explain the substance of the charge to the child in simple language and ask whether he admits it, rather than putting it to him and asking how he pleads. The High Court has said that "where the defendant is not represented or where the defendant is of tender age or for any other reasons there must necessarily be doubts as to his ability finally to decide whether he is guilty or not, the magistrate ought . . . to defer a final acceptance of the plea until he has a chance to learn a little bit more about the case, and to see whether there is some undisclosed factor which may render the unequivocal plea of guilty a misleading one" (*R.* v. *Blandford Justices, ex p. G.* [1967] 1 Q.B. 82). They can allow the child to change his plea, if this seems right, at any time before the final order is made (*S.* v. *Recorder of Manchester* [1971] A.C. 481), and in some cases should themselves take the initiative.

If the charge is not admitted, the prosecution opens its case and calls witnesses, who may be cross-examined. If the child is not legally represented, the court must allow his parent to help him, and if the parent cannot be found or required to attend, the court may allow any relative or other responsible person to do so. If the child is neither legally represented nor helped, the court is allowed to translate assertions made by the child into questions for the purpose of cross-examining witnesses. This is all very well, but many parents are equally unfamiliar with the concept of cross-examination and may have to be restrained from simply putting forward their child's version of events. The danger then is that they will see no point in doing so at the right time, after the prosecution case is finished.

Formality is always much more a matter of personalities and atmosphere than procedural rules. Some magistrates think it right to preserve a stern unbending countenance, perhaps in a deliberate attempt to strengthen the deterrent effect of the court appearance. Parents having trouble with a child may build up an appearance as an awe-inspiring experience and be disappointed if the court seems to bend over backwards to be kind to the child. Other magistrates prefer to reject formality in favour of the Scottish model of a general discussion between themselves, the professionals and the family on the best way of helping the child out of his difficulties.

In Scotland, the children's hearing deals only with the treatment of those whose guilt is admitted, or proven elsewhere. This distances the circumstances of the offence from the choice of treatment, but there may be a greater risk of admissions in the hope of a quick and sympathetic disposal. In England, there is no reason why juvenile courts should not adopt a sympathetic appearance, but the central issue of innocence or guilt should not be lost sight of in the general concern for the child's welfare. Otherwise he will not receive that vital reassurance that nothing unpleasant can be done to those who keep the rules.

Some courts positively dislike legal representation for children, not only because it tends to impose more formality on the proceedings, but also because a lawyer will fight for what his client regards as the best result, whether or not it is what the court or the professionals think he needs (*Anderson*, 1978). It has been suggested that legal aid is unnecessary for juveniles, because the court must always "have regard to the welfare of the child" (1933 Act, s. 44). Legal aid is however available, subject to his parents' means, at the discretion of the court. It is mandatory in murder cases, certain custodial remands, and before the court can make an order for care, detention or youth custody (unless refused by the child or on grounds of means). It is almost always granted in the Crown Court, but magistrates vary very considerably in their approach.

4. *Disposal*

If guilt is admitted or proved, the court must allow both the child and his parents to make a statement; and before deciding on an order it must consider all the background information about the child's general conduct, home surroundings, school record and medical history. The police will supply their records, including cautions. The rest may be supplied by a social inquiry report.

(i) Social Inquiry Reports

Anyone prosecuting a juvenile must give notice to the local authority for the area where he lives (or, if he lives nowhere, where the offence was committed). If the child is 13 or over, notice must also be given to a probation officer for the court's area. It is then normally the duty of the local authority to make investigations and produce a home surroundings report, unless this seems unnecessary (1969 Act, s.9); but if the child is 13 or over, this duty falls instead on the probation service in those areas where arrangements are in force for it to do so (s.34(3)). Either must comply with any request from the court for specific information or investigations (s.9 or Powers of Criminal Courts Act 1973, Sched. 3, para. 8). A report should usually be obtained in all but trivial cases, and certainly the courts should not consider making a supervision order or removing a child from home without one.

Any written report from a local authority, probation officer or doctor can be received and considered by the court without being read aloud (r. 10), and in any event the court may ask the child or his parents to withdraw. If either of these happens, the court must tell the *child* the substance of anything which bears on his character or conduct and seems relevant to the order, unless this is impracticable having regard to his age and understanding (but should a child be prosecuted at all if he cannot understand the information on which the court's order will be based?); and the *parent* must be told of any relevant information bearing on his own character or conduct, or the character, conduct, home surroundings or health of his child. The object of this is to make sure that orders are not made on the basis of factual information contained in reports which the family has had no opportunity of seeing and challenging. This is an essential principle of open justice, however embarrassing it may be to a social worker for his client to realise that he has revealed damaging information. Sometimes there may be information about the parents, or the home, or his own health, which ought not to be revealed to the child, and the rules allow some discrimination. There is very little which may lawfully be kept from the parents and the best practice should be to give them a copy. However, this may be thought to be a decision for the court, rather than for the reporter.

There is no statutory form for these reports, but many authorities will give their workers guide-lines. It is usual for them to include details of the family structure and of the physical and material conditions in the home. There often follows an examination of the parents' characters, their relationships with one another and with this and other children, and their attitude to this offence. The child's own character and personality are covered, including any relevant medical and psychiatric history, his school record and attendance, his work record if he is old enough, his criminal record if he has one, and his attitude to this offence and the circumstances in which it was committed. If he is already in some residential establishment, the report may be made from there. It may well conclude with a recommendation for the treatment which the reporter feels most appropriate to the case.

This can place the social worker in a difficult position. He is there to provide essential objective information to the court, but he will often already be involved with the child or his family. He could be reluctant to forfeit their trust by revealing certain things about them or making a "hostile" recommendation, particularly as he may have to carry out any order which the court makes. He may feel obliged to be something of an advocate where a child is not represented. Yet he may also have been involved in the decision to bring the child before the court and his professional orientation is likely to be towards meeting the child's needs as he sees them rather than achieving what the child will see as a good result. Nor are recommendations which the court thinks unrealistic the best way of helping either the child or the court.

(ii) The Orders Available

Social workers may find it difficult to make realistic recommendations to juvenile courts because there is so much uncertainty about what the court should be trying to do. The choice of orders reflects that uncertainty. It ranges from the purely penal to the purely therapeutic, through orders which are meant to be therapeutic but are seen by many children and an increasing number of commentators as also penal. Care and supervision orders were based on the therapeutic notion that, if a serious attempt is to be made to cure the offender or his circumstances, then the people responsible must be given a freer hand, both in the choice of methods and in the time needed to complete the task. Unlike fines, detention, youth custody and community service, they cannot reflect the gravity of the offence in their size or length on the so-called "tariff" principle. Indeed, many offenders might prefer the supposedly more serious "short, sharp shock" of detention to the demands of supervision and intermediate treatment.

Nor are the courts given much firm guidance on how to choose between the orders available. The rules refer to dealing with the child in his "best interests" (r. 10(1)(*b*)). Section 44(1) of the 1933 Act requires the court to "have regard to the welfare of the child" but stops short of making it the first and paramount consideration, because a criminal court must sometimes give priority to the protection of the public. Both the welfare of the child and the protection of the public provide logical justifications for the complete abandonment of any tariff. They rather suggest that it should be replaced by a "ladder," which the child climbs at each successive court appearance. The less drastic orders have obviously failed to meet either *his* need for a more constructive upbringing or *our* need for him to stop committing offences. More drastic steps are therefore needed, however trivial the occasion for invoking them.

Recent changes in the criteria for care orders have tried to cut down on this risk. Generally, however, the therapeutic approach has been retained for younger juveniles, but is being supplanted for the older offenders, with the introduction of more and more penal disposals of determinate length.

(a) *Binding over and deferring sentence*

Juvenile courts, as magistrates, have the ancient common law power to bind over those who disturb the peace not to do so again within a specified period, on pain of committal to custody for up to six months. No finding of guilt need be involved. They also have power (under the Powers of Criminal Courts Act 1973, s.1) to defer making an order for up to six months, with a view to taking an offender's later conduct into account. The idea is not only to discourage further offences, but to encourage even better behaviour, such as making amends to a victim, by the hope of a lower order. But if there is no tariff in a juvenile court, it is hard to measure the size of this carrot. Both powers require the offender's consent.

(b) *Discharge*

An absolute discharge means that the offence has no further consequences, a conditional discharge that it has no further consequences provided that the child does not offend again within a specified period of up to three years (Powers of Criminal Courts Act 1973, s.7). If he does, he may be sentenced again for the original offence (s.8) and this must be explained to him in ordinary language when the order is made. Offences for which an offender is discharged are not treated as convictions for any purpose apart from driving penalties (s.13). Discharges are the lowest rungs on the ladder, with minimal deterrent or therapeutic effect. Their continued popularity with juvenile courts must indicate either that a beneficial effect is attributed to a court appearance alone or that many children are still being needlessly prosecuted.

(c) *Fines and other payments*

A fine can hardly be anything other than a punishment, but it is remarkably popular in juvenile courts, perhaps because it is next on the ladder and perhaps because it has a built-in tariff. The court may fine a child up to £100 and a young person up to £400 (Magistrates' Courts Act 1980, s.36), unless a lower maximum is laid down for the offence. It may also order him to pay costs, but not more than the amount of any fine (Costs in Criminal Cases Act 1973, s.2(2)), or compensation to a victim for any personal injury, loss or damage, up to £2,000 for each offence (Powers of Criminal Courts Act 1973, s.35). Compensation can now be ordered without imposing any other penalty. The main problem with all these orders is ensuring that they are paid, and paid by the right person, whether the court thinks this is the child himself or his parents.

The 1969 Act abolished all sanctions against juvenile fine defaulters, leaving only the unlikely remedies of attachment of earnings, seizing his goods, or a fine supervision order. In 1977 the possibility of an attendance centre order was restored, and powers to bind over a parent or guardian (with his consent) to see that the defaulter pays, or to order the parent or guardian to pay the remaining sum himself were introduced (now Magistrates' Courts Act 1980, s.81). None of these can be ordered without a personal inquiry into the defaulter's means, and an attendance centre order can only be made if he has actually had the money to pay but failed to use it for that purpose.

However, the court must now order the parent or guardian to pay
the fine, compensation or costs at the outset, unless he cannot be
found or it would be unreasonable in the circumstances to do so
(1933 Act, s.55; under the Criminal Justice Bill 1987, cl. 87, the
same would have applied to fines imposed for breach of attendance
centre or community service orders). He should be given a hearing,
unless he was required to attend the trial and did not do so, and can
appeal against the order. A local authority is not a parent or guardian for this purpose, whether the child is in voluntary or compulsory
care (*Leeds City Council* v. *West Yorkshire Metropolitan Police* [1983] 1
A.C. 29). A person to whom a child has been sent "home on trial"
may qualify. A "guardian" includes someone who for the time being
has "charge of or control over" the child (1933 Act, s.107(1)).
Parents are ordered to pay getting on for half of the fines imposed
upon children under 14 for indictable offences and more than a
quarter of those imposed on young persons (*Home Office*, 1986a).

(d) *Parental recognisances*

Another way of holding parents responsible for their children's
misdeeds is to ask them to promise, for a specified period of up to
three years or until the child reaches 18 if earlier, to take proper care
of him and exercise proper control over him (1969 Act, ss.7(7)(*c*)
and 2(13)). The order may only be made with the parent or guardian's consent, but if he fails to keep his promise, he may forfeit a
specified sum of up to £1000.

(e) *Supervision and intermediate treatment orders*

Originally, the same order was to apply both to offenders and to
children found in need of care or control. Changes made in 1977 and
1982 have, however, restored the order made in criminal proceedings to something more like probation. The court may place an
offender under the supervision either of the local authority (for the
area where he lives or some other authority which agrees to supervise him) or of a probation officer for the court's area; an offender
under 13 must be supervised by the local authority, unless a probation officer is already working with another member of the household and the authority asks that he should also supervise the child
(1969 Act, ss.7(7)(*b*), 11 and 13). Some consider that probation officers are more suited to work with offenders (*House of Commons*, 1975),
but the Home Office does not agree.

The supervisor's duty is to "advise, assist and befriend" the child
(s.14) and to this end the order can require the child to inform the
supervisor immediately of any change of address or employment, to

keep in touch with the supervisor as he directs, and to allow the supervisor to visit him at home (s.18(2)(*b*) and r. 28(2) and (3)). The Probation Rules 1984 require a probation officer to advise, assist and befriend the person supervised (r. 33); keep records on him (r. 31(1)) and report to the court if so requested; and to apply for discharge or variation if appropriate (r. 39(3)). There are no similar rules about the conduct of supervision orders (made in criminal proceedings) by local authority social workers, although the same result may be achieved by administrative instructions within the authority.

The court may also order the child to live with a named individual who agrees to this (s.12(1)), but a care order is generally a preferable method of removing the child from home. More important are the court's powers to authorise intermediate treatment. This is intended to make a more positive contribution towards widening the child's horizons and bringing him into contact with a different environment, interests and experiences, which may be more beneficial to him than a life of crime.

In true therapeutic spirit the court may simply decide whether this should be a possibility, and fix the maximum duration; then the supervisor can decide whether, in what way and for how long to make use of that possibility (s.12(2)). He may require the client from time to time to do all or any of the following: to live at a specified place or places for a specified period or periods; to present himself to a specified person or persons at a place or places for a specified period or periods; or to participate in specified activities on a specified day or days. The total time required cannot be more than 90 days or a shorter period laid down by the court; days on which the supervisor's instructions have been disobeyed are ignored (s.12(3)). There is no statutory form for giving instructions, although the Home Office (1970) has recommended writing them down, to avoid any later doubts and arguments.

The original idea was to avoid the impression that the court was ordering the child to do anything. It was hoped that the supervisor would be able to persuade the child that a particular activity was a good idea, as indeed most of them are; examples are outward bound centres, summer camps, sporting activities, scouting, handicrafts, evening classes, youth clubs, voluntary social service and community work. Most of these activities are suitable only for genuine volunteers. The D.H.S.S (1977) recommends that the whole family should be involved and that schemes should cater not only for children under statutory supervision but also for other children under the general power to provide help which will reduce the need to bring them before the court or take them into care. This may also

help to reduce resentment in the families of children who have not
committed offences; they may be equally unable to give the children
all the opportunities for exciting activities that they would wish.
However, although supervisors may be reluctant to emphasise the
point, children under supervision orders are legally required to participate, and supervisors should keep records of what has been
required and performed and of their clients' progress.

On the other hand, the court may now impose its own requirements on the child. These may be "positive," requiring him to do
any of the things a supervisor may be authorised to require
(s.12(3C)(*a*); under Criminal Justice Bill 1987 to become
s.12A(3)(*a*)), or "negative," requiring him *not* to participate in
specified activities (such as going to football matches) on a particular day or days or throughout all or part of the order (s.12(3C)(*c*); to
be s.12A(3)(*c*)). The total number of days in the former case cannot
exceed 90 (s.12(3E); to be s.12A(4)). The court may also impose a
curfew or "night restriction" order (s.12(3C)(*b*); to be s.12A(3)(*b*)).
This requires the child to stay at a particular place or places, which
must include his home, for up to 10 hours between 6.00 p.m. and
6.00 a.m., though he can leave if accompanied by his parent or
guardian. The curfew cannot be imposed for more than 30 nights or
more than three months from the date of the order (s.12(3H) to
(3N); to be s.12A(7) to (12)). None of these requirements can be
imposed without the consent of the parent or guardian of a child
under 14 or of a young person himself; the supervisor must be consulted about their feasibility; and the court must think them necessary to secure good conduct or prevent more offending (s.12(3F); to
be s.12A(5)). Anything requiring co-operation from another person
needs that person's consent as well (s.12(3G); to be s.12A(6)). The
Criminal Justice Bill 1987, would also have allowed the court to
require an offender of school age to comply with the arrangements
made by his parents for his education; his consent would not be
needed, but the approval of the L.E.A. to the arrangements would
(1969 Act, proposed new s.12C).

Last, there is power to require psychiatric treatment. The court
must have evidence from an approved specialist in mental disorder
that the child's mental condition is "such as requires and may be
susceptible to medical treatment" but is not such as to warrant a
hospital order. It may then require him for a specified period to sub-
mit to in-patient treatment at any hospital other than a special hospital, or out-patient treatment at any specified place, or any
treatment by or under the direction of a specified doctor (s.12(4); to
be s.12B(1)). The requirement cannot be made without the consent
of a child who has reached 14 and cannot in any event last beyond

the age of 18 (s.12(5); to be s.12B(2)). It cannot be inserted into an existing order which has lasted for more than three months (s.15(1)) or without the consent of a child who has reached 14 (s.16(7)). If a doctor in charge thinks that a change should be made in an existing requirement, he must report to the supervisor, who must refer it to the court, which can then cancel or vary the requirement (s.15(5)).

Before the child reaches 18, the court may add, vary or discharge any requirement which was or could have been made at the outset, apart from a curfew or pyschiatric treatment; it may also discharge the order or substitute a care order (s.15(1)). This used to be the only sanction for under-17-year-olds who failed to comply with an order. Now the court may impose a fine of up to £100 or an attendance centre order (s.15(2A) and (4)). Those aged 17 or more may also be re-sentenced for the original offence (s.15(2) and (4)); under the Criminal Justice Bill 1987, the same would apply to those who disobey the court's order to take part in activities (under the new-s.12A(3)(a)) having been told (under new s.12D) that it was imposed instead of a custodial penalty (new s.15(4A)).

In criminal proceedings, supervision orders last for three years or a shorter specified period and need not expire when the child reaches 18 (s.17(a)), although no new requirement for intermediate treatment may be made after the child reaches 18. If he is under 18, either party may apply for discharge, but a care order may then be substituted (s.15(1)); and if he is 17 or over, the duration of the order may be shortened or even extended if a shorter period than three years was originally specified (s.15(2) and (3)(a)). If an application for discharge is refused, no-one may apply again within three months without the court's consent (s.16(9)).

(f) *Attendance centre order*

This can be imposed for any offence punishable in the case of an adult by imprisonment, for fine default, and for breach of a supervision order (Criminal Justice Act 1982, ss.17 to 19). Unless there are special circumstances it cannot be imposed on an offender who has already suffered a more serious deprivation of liberty (this does not include a care order). The normal length is 12 hours, unless this would be too much for a child under 14 or too little for an older one. The maximum is 24 hours for anyone under 17. Attendance centres open on Saturdays, senior centres (over 16s) usually for three hours, juniors for two. There are 127 of them, most for boys of 10 to 16, but there are seven for girls and 13 mixed.

The object is to interfere with football matches but not with school or work. Centres are provided by the Home Office, usually by arrangement with local police but sometimes with social services or education authorities. Schools and similar buildings are used. The regime includes physical training, "disciplinary tasks," craftwork and lectures. Registers are kept and the attenders must be orderly and obedient (Attendance Centre Rules 1958). Disobedience or absence may result in return to court to be dealt with again for the original misdeed. But orders may also be discharged; and if made for default in payment, they lapse automatically if payment is made, *pro rata* for part payment.

The Home Office considers that centres have three aims: to vindicate the law by loss of leisure; to bring the offender under the influence of representatives of state authority; and to teach the more constructive use of leisure. The child may perceive more of the first two than the last, but will appreciate the defined and limited nature of an order which has all the hallmarks of traditional punishment. As orders can only be made if a place in a reasonably accessible centre is available, facilities are being expanded for a treatment which is apparently popular with almost everyone.

(g) *Care order*

This again may only be imposed for an offence punishable with imprisonment in an adult (1969 Act, s.7(7)(*a*)); the child must be in need of care or control which he is unlikely to receive otherwise and the offence must be serious enough to warrant what is not intended as a punishment but is nevertheless a serious interference in his life (s.7(7A)). It is virtually the only quasi-custodial disposal available for children under 14.

The order lasts until an offender reaches 18, unless he was already 16 when it was made, in which case it lasts until he is 19 (s.20(3)). The local authority may apply for an order which would normally lapse at 18 to be extended to 19, on the ground that the child is in a community home or youth treatment centre and should be kept there for his own or the public's good because of his mental condition or behaviour (s.21(1)). The order may be discharged at any time on the application either of the authority or of the child (s.21(2) or of his parents (s.70(2)), and if the child is under 18, it may be replaced with a supervision order; but this should not be done if the child is in need of care or control, unless the court is satisfied that he will receive it, whether under a supervision order or otherwise (s.21(2A)). An unsuccessful application for discharge cannot be repeated in under three months without the court's consent (s.21(3)(*b*)). The effect of an order is to transfer parental powers and duties to the local authority. The responsibilities of the local authority are dealt with in Chapter 9.

As a disposal made in criminal cases, the care order has two controversial characteristics which arise from its therapeutic aims. It may go on for a very long time indeed, usually for as long as the social workers think it necessary, and the placement of the child during that time is entirely in their discretion. Hence it could be attacked from all sides: by magistrates who were sorry that they no longer had power to insist on a definite period of detention in a secure home; by traditional libertarians who disliked the power to decide upon custodial treatment by bureaucratic machinery without due process of law; by more radical theorists who found the notion that care orders can cure either the child or his family of their pathology even more sinister than the old retributive principle; by those retributionists who felt that a serious offence should receive a commensurate mark of society's disapproval; and by the children themselves, who could see only an indefinite period away from home in prospect, whatever might actually happen.

The order could still be defended if there were evidence that the children's needs were being individually and properly assessed and suitable treatment then devised, but such evidence is hard to find. Significantly, for Northern Ireland it has been recommended that custodial measures should always be related in length to the gravity of the offence, even if they also aim to treat the child (*Black*, 1979). In England, however, the Government was worried that the courts' lack of confidence in both care and supervision orders might help to explain the rise in their use of sterner measures. Thus if a child who is in care as a result of a criminal offence commits a further imprisonable offence, the court may now prohibit the local authority from sending him "home on trial" altogether, or specify the person to whom he may go, for up to six months (s.20A). Such orders are rare; there has still been a considerable fall in the use of care orders; numbers more than halved between 1982 and 1984/85, when they accounted for only 4·2 per cent. of disposals of children under 14 for indictable offences and 1·9 per cent. of young persons' (*Home Office*, 1986a).

(h) *Hospital and guardianship orders*

These may only be imposed for imprisonable offences (Mental Health Act 1983, s.37). The child must be suffering from mental illness, psychopathic disorder, or significant or severe mental impairment. For a hospital order, psychopathic disorder and significant impairment must be "treatable." For guardianship, the child must be 16. Either may be combined with a care order, but not with a fine, supervision, detention or custody (s.37(8)).

Both last initially for six months but may be renewed by the medical authorities for another six months and then for 12 months at a time. They may therefore last indefinitely, subject to review by a Mental Health Review Tribunal. However, under a care order the authority will usually be able to "volunteer" a child for treatment, at least if he is under 16, or do anything which a Mental Health Act guardian could do. These orders are therefore hardly ever imposed upon juveniles.

(i) *Community service order*

These have now become available for 16-year-olds found guilty of imprisonable offences. The order is for between 40 and 120 hours of unpaid work for the community (Powers of Criminal Courts Act 1973, s.14), normally to be completed within 12 months of the order. Work is organised by the probation service. If the offender fails to report for work as required, or to do it satisfactorily, he may be fined or dealt with again for the original offence. (s.16). Also, the order may be revoked and a different one substituted if his circumstances change or he commits a further offence (s.17). This must be explained to him at the outset and his consent obtained.

Community Service is definitely intended as a punishment, although it is more constructive and decidedly cheaper than the custodial alternatives. At its best, it has been remarkably successful, despite the risk that both courts and offenders will regard it as a soft option. It is now imposed in a higher proportion of eligible cases than is a care order.

(j) *Detention centre and youth custody orders*

These can only be imposed where nothing else will do, because the offender has not responded to other measures, or the public require protection, or the offence is so serious that a non-custodial penalty cannot be justified (Criminal Justice Act 1982, s.1(4)). The last is a pure "tariff" principle; for older offenders, there are well-developed guide-lines as to what requires immediate custody (such as unprovoked street violence or domestic burglaries at night) and these may be applied by adult and even juvenile courts to these older juveniles. The court must have a social enquiry report unless it thinks this unnecessary (s.2(2) and (3)) and must explain its reasons for thinking that nothing else will do (s.2(4)).

Detention centre orders may be imposed for imprisonable offences upon boys of 14 to 20 (s.4). The order must be for at least 21 days and not more than four months, but up to a third may be remitted for good behaviour and time spent in custody before trial or disposal is deducted. It is intended as a "short, sharp shock" and so can only be imposed upon those who have already served youth custody if there are special circumstances (s.4(5)(*b*) and (6)). The shock is now sharper, with "basic and demanding work," minimal association and privileges (*Home Office*, 1985b); it should not be imposed upon those whose physical or mental condition makes it unsuitable (s.4(5)(*a*)).

Youth custody may be imposed upon boys or girls of 15 to 20 for imprisonable offences meriting more than four months' detention (s.6). The maximum is the maximum for the offence, but for offenders under 17 it cannot be more than 12 months in all. Magistrates cannot impose more than six months for a single offence, but may commit the offender to the Crown Court for this purpose. The minimum is normally four months, but custody may by used for boys who are not fit enough for detention, in which case the minimum is 21 days. The usual rules as to remission and time spent in custody on remand apply. Furthermore, if the order is for nine months or more, the offender is eligible for parole after six. Youth custody is a determinate replacement for borstal training (and imprisonment for 17 to 20-year-olds). It should be more constructive than many prisons, but courts should not use it to ensure that the offender receives training (*Home Office*, 1983).

On release from either detention or custody, the offender is subject to supervision, normally for three months or the remainder of his term (s.15). This is seen as an integral part of the sentence and he may be fined or given up to 30 days' detention or custody if he breaks its requirements.

Neither sentence has been particularly successful in deterring the individual concerned, as reconviction rates are high, although of course they may have deterred others. Unlike imprisonment for adults, neither can be suspended and some think that this should be possible (see *Home Office*, 1986b). Yet if they are to be regarded as genuinely last resorts, and not as junior imprisonment, it may be necessary to single them out in this way. They account for a higher proportion of eligible offenders than do care orders, and in the higher courts they seem to be used in just the same way as imprisonment for adults.

(k) *Long detention*

A child or young person who is found guilty in the Crown Court of an offence for which an adult could be sentenced to 14 or more years in prison (life is more) may be ordered to be detained subject to the directions of the Secretary of State for a fixed period of no longer than the maximum term of imprisonment for the offence (1933 Act, s.53(2)). Only young persons of 14 or more may be committed for trial in the Crown Court simply so that this will be possible; thus unless a child under 14 can be committed there for some other reason, this power will not apply and the most which can be ordered, however serious the offence, is local authority care. A juvenile found guilty of murder must be ordered to be detained during Her Majesty's Pleasure (1933 Act, s.53(1)). The effect is much the same as an order for life detention.

Long detention is only suitable if nothing else will do. It should not be used to get round the restriction on the length of youth custody (*R. v. Horrocks* [1986] Crim. L.R. 412). Two years should usually be the minimum, because otherwise youth custody would do (*R. v. Dewberry and Stone* [1985] Crim. L.R. 804). The usual "tariff" principle may apply, although the period should, if anything, be shorter than for an adult and the court should not take account of the Home Secretary's power to order an earlier release (*R. v. Burrowes* [1985] Crim. L.R. 606), but should bear in mind that the rules about remission and time spent on remand do not apply (see generally *R. v. Fairhurst* [1986] 1 W.L.R. 1374).

The Home Secretary decides where he shall be held; until he is 19, this might be in a youth treatment centre or community home (1969 Act, s.30); otherwise he may go to a youth custody centre or prison. He may be released on licence at any time if this is recommended by the Parole Board (for life detainees, after consultation with the Lord Chief Justice and, if possible, the trial judge) (Criminal Justice Act 1967, s.61); a released detainee remains subject to recall for the whole of the remainder of the term ordered (1967 Act, ss.61 and 62). Otherwise there is no supervision after release.

Now that older juveniles are increasingly subject to similar treatment to that given to 17-to-20-year-olds, these orders could well be brought into line with other custodial penalties. The original aim in 1969 that social services departments would take responsibility for handling most juvenile offenders upon welfare principles seems largely to have disappeared (but *cf. Tutt* 1987).

5 Child Abuse

The law has known for a long time that people are capable of treating children badly, although its notions of what is bad for children have varied with those of society at large. Its first response was simply to punish the wrongdoer, and the special vulnerability of children made it necessary to devise special offences to protect them. Its second response was to provide ways of removing them from the harmful environment. The third response was to try to improve that environment, to prevent the harm and preserve what was good. This came about before the recent wave of concern over "non-accidental injury," and choosing what to do in any individual case presents serious difficulties in principle and practice.

1. *Punishing the Abuser*

It is not possible here to discuss all the offences with which people who maltreat children may be charged, but some account of the one most frequently used may be helpful. The offence of "cruelty to a child" under section 1 of the Children and Young Persons Act 1933 recognises that the ordinary offences against the person are not enough. Children have positive needs and it is just as cruel to neglect these as it is to batter them. In punishing that neglect, therefore, the section imposes duties upon people who are responsible for children which they would not normally have towards adults.

The victim must be under 16 and the defendant must both be of or over 16 and have "custody, charge or care" of his victim. Each parent if they are or have been married to one another, the mother if they have not, a legal guardian, and anyone else legally liable to maintain the child is presumed to have "custody" (s.17); thus they cannot abdicate responsibility by desertion, private agreement, or even, it seems, a court order. A person has "charge" if it has been entrusted to him by a person with "custody." A person has "care" if he has actual possession or control. This could include an unmarried father, step-parent or cohabitant living with the family.

The defendant must be shown to have assaulted, ill-treated, neglected, abandoned or exposed his victim. These are not water-tight compartments and a particular case could be described in more than one way. Conduct of all five types must be "likely to cause unnecessary suffering or injury to health." This can define what is meant by "exposes," but it can limit the scope of "abandons" or "assaults" or even "neglects" if in fact no harm is likely. But the fact that likely harm has been prevented by the action of someone else is no defence (s.1(3)(a)). A parent or other person legally liable to maintain is deemed to have neglected in a manner likely to injure health if he has failed to provide his child with adequate food, clothing, medical aid or lodging, or being unable to do so, has failed to seek the assistance of the state (s.1(2)(a)). However, conduct of all five types must also be "wilful": a person accused of neglect, for example to provide necessary medical aid, must either have been aware of the risk to the child's health or simply not have cared about any possible danger. Stupidity or fecklessness may therefore assist the defence. The majority of the House of Lords in *R.* v. *Sheppard* [1981] A.C. 394 rejected the idea that neglect should be an offence of strict liability to be judged on the objective standard of the "reasonable parent." Criminal penalties cannot deter people who have genuinely not foreseen the harm which their neglect may bring (the objective standard does apply to procedures designed to protect the child, see below). However, a sincere religious belief that medical aid to prevent a known risk to the child's health is sinful is still no defence (*R.* v. *Senior* [1899] 1 Q.B. 283). It may still be difficult to define neglect to make "adequate" provision for a child's physical needs; battery may be easier to recognise and prove, even though lawful chastisement (see Chapter 1) is a defence (s.1(7)).

2. *Prevention*

Local authorities have a duty to provide families with "advice, guidance and assistance" (including assistance in kind or, exceptionally, even in cash) in order to reduce the need to bring care proceedings to protect the child (Child Care Act 1980, s.1(1)). Prevention and care in the home are clearly placed before removal. Voluntary supervision is in any event often thought better than an order. For pre-school children, it may be combined with day care (see Chapter 2) to reduce the stress on a troubled parent. For older children, voluntary intermediate treatment can be provided under this section. If it is thought necessary for the child to leave home, many social workers prefer to arrange a voluntary reception into care under the Child Care Act 1980, rather than to risk the hostile step of care proceedings. The temptation is obvious, particularly if only a short break seems needed, but there are disadvantages. The parent may feel under as much pressure to agree as does a juvenile offender faced with the choice between a caution and prosecution. The authority may find itself in difficulties if the parent wishes the child to come home too soon. Long-term planning in the child's best interests may be impeded. Little may be gained by pretending that what is essentially an authoritarian intervention is in fact quite voluntary.

3. *Care Proceedings*

Families, including the children in them, deserve some protection from officious interference from the state, however benevolent its intentions (*Goldstein, Freud and Solnit,* 1980). If a family is not prepared to accept help voluntarily, the authorities can only intervene after taking legal proceedings giving them the right to do so (*Havering London Borough Council* v. *S.* [1986] 1 F.L.R. 489, where the authority had acted "unconstitutionally" by removing a new-born baby without any order and had to pay the costs of doing so). This is usually done by care proceedings under section 1 of the Children and Young Persons Act 1969, but these have been made to serve three quite different purposes, to which they are not equally well-suited. They are now most often used to protect children who are the victims of physical or sexual abuse or neglect in their own homes. However, they were originally devised to deal with children who were seen more as "threats" than as "victims," because they were being troublesome in ways which were not criminal, but were thought to lead to a criminal career if allowed to continue unchecked (*Eekelaar, Dingwall and Murray,* 1982). This elision between the "deprived" and the "depraved" was taken a step further in the 1969 Act, under which the original plan was that care proceedings should largely take the place of criminal proceedings against juvenile offenders. This means that care proceedings are far more like criminal proceedings against the child than a private custody dispute between two adults who are offering the child alternative homes. One of the main aims of the recent Review of Child Care Law (R.C.C.L., 1985; D.H.S.S., 1987) was to change all that.

(i) Who is Involved?

Care proceedings can only be brought by the police, a local authority, or the N.S.P.C.C. (s.1(1)). The local authority for the area where the child lives or is found has a positive duty to make inquiries if it receives information suggesting that there are grounds for bringing proceedings, unless satisfied that inquiries are unnecessary (s.2(1)). Provided that the applicant can after investigation obtain enough evidence to prove the case, there is no need to disclose any informant's name in the care proceedings themselves, nor can they be made to disclose it in any other civil proceedings in which it might be relevant; the public interest in disclosure is outweighed by the public interest in protecting children from harm (*D.* v. *N.S.P.C.C.* [1978] A.C. 171). It is proposed to strengthen the local authority's duty, to ensure that it makes minimum inquiries to enable it to decide what action, if any, to take and to place greater emphasis on co-operation with other agencies (R.C.C.L., 1985; *Blom-Cooper*, 1985; D.H.S.S., 1987). The local authority already has a positive duty to bring proceedings if it thinks that the grounds exist, unless satisfied that this is neither in the child's nor the public interest (s.2(2)), but education and health authorities have some-times been worried about the reluctance of social services depart-ments to take action. Any applicant other than the local authority for the area where the child lives (or, if he does not seem to live any-where, where the facts arose) must first inform that authority (s.2(3)). If the proceedings succeed, of course, the social services authority will have to implement any order made. Hence, it is now proposed that only the N.S.P.C.C. (which rarely does so) and social services departments should be able to bring proceedings (R.C.C.L., 1985; D.H.S.S., 1987).

Like prosecutions, care proceedings are at present brought "against" a "child" under 14 or a "young person" of 14 but under 17 ("child" will here be used for both). They cannot be brought against a 16-year-old who is, or has been, married (s.1(5)(*c*)). The child must be physically brought before the court; the only exception is where he is under five and either his parent or guardian is there or the court is satisfied that the parent or guardian has been given reasonable notice (s.2(9)), but even then the court may insist on the child's appearance. The child, unless he is conducting his own case or the evidence relates to his own character or conduct, may be asked to leave, in his own interests, while some or all of the evidence is being given (Magistrates' Courts (Children and Young Persons) Rules 1970, Part II, r. 18(1)).

The child's presence may be secured by a simple summons, but if necessary a warrant can be obtained from a magistrate (s.2(4)). If, as is likely, a child arrested under such a warrant cannot be brought to court immediately, he may be taken to a "place of safety" and detained there for up to 72 hours. If he cannot be brought before a full court within that time, he must be brought before a magistrate, who may either make an interim order or release him (s.2(5)). In many cases, however, the child will already be subject to a place of safety order under section 28 (see below), which has become the common way of embarking upon care proceedings in abuse and neglect cases.

As the child is the respondent to the application, his parents or the other people with whom he may be living are not parties to the proceedings. However, notice of them must be given to any parent or guardian whose whereabouts are known; "guardian" has the wide meaning given it under the 1933 Act, of any person having "charge of or control over" the child (s.107(1)); in variation or discharge applications it includes the person who was such a "guardian" when the order was originally made (1969 Act, s.70(2) and r. 13(2)). Notice must also be given to any foster parent or other person with whom the child has had his home for not less than six weeks, ending not more than six months before the application in question (again provided the applicant knows his whereabouts); to the appropriate local authority if it is not the applicant; to the probation officer, if the child is 13 or more; and, if the application is for the discharge or variation of a supervision order, to the supervisor (r. 14).

The provision about foster parents was introduced following the case of Maria Colwell, who was killed by her step-father having been returned to her mother after six apparently happy years with her paternal uncle and aunt (see *Field-Fisher*, 1974). The rules give them a right to be notified and to make representations to the court, but no more (r. 14C). Under the Children and Young Persons (Amendment) Act 1986, grand-parents will be able to apply to be made full parties to care proceedings, but rules have yet to be made prescribing the circumstances in which the court may allow this (s.3(2); 1969 Act, s.32C).

The Maria Colwell case also focussed attention on the position of the child's own parents in the proceedings, which up till then had tended to be confused with that of the child. It is obviously right that they should be notified of the proceedings and that the court should be able to compel them to attend unless this would be unreasonable (1933 Act, s.34). It is not so obviously right that they should be allowed to act for their child in the proceedings, at least in child abuse cases, but the rules originally provided for them to do so in all but three situations: where the parent himself had asked for the proceedings to be brought because the child was beyond his control; where the child himself had requested otherwise; and where either the child or his parents was represented by a lawyer (r. 17). These rules were clearly based on the criminal model and quite unsuitable for allegations of parental abuse or neglect.

If there was no lawyer, the parent might be representing the very person with whom he was in conflict; but if there was a lawyer, the

position was equally unsatisfactory. He would often be approached
first by the parents, but if legal aid were granted, it was granted to
the child and not to them (*R.* v. *Worthing Justices, ex p. Stevenson* [1976]
2 All E.R. 194). The court, and not the parents, chose who the lawyer should be (*R.* v. *Northampton Justices, ex. p. McElkennon* (1976) 120
S.J. 677). The lawyer had then, if he knew his job, to attempt to represent the child. He might not take his instructions from the parents
if he thought they were in conflict with the interests of his client (*Re
S. (a minor) (care order; education)* [1978] Q.B. 120). The parents might
instruct their own lawyer, but they had to pay for him themselves as
no legal aid was available for them. Whether they had their own
lawyer or not, they were only entitled to take a very limited part in
the actual hearing. They might meet any allegations made against
them by calling or giving evidence and cross-examining the applicant's witnesses (r. 14B) How much more the court might allow
them to do without the agreement of all concerned is not clear.

This remains the basic position in all care proceedings. However,
if there appears to be any conflict of interest between parent and
child in the proceedings, including discharge applications and
appeals, the court may (and if an application to discharge a care or
supervision order is unopposed, must) order that the parent is not to
be treated as representing the child (1969 Act, s.32A). The court
must then appoint a guardian *ad litem* for the child, if this is in his
interests (or in unopposed discharge application unless it is not
necessary) (s.32B; r. 14A). The guardian must be chosen from
panels of experienced social workers set up by local authorities
under section 103 of the Children Act 1975 , but must be independent of the local authority involved in the proceedings. He is
expected to investigate all the circumstances, interview everyone he
thinks appropriate, and ask to inspect any relevant records (local
authorities may refuse access, but this is not recommended by the
D.H.S.S.). He should try to discover the child's own point of view,
and ensure that the court knows it. Unlike a lawyer, however, who is
committed to representing his client's wishes, the guardian is committed to his client's best interests, which may not be quite the same.
He must also make a written report to the court, which will be
covered by the same rules as a social inquiry report (see later). At
the end of the case, he should decide whether to appeal (r. 14A(6)
and (7)).

Unless a solicitor for the child has already been appointed, the
guardian must consult the court and instruct one, except where the
court rules against this. Guardian and solicitor should act together
in deciding how to conduct the case, but the solicitor should take his
instructions from the guardian unless he thinks that the child wishes

to instruct him and is old enough to do so (r. 14A(*b*), (*c*) and (*d*)). This decision can be difficult as the guardian will then have no legal representative.

If a separate representation order is made, the parent can no longer represent the child (r. 17) but he can then make representations to the court as well as meeting allegations against himself (r. 14B). More importantly, he may be granted legal aid on his own account. However, he still does not have all the rights of a full party to the proceedings; for example, he cannot appeal if the guardian *ad litem* chooses not to do so (*A.R.* v. *Avon County Council* [1985] Fam. 150); the Children and Young Persons (Amendment) Act 1986 (s.3(1); 1969 Act, s.32A(4A)) provides for parents to become full parties if a separate representation order is made, but is not yet in force. The Review of Child Care Law (1985) suggested that parents should always be full parties to the proceedings, as it was their parental status which was mainly at stake.

But why was further protection for the child thought necessary when that is that the applicant is trying to achieve? The local authority social workers are in a most ambiguous position. The whole form of care proceedings places their agency in opposition to both parents and child and then expects it to become a substitute parent. The individual worker will have played a part in the decision to proceed, will have to give evidence against the parents, and may even have to represent the authority as an advocate. He will then have to carry out the court's order to supervise or remove the child. On top of this he may be expected to provide an impartial home surroundings report as agent for the court. In doing all these things he is bound to reflect both the decisions of his superiors and his own professional loyalties and views. The family-centred, preventive approach to social work means that the parent is as much the client as is the child. The worker can only help to keep the family viable and prevent abuse while the child is in the home if he can form some relationship with the parents. He may find it personally difficult to "betray" them by removing what may be all they have, their child. That relationship cannot be lightly put at risk in the hostile climate of care proceedings, which could fail.

Hence, even if the proceedings become in essence a dispute between the applicant and the parents, the consequences for the child are so serious that he should always have someone who is committed to his interests alone (R.C.C.L., 1985; D.H.S.S., 1987). It may be more important for that to be a social worker who is able to assess his interests and what can be done to protect them, rather than a lawyer who would have to turn elsewhere for advice.

(ii) Interim Orders

Care proceedings are often preceded by a place of safety order under section 28 of the 1969 Act (see below). Before it expires, a court or a single magistrate an make an interim care order under section 28(6)). Interim orders can also be made if the child is brought before a court other than the one for the area where he lives (s.2(11)), by a court or single magistrate after a child has been arrested under a warrant to secure his attendance (s.2(4)), or by a court which is not yet in a position to decide what order, if any, ought to be made (s.2(10)). The child must always be present at he making of an interim order, unless he is prevented by illness or accident (s.22(1)); these are not excuses for absence from the proceedings proper and so may be reasons why an interim order is needed. However, the case may always be adjourned without an interim order instead.

An interim order places the child in the care of the local authority for a specified period of up to 28 days (but if made by a single magistrate, this dates from when the child was first in custody in connection with the proceedings) (s.20(1)). Either side may apply for it to be discharged earlier (s.21(2)); and the child may apply to the High Court for discharge, rather as a remanded child may apply for bail, but if this is refused the local authority cannot then send him "home on trial" (s.22(4)). If a boy of 15 or 16 is certified unruly (see p. 59), he can be sent to a remand centre instead of care (s.22(5)). Otherwise, the authority must bring the child before the court when or before the order expires (s.22(2)). The court may then either deal with the case or make a further interim order (s.22(3)).

There are no prescribed grounds for interim orders and courts vary in what they require (*Farmer and Parker*, 1985a). The court should not act as a rubber stamp or grant too many orders before hearing the case (see *R.* v. *Birmingham Juvenile Court, ex p. S. and P.* [1984] 1 W.L.R. 618). But contests seem rare and successive orders common in abuse and neglect cases. To encourage a tight but realistic time-table and avoid ritualistic successive hearings, it is now proposed that interim orders or adjournments should last up to eight weeks in all before the hearing, which should only be further postponed in exceptional circumstances (R.C.C.L., 1985; D.H.S.S., 1987).

(iii) The Grounds

The applicant must prove, first, that one or more of seven "primary conditions" relating to the child is fulfilled, and secondly, that the child is in need of care or control which he is unlikely to receive

unless the court makes an order (s.1(2)). Care proceedings are civil
rather than criminal; apart from the offence condition, the case may
be proved on the balance of probabilities rather than beyond reasonable doubt. The civil rules of evidence apply, so that both the child
and his parents may be compelled to give evidence, but the rule
against hearsay evidence still remains, although the High Court has
encouraged a flexible attitude towards it (see *Humberside County Council* v. *D.P.R.* [1977] 1 W.L.R. 1251).

The seven primary conditions are:

(a) The child's proper development is being avoidably prevented or neglected, or his health is being avoidably impaired or
neglected, or he is being ill-treated.

This can cover child abuse in its broadest sense, including
emotional or psychological deprivation (*F.* v. *Suffolk County Council*
(1981) 2 F.L.R. 208). It is wider than the criminal offence of
"cruelty to a child," because there is no need to prove any intention
or indeed which person was responsible for the neglect or ill-treatment shown. If a parent is also to be prosecuted, however, some
courts take the view that care proceedings should be adjourned until
the outcome is known, for a parent may well feel aggrieved if a care
order is made and he is later acquitted, while his conviction could be
useful evidence in the care proceedings. But as the questions for each
court are quite different, it may sometimes be proper to hear the care
proceedings first.

Almost anything can prevent a child's proper development or
impair his health, but this must be "avoidable." This must mean
avoidable by someone, even if not by the parents, for otherwise the
child of a totally inadequate parent would be left unprotected. But
there are some problems which it is difficult for anyone to avoid. A
subnormal mother caring in unsuitable accommodation for two tiny
children with fragile bones may find it well-nigh impossible to prevent fractures, but given that a foster home would be virtually unob-
tainable, could a children's home do any better?

The condition is phrased in the present continuous tense. This
suggests that the applicant must prove a course of conduct which is
still going on or at least has persisted until just before action was
taken to protect the child (*M.* v. *Westminster City Council* [1985]
F.L.R. 325). A single incident some time ago may not be enough.
But if the child is still suffering the consequences, it does not matter
that they are the result of action taken in the past, such as hard
drugs taken by the mother during pregnancy (*Re D. (a minor)* [1986]
3 W.L.R. 1080). However, the condition cannot be invoked to prevent the discharge from voluntary care of a child whom the authority fears may suffer if he goes home (*Essex County Council* v. *T.L.R.*

and K.B.R. ((1978) 143 J.P. 309). It does not apply if nothing has yet happened to him.

(b) It is probable that condition (a) *will* be satisfied "having regard to the fact that the court or another court has found that [it] is or was satisfied in the case of a child or young person who is or was a member of the household to which [this child] belongs."

Other children in households where there has already been abuse may thus be protected before anything has happened to them. This is so even if the first child has died, so that no proceedings were ever taken in respect of him (*Surrey County Council* v. *S.* [1974] Q.B. 124). "Household" refers to people rather than places, so that it does not matter if the family has moved in the meantime (*R.* v. *Birmingham Juvenile Court, ex p. S. (a minor)* [1984] Fam. 93). There should however be a likelihood of harm to this child as well; some parents make one the scapegoat, leaving the others in no danger.

(bb) It is probable that condition (a) *will* be satisfied "having regard to the fact that a person who has been convicted of an offence mentioned in Schedule 1 of the Act of 1933," including someone discharged or placed on probation, "is, or may become, a member of the same household as the child."

The Schedule covers virtually every offence of a violent or sexual nature against a child; the child involved may have been quite outside this child's household. Risk to this child must still be shown.

(c) He is exposed to moral danger.

Moral danger need not be limited to sexual danger, for it could cover such things as "bad associations." It is in practice used in cases of sexual abuse in the home, or where older girls are indulging in premature and promiscuous heterosexual intercourse or boys in homosexual practices. In the second two cases, the children may perceive the intervention as punitive rather than protective; indeed, the effect of institutionalising teenage girls, particularly upon their chances of later leading an ordinary married life, has not always been happy (*Smart*, 1976). The condition raises a moral problem which is not so apparent in cases of physical abuse. Should we attempt to impose a moral code upon sections of the population who do not share it, particularly by action which can seem to punish a victim who has committed no crime?

In *Alhaji Mohamed* v. *Knott* [1969] 1 Q.B. 1, a 26-year-old Nigerian student came to this country with his 13-year-old Nigerian wife, to whom he was validly married under Nigerian Moslem law. He took her to be fitted with a contraceptive. The doctor thought she was very young and informed the local authority, which brought care proceedings. They succeeded in the juvenile court, but on appeal the High Court did not agree that marital relations between two people whose marriage was valid in their own country could place the girl in moral danger: " . . . it could only be said that she was in moral danger if one was considering somebody brought up in and living in, our way of life, and to hold that she is in moral danger . . . can only be arrived at . . . by ignoring the way of life in which she was brought up, and [her husband] was brought up" (Lord Parker). But why should this not apply equally to different standards of child-rearing?

(d) He is beyond the control of his parent or guardian.

This is the successor to a long line of powers to deal with refractory children, who could originally be brought to court by their own parents. Nowadays, this is impossible, but the parent may make a written request to the local authority for proceedings to be brought, and if the authority refuses or fails to do so within 28 days, the parent can apply to the juvenile court for an order directing it to do so (1963 Act, s.3). However, the condition is more likely to be invoked where children are troublesome but cannot be proved to have committed offences, perhaps because they are under the age of ten. They will not necessarily perceive the difference.

(e) He is of compulsory school age and is not receiving efficient full-time education suitable to his age, ability and aptitude and to any special educational needs he may have.

Proceedings under this condition may only be brought by the local education authority; the condition is automatically fulfilled if an attendance order has been broken, or a registered pupil is not attending regularly, or the child is with someone habitually wandering from place to place, unless the parent can show that the child is still being properly educated (see further in Chapter 1) (s.2(8)). Education cases are different in other ways: separate representation is rare, adjournments with the threat of later removal (the "Leeds" system) may be more common, and if a care order is made, the child may remain at home. The fact that a child is not going to school may also be highly relevant to proceedings under condition (a). It may be a symptom of abuse or neglect in the usual sense; or the result of the parents' opposition to the normal school system; or an aspect of the child's own troublesome behaviour.

(f) He is guilty of an offence, excluding homicide.

This is hardly ever used, because the much simpler alternative of prosecution is still available. But the Act does provide that children brought before the court in care proceedings should be no *worse* off than if they had been prosecuted (s.3): it cannot be used for children under 10, the *doli incapax* presumption applies between 10 and 14, and the stricter rules of evidence and burden of proof apply; the same offence cannot be used twice, whether in care or criminal pro-

ceedings. There is a separate right of appeal against a finding that
the condition is proved, even if no order is made. The court can also
order the payment of compensation, whether or not it makes any
other order; and if the child is 14 or over, it may bind him over for up
to a year to keep the peace or be of good behaviour, instead of making another order. Proceedings under this condition cannot be
brought by the N.S.P.C.C.

The care or control test. Once one of the primary conditions has been
proved, the court must still be persuaded that the child is in need of
care or control which he is unlikely to receive unless the court makes
an order. This is a separate requirement, designed to limit compulsory intervention to cases where it is clearly needed. Courts and
applicants should beware of assuming that it is automatically fulfilled once a primary condition has been shown. In *Re S. (a minor)*
(care order: education) [1978] Q.B. 120 a 12-year-old boy had been
deliberately kept away from school by his parents since leaving his
primary school, because they were opposed to comprehensive education. Primary condition (e) was clearly satisfied and the juvenile
court made a care order. He was placed in a small children's home
and sent to school. The Crown Court allowed his appeal, holding,
first, that the care or control test had not been satisfied and,
secondly, that even if it had, the court would not have made a care
order. It was clearly worried about the damage involved in uproot-
ing a happy and well-brought-up child from a good home and placing him in an institution with children from very different
backgrounds. However, the authority eventually succeeded in the
Court of Appeal. The Crown Court had applied too narrow a test by
suggesting that to be "in need of care" the boy had to be neglected in
his day-to-day physical or emotional needs. The Act defines "care"
to include "protection and guidance" (s.70(1)), and education,
which is needed for his intellectual and social development, can certainly come within it. Even if the home is otherwise extremely good,
the court should make a care order if this is the only way to secure it.
"Control" is defined to include discipline, but that was not a problem in this case.

The case illustrates, not only that the care or control test should
not be a formality, but also that even when the grounds are proved
the court has a discretion whether or not to make any order. The
defined grounds must first be proved. Thereafter the court must
have regard to the welfare of the child (1933 Act, s.44(1)), and it has
been said that at this point the child's welfare is the paramount consideration (*Re C. (a minor) (justices' decision: review)* (1979) 2 F.L.R.
62). If the only order possible will do the child more harm than
good, then in theory no order should be made. It is hard to know

how the court can decide this without being given at least some idea of how the authority intends to look after the child if a care order is made.

But when *should* the authorities be able to intervene compulsorily in family life? A main aim of the Review of Child Care Law (1985) was to provide a single set of grounds, and possibly also procedures, to replace the present complexities of care proceedings, resolutions under the Child Care Act, and committal to care in family proceedings. The call was for simplicity but without sacrifice to the protection given by the present criteria, not only to children but also to their families (*House of Commons*, 1984). The existing criteria focus on the present rather than the future and so cannot be used for children already in care or some others who are obviously at risk in their own homes. On the other hand, specific conditions, such as the so called "status offences" of "moral danger," "beyond control" or lack of education, not only blur the distinction between protection and punishment but can lead almost automatically to an order, even if putting the child in care is unlikely to be the most constructive way of dealing with the problem.

Leaving every case to be governed by the "first and paramount" consideration of the child's welfare would increase the risk, not only of subjective and inconsistent judgments, but also of children being removed or kept simply because the authorities might be able to do better than the parents could. It is proposed, therefore, that children should only be removed or kept if they are suffering harm, or are likely to do so; if the harm is the result or the likely result of inadequate standards of care from their family (or if the child is beyond control and so unable to benefit from that care); and if the order proposed is the most effective means of safeguarding and promoting his welfare in the future (R.C.C.L., 1985; D.H.S.S., 1987).

(iv) The Orders Available

Once the case is proved, the court must consider all the background information necessary to enable it to deal with the case in the child's "best interests" (r. 20). Now is therefore the time to consider the social inquiry and, if there is one, the guardian *ad litem's* report, which should not be used to help in proving the applicant's case. The rules relating to these reports are identical to those in criminal proceedings (see Chapter 4). Once again, the criminal model of separate "proof" and "disposal" stages does not make the task of applicant or court any easier. The court may choose between the following orders (s.1(3)):

(a) *Parental recognisances*

This is the same as the order which may be made in criminal proceedings; it is scarcely ever used and may well be abolished
(R.C.C.L., 1985).

(b) *A supervision order*

This is one of the two principal protective measures available; it
began virtually identical to the order which could be made against a
juvenile offender, but there are now several differences between
them.

The first is that a supervision order made in care proceedings or on
the discharge of a care order cannot last beyond the child's eight-
eenth birthday (s.17(*b*)). Secondly, although the order may include
requirements for residence with a named individual (s.12(1)), for
intermediate treatment at the discretion of the supervisor (s.12(2)
and (3)) or for psychiatric treatment (s.12(4)), none of the extra
requirements (see p. 70, above) introduced to encourage better
behaviour in offenders can be included. Thirdly, there are no sanctions for failing to co-operate apart from the substitution of a care
order. Lastly, as well as the usual requirements for the *child* to inform
his supervisor of any change of address or employment and to keep in
touch with the supervisor as required (including receiving visits at
home if asked), the order may require the child to be medically examined in accordance with arrangements made by the supervisor.

It is unfortunate that these requirements are technically
addressed to the child rather than to his parents. They probably
have no right in any event to object to a medical examination which
can do their child no harm. But as occupiers of the child's home, can
they not refuse to allow the supervisor in? If the supervisor becomes
seriously concerned, his short-term solution is to seek a warrant
under section 40 of the 1933 Act (see below); refusal to comply with
requirements, in an order obtained on conditions (a) to (c), for the
supervisor to visit or the child to be medically examined is now automatically good reason for such a warrant (1969 Act, s.14A). The
only long-term solution is to apply for the supervision order to be
replaced by a care order, which may do more harm than good and
could in any event have been made in the first place, even if it was
planned to leave the child at home. Thus some social workers feel
that an order is no more use than voluntary supervision and certainly not worth the damage caused by the proceedings to their relationship with the parents.

It is now proposed to replace the requirement to live with a
named individual by a general power to grant custody to non-

parents in care proceedings, provided either that the grounds have been proved or that they qualify for custodianship (R.C.C.L., 1985; D.H.S.S., 1987). It is also proposed to broaden the range of possible requirements in supervision orders, and to apply them to parents as well as to children; thus, for example, a parent might be required to take the child to a clinic or day centre so that the child could be treated or participate in the centre's activities. The hope is to turn supervision into a more attractive alternative to a care order, especially where it is planned to leave the child at home.

The order is at present quite unspecific about the supervisor's own duties. This is in stark contrast to the regulations on boarding-out (see Chapter 9), and some have criticised the law for providing such detailed protection for children who are placed with officially approved foster parents and so little for children who have been proved to be at some risk in their own homes (*Field-Fisher*, 1974). The Act gives power to the Secretary of State to make regulations about the conduct by local authorities of supervision orders made in care proceedings or on the discharge of a care order (s.11A), but none have yet been made.

(c) *A care order*

This is the principal means of removing a child from a damaging home. It used also to be the principal custodial treatment available for juvenile offenders. There are no differences in their legal effects, save that in non-criminal cases the court cannot later add a restriction on sending the child home on trial if he commits a further offence. The local authority's powers and responsibilities, for example over the choice of placement, ending parental contact, or locking the child up, are discussed in Chapter 9. In child abuse cases, the difficult question is always whether to plan for the child's eventual return home or to attempt to provide him with some alternative source of comfort, stability and security.

Care orders last until the child is 18 (or 19 if he was 16 when it was made), but the local authority, the child, or a parent "on his behalf" (s.70(2)) may apply for it to be discharged (s.21(2)). The order may be ended if "appropriate" and if the child is under 18, a supervision order may be substituted; but the court must not do this if the child is under 18 and still in need of care or control unless satisfied that he will receive it (s.21(2A)).

In the report on the Maria Colwell case, "it was put to us and we accept that there was a strong presumption that the magistrates would return a child to the parent once the parent's fitness was proved, unless it could clearly be shown not to be in the best interests of the child" *(Field-Fisher, 1974)*. Yet when parents seek to recover their children from other individuals (see Chapter 10), there is no presumption in their favour and the child's welfare is the paramount consideration. Any uncertainty about whether the court will consider the *child's* present needs, rather than his *parents'* present circumstances, could obviously make it more difficult for local authorities to make long-term plans for children removed from damaging homes *(Adcock and White*, 1980a).

In reality, however, the number of discharge applications is small in proportion to the number of orders; most are made by local authorities and even those by parents are rarely opposed; many relate to teenagers who are more likely to be offenders or truants than victims of abuse; and most are already "home on trial" *(Farmer and Parker*, 1985b). Children may remain at home on trial for long periods without anyone applying for the order to be discharged, even though the local authority has a duty to consider this at its statutory six-monthly reviews (s.27(4)). The spectre of uncertainty caused by parents' exercising their three-monthly right to apply for discharge may be much more apparent than real. The risk that the parents rather than the child become the focus of social work activity while the child is home on trial may be greater *(Blom-Cooper*, 1985). In any case, it seems right that once the authorities have intervened in a child's upbringing their continued right to do so should depend upon his present welfare rather than upon whether past conditions still hold good (R.C.C.L., 1985; D.H.S.S., 1987).

One factor hampering parents is that discharge is such an all-or-nothing event. Supervision is apparently rarely thought an acceptable half-way house, although it might be if strengthened; nor can the court order a phased return home to smooth the transition for the child. Hence the parents who apply precisely because access is being reduced in preparation for a permanent substitute home will be at the greatest disadvantage. Plans to enable them to challenge the reasonableness of access without having to ask for the child back straightaway may help with this (R.C.C.L., 1985; D.H.S.S., 1987), but ought not to stand in the way of permanence if this is right for the child.

(d) *A hospital order and* (e) *a guardianship order*

The requirements of section 37 of the Mental Health Act 1983 must also be met (see Chapter 4) and these orders have the same effect. In care proceedings a hospital order may be combined with a care order (s.1(4)). If so, the authority becomes the "nearest relative" and will be responsible for the child if he is discharged from hospital before 18 (or sometimes 19). Much the same result could be achieved by a care order, for the authority could then arrange informal admission to hospital, at least for an under 16-year-old (see Chapter 1) and subject to the limits on secure accommodation (see Chapter 9). But a hospital order may be renewed indefinitely, while a care order is bound to end some time.

(v) Appeals

The present structure of appeals in care proceedings clearly shows how they have been confused with criminal proceedings against the child. Appeals are heard by the Crown Court, which is mainly a court for the trial of serious adult crime. More seriously, it is only possible to appeal against the *making* of an order: the child may do so (s.2(12)); his parents may do so on his behalf (*B. and another* v. *Gloucestershire County Council* [1980] 2 All E.R. 746) unless there has been a separate representation order, in which case at present they cannot appeal at all (*A.-R.* v. *Avon County Council* [1985] Fam. 150) but will be able to do so once the Children and Young Persons (Amendment) Act 1986 is in force; the local authority may only appeal if it considers that a different authority should have been named because the child lives elsewhere (s.21(5)). There is no right of appeal against the *refusal* of an order. Again, it is only possible to appeal against the *dismissal* of an application to discharge a care or supervision order or against certain variations which are thought disadvantageous to the client (ss.16(5) and 21(4)). It is not possible to appeal against the *granting* of such a discharge. Either side may appeal to the High Court on a pure point of law and local authorities may take a "second bite at the cherry" through wardship (see below). It is proposed, however, to give all parties the same rights of appeal, to be heard in the Family Division of the High Court (R.C.C.L., 1985; D.H.S.S., 1987).

4. *Emergency Protection*

Social workers, health visitors and other professionals concerned with the welfare of children have no general power to enter other people's property without their consent, still less to force their way in or remove the children. Social workers have some powers to enter the homes of child-minders, foster parents and prospective adopters, but even then they may need a warrant to authorise forcible entry. However entry has been gained, it may also be necessary to obtain authority to remove the child to a place of safety for the time being.

(i) Entry Warrants

Under section 40 of the Children and Young Persons Act 1933, any person who is acting in the child's interests may apply to a single magistrate at any time or place. The applicant must show, on oath, reasonable grounds to suspect that a child or young person has been or is being assaulted, ill-treated or neglected in a manner likely to cause unnecessary suffering or injury to health, or that any of the offences listed in Schedule 1 of the Act has been or is being committed in respect of him. The magistrate may then issue a warrant authorising a *policeman* to enter *specified* premises, by force if need be, to search for the child, and if the suspicions are justified, to remove him to a place of safety. The officer may be authorised to arrest any offenders at the same time. The applicant is allowed to go too, unless the magistrate directs otherwise; the magistrate may also direct that a doctor may go with them.

The child may be kept in the place of safety for any specified period up to 28 days (1963 Act, s.23(1)). Thereafter he must be released or, if the grounds exist, received into care under the Child Care Act 1980; or he may be brought before a juvenile court, which may then make an interim order or release him (s.23(5)). It is the *local authority* which must bring him before the court (although he need not be physically present if he is under five or prevented by illness or accident, s.23(4)); the local authority must also pay for his accommodation in the place of safety, unless it is an N.H.S. hospital (Child Care Act 1980, s.73(2)); hence the occupier of the place of safety, if it is not the local authority, must tell the authority of his reception as soon as possible (1963 Act, s.23(3)). There is no statutory duty to tell the child or the parents anything. A place of safety is a community home which is either provided or controlled by a local authority, any police station, any hospital or surgery, or any other suitable place, the occupier of which is willing temporarily to receive the child (1933 Act, s.107(1)).

Various things are automatically reasonable cause for the suspicions required to get a warrant. These include refusal to allow the local authority to visit a privately fostered child or to inspect a private foster home (see Chapter 2); similar refusals in the case of children protected under the adoption legislation (see Chapter 11); and refusal to allow D.H.S.S. representatives to enter community homes, voluntary homes, places where children in care are accommodated, places where children are boarded-out by voluntary organisations, or places where privately fostered or "protected" children are living (Child Care Act 1980, ss.74 and 75). The presumption now applies to refusal to allow visiting or medical examination under a supervision order made on conditions (a) to (c) (1969 Act, s.14A), but not to refusal to allow visiting and removal by the local authority or voluntary organisation of a child boarded-out by them. In all cases, removal is only possible if the suspicions prove well-founded after entry has been gained.

(ii) Place of Safety Orders

Under section 28(1) of the Children and Young Persons Act 1969, any person (usually but not necessarily a social worker) may apply to a single magistrate at any time or place. The applicant does not have to *prove* anything and need not even swear an oath. He must simply satisfy the magistrate that he has reasonable cause to believe that any of primary conditions (a) to (e) in section 1(2) of the Act is satisfied; or that a court would find condition (b) satisfied; or that a child is about to be taken abroad as an entertainer without a licence. The magistrate may then give the *applicant* "authority to detain [the child] and take him to a place of safety," where he may be kept for 28 days or a shorter specified period. Although the section talks of detaining *and* taking, there is no reason to think that both must be necessary; an order should be obtainable even though the child is already in a place of safety, such as a hospital.

There is no need to tell the parents beforehand, but the detainer must, as soon as practicable afterwards, explain the reasons to the child and take such steps as are practicable to explain matters to his parent or guardian. There is no right of appeal against the order (except by asking the High Court to quash it for invalidity), nor is there any power to renew it. An application for an interim order (see above) may be made either to a court or a magistrate before it expires (s.28(6)). The court or magistrate could instead direct the child's immediate release, even though the place of safety order had not yet expired. It has therefore been held that a *parent* may apply for an interim order under this subsection, even though he hopes that the application will fail and the child be sent home (*R. v. Lincoln (Kesteven) County Justice, ex p. M.* [1976] Q.B. 957) but this should not normally be used as a disguised form of appeal against the order (*Nottinghamshire County Council v. Q.* [1982] Fam. 94).

Place of Safety Orders seem to have become the normal way of beginning care proceedings, at least in child abuse cases, and there is understandable concern that children can be removed and kept away from home for such a long time without any opportunity to challenge the order or test the evidence (*House of Commons*, 1984). On the other hand, children undoubtedly need emergency protection and the order may enable a crisis to be resolved without having to take the drastic step into full care proceedings. The proposal now is to limit orders to cases where there is a risk of damage to the child unless he is removed for a short period; this should be no more than eight days, extendable by a court for a further seven days if the authority is not ready to proceed; normally the authority should have decided whether or not to bring care proceedings before the original order expires (R.C.C.L., 1985; D.H.S.S., 1987). Coupled with the proposed limits on interim orders (see above), the aim is to cut down the delays which can be so damaging for the child and so prejudicial to his parents.

(iii) Police Detention

Section 28(2) of the Children and Young Persons Act 1969 allows a police officer to detain a child or young person without any order or warrant, if he has reasonable cause to believe that any of primary conditions (a) to (d) is satisfied; or that a court would find condition (b) satisfied; or that a vagrant is taking a school age child about with him and thus preventing the child's proper education. After detention, the child's case must be considered by a senior officer, who after enquiries may either release him or arrange for him to be kept in a place of safety (s.28(4)). The detention cannot last longer than eight days (s.28(5)). The child, and if practicable his parent or guardian, must be told of the reasons for it (s.28(3)) and of a special right to apply immediately to a magistrate for release (s.28(4) and (5)). If the child has to be detained longer before care proceedings can be started, an interim order under section 28(6) may be sought.

As the police are always available, the power is useful for picking up children who have been abandoned or have run away from home. Responsibility is quickly passed on to social services or back to the parents. It is therefore proposed to limit detention without an order to 72 hours; the grounds would be the same as is proposed for section 28(1) (R.C.C.L., 1985; D.H.S.S., 1987).

5. *Wardship*

Making the child a ward of the High Court has many advantages over the usual juvenile court procedures. It may be done by anyone who is personally or professionally concerned about the child's welfare. The child's parents will be full parties to the proceedings and may have legal aid, subject to the usual means test. Any other person or agency with an interest in the case may also be made a party or given a hearing. The child may be separately represented by the Official Solicitor or some other person as guardian *ad litem*. An independent welfare officer's report may also be obtained. If the child's custody or upbringing is in issue, the decision is governed by the "first and paramount consideration" of his welfare (Guardianship of Minors Act 1971, s.1; see Chapter 3). The hearing takes place before (usually) a High Court judge, who is not bound by rigid rules of procedure and evidence. Evidence is exchanged in affidavit form beforehand, followed by oral examination at the hearing. The hearsay rule will not apply if proper notice has been given. If the circumstances warrant it, the Official Solicitor's report may be kept confidential (*Official Solicitor* v. *K.* [1965] A.C. 201). The judge may, if he sees fit, interview the child in private.

A successful application places the child under the guardianship of the court, which will then decide what is best for him. The object may be to challenge a single aspect of the child's upbringing, such as the proposed sterilisation of a handicapped girl whose upbringing was otherwise excellent (*Re D (a minor) (wardship: sterilisation)* [1976] Fam. 185); or to save the life of a Down's syndrome baby whose parents would not agree to an operation (*Re B. (a minor) (wardship: medical treatment)* [1981] 1 W.L.R. 1421); or to decide the future of a child born as a result of a surrogacy arrangement (*Re C. (a minor) (wardship: surrogacy)* [1985] F.L.R. 846); or to control a particularly recalcitrant 17-year-old girl (*Re S.W. (a minor) (wardship : jurisdiction)* [1986] 1 F.L.R. 24); or to remove the child from home or to keep him in a foster home; or whatever the applicant thinks best. The court's powers have never been precisely defined by statute, but the Family Law Reform Act 1969 gives power, in "exceptional circumstances," to place the child under the supervision of a local social services authority or probation officer (s.7(4)) or to commit the child to care if it is impracticable or undesirable for him to be or continue in the care of either parent or any other individual (s.7(2)). The court may also grant "care and control" to a local authority as part of its inherent non-statutory powers (*Re C.B. (a minor)* [1981] 1 W.L.R. 379); this is often done on an interim basis, although the extent of the local authority's responsibilities is not very clear. The child becomes a ward of court the moment an application is made (but will cease to be one unless an appointment for a hearing is obtained within 21 days). Thereafter no important step may be taken without the court's leave, so that an interim order should be obtained before the child is moved, whether from or presumably to his parents (see *Havering London Borough Council* v. *S.* [1986] 1 F.L.R. 489). Nevertheless, the protection available can be swift and all-embracing.

Thus local authorities have been encouraged to use wardship as an alternative to care proceedings in cases where they are unsure of their chances of success; or where they have been unsuccessful in care proceedings but have no right of appeal (*Re C. (a minor) (justices' decision: review)* (1979) 2 F.L.R. 62; or where they are aggrieved by a juvenile court's decision to discharge a care order but again have no right of appeal (*Re D. (a minor) (justices' decision: review)* [1977] Fam. 158). The price they have to pay is the court's power to direct how they should carry out their responsibilities under the Child Care Act and the need to refer all important decisions to the court. In practice, the court does not interfere in day-to-day matters and the fact that a child is a ward of court should not prevent social workers from obtaining a place of safety order if this is necessary for the child's immediate protection (*Re B. (a minor)* (1979) 124 S.J. 81). It is most often used to decide whether a child should be placed with long term foster-parents, perhaps with a view to adoption, or to arrange for a phased attempt to reunite the family.

A simpler alternative to wardship where the child's parents are divorced is for the authority to seek leave to apply in the divorce proceedings for committal to care (see Chapter 3). Some authorities are now choosing to do this, particularly in sensitive cases such as sexual abuse which they would prefer to have dealt with by a judge. At present, the grounds and effects are the same as in wardship, except that important steps do not invariably have to be referred to the judge. It is proposed, however, to assimilate these committals to ordinary care orders, while leaving wardship as it is to deal with the truly exceptional case (R.C.C.L., 1985; *cf. Law Commission*, 1987b).

6. *What to do?*

The problems presented by this diversity of responses may be illustrated by the following example. A two-month-old baby is brought to the casualty department by his 17-year-old mother and 19-year-old father. He has bruises and minor scratches on his face. His mother says she noticed them when she got home from shopping having left the baby with his father. The father says the baby must have hurt himself on the rattle stretched across his cot. The bruises seem more consistent with a blow from an open hand. The baby is well-nourished and normally developed and his mother looks after him well in hospital. The father is unemployed, emotionally unstable, and has a minor criminal record. He is currently on probation. They live on supplementary benefit in a one-roomed flat, disowned by both sets of parents.

The first step in all cases of reasonable suspicion of non-accidental injury is to admit the child to hospital. If there is parental opposition, a place of safety order should be obtained. When suspicion is less firm than here, any professional concerned, such as a social worker or health visitor, should discuss with a senior colleague whether the risk of *not* arranging hospital admission is acceptable and whether a case conference should be called. The next step is to call a case conference. This should include the people with statutory responsibilities for the child, those concerned with services likely to be relevant, and those with helpful information about the child and his family. In this case, it may involve the hospital doctor and social worker, a senior social worker from the local authority, a field social worker with knowledge of the family, the father's probation officer, the health visitor, and the G.P. (but it is always difficult to get the G.P. there). For older children, teachers and the educational welfare officer should be there. More controversial is the presence of the police or a local authority solicitor.

The object of getting all these people together is to pool information and ideas, to make sure that nothing relevant is over-looked, to encourage collective decisions and to discourage inconsistent and ill-planned action (*Hallett and Stevenson*, 1980). But what is such a case conference to do?

Prosecution is still within the discretion of the police and other professions are sometimes reluctant to involve them, partly because of confidentiality and partly because they see prosecution as an inappropriate response (see *Maidment*, 1980). Much abuse is thought to be the result of environmental stresses or personal factors which make nonsense of a theory of punishment based on free will. Nevertheless, it is clearly necessary to retain the notion that child abuse is a crime, not only to deter the rational but also to define the limits of acceptable behaviour towards children. If it is a crime, if is often difficult to find justifications for treating it any differently from many other offences where deterrence may be just as unrealistic and mitigation just as strong. A humane and discriminating prosecution policy may however be justified in the interests of the victims themselves. This baby will not be helped if his parents are deterred from confessing their difficulties by a fear of punishment, nor if that punishment destroys the hope of maintaining a viable family unit. Many police forces accept this and are willing to be guided by the advice of a case conference, to which they in their turn have much useful information to offer.

The question of care proceedings is even more difficult. To take this baby away is the only sure means of preventing the injury happening again, for the mother cannot be forced to leave the father. Yet this will deprive him of the care of a good and loving mother, and no social worker can guarantee that the substitute care provided will be anything like as good. Even if it is good, the authority will have to choose between encouraging the mother to maintain contact, in the hope either that she will leave the father or that their circumstances will improve, or accepting that a baby removed as early as this should be given a normal chance in life by making plans for adoption. Even if it is accepted that good substitute parenting is better than bad natural parenting, how can one distinguish between the completely unsatisfactory home and the one which could function much better with adequate housing, day care, and social work support? And how ready are either social workers or the courts to put the interests of the child before those of the parents in quite such a dramatic way? Social workers cannot, and should not, be sure that the courts will support them if they seek to terminate access or free the child for adoption.

Indeed, the chances of success in any proceeding seem to be one of the most important factors governing the management of a case. It is not always easy to decide whether an injury is non-accidental, still less to prove it in court. If a lawyer attends the case conference, the others may resent his concern to collect and assess the evidence while they wish to concentrate on substantive issues. Yet unsuccessful proceedings can do more harm than good, both to access and to future work with the family. Social workers who are unsure of their evidence may be tempted to use voluntary measures irrespective of their suitability to the case (*Lawson*, 1980). It would be ironic if a parental admission meant that compulsory measures were *more* likely than if they kept silent.

There may be another reason for a lawyer's presence. Case conferences can also have an adjudicatory function, if they have to decide whether a child shall be placed on or taken off the register of those "at risk." These child protection registers are an invaluable resource and constitute no invasion of the parents' rights, so that there is no legal requirement to observe the rules of natural justice in making these decisions. But they will have serious implications for both child and parents and should obviously be taken as fairly as possible in the circumstances. In practice, the decisions of case conferences are usually more important than those of courts.

Part III
Anomalous "Parents"

6 Unmarried Parents

The proportion of live births registered as illegitimate rose steeply in the swinging sixties, fell off a little after the Abortion Act 1967, and then resumed a gentler climb. By 1985, it had reached one-fifth of the total. Many children are born into non-marital unions which prove at least as stable as many marriages. Among the reasons suggested for this are better contraceptive and abortion facilities, which make it more likely that the child is not unwelcome; fewer financial and social pressures upon the mother; diminishing stigma and disability for her child; and an increasing tendency either to postpone marriage or to reject it altogether in favour of cohabitation. At the age of 11, two in five of the illegitimate children in the National Child Development Study (all babies born in a single week in 1953) who had not been adopted by strangers were living with both natural parents (*Lambert and Streather*, 1980).

The institution of marriage may well have been devised by early societies in order to establish a relationship between man and child (*Mair*, 1971). A man may derive spiritual, emotional and material advantages from having children, but whereas motherhood might easily be proved, fatherhood might not. A formal ceremony between man and woman, after which it is assumed that any children she may have are his, was the simplest method of establishing a link. It also enabled him to limit his relationships to the offspring of a suitable selected mate. A legal system which wishes to facilitate the orderly devolution of property and status within patrilineal families therefore places great emphasis on the concept of legitimacy. A legal system which is no longer so concerned about material provision for future generations of the few, and is far more concerned about the welfare of all young children, is likely to find the concept more and more distasteful. Abolishing it for the sake of the child, however, presents a problem. The main distinction is that a mother's husband enjoys an automatic legal relationship with her children, whereas any other would-be father not only has some difficulty in establishing the link, but also finds that it has only limited legal consequences; and so, of course, does the child. Abolishing the distinction by conferring automatic parental status on all fathers (as has happened in some countries) is not necessarily in the best interests of the

children, most of whom are still brought up by their mothers alone
(*One Parent Families*, 1980; *cf. Law Commission*, 1979).

Under the Family Law Reform Act 1987, therefore, it is intended
to remove as many as possible of the differences which affect the
child's legal rights, but not to give the father automatic powers over
his upbringing. In future legislation and legal documents, there will
be no need to make special mention of children of unmarried
parents, or relationships traced through them, because everyone will
be included in such terms as "child," "parent" or "relative," unless
a contrary intention appears (s.1).

One object of this is to avoid having to use any adjectives such
as "illegitimate" or "non-marital" when describing the child.
Future distinctions should refer to whether or not the parents were
married to one another at the relevant time, and not to the child at
all. Once this happens, "it would be a matter for argument
whether it was any longer justifiable to refer to a legal status of
illegitimacy . . . " (*Scottish Law Commission*, 1984). But because
there have been legal differences in the past and will continue to
be a few in the future, it is still necessary to put some people in
one category and some in another.

1. *Sheep or Goat?*

Strictly speaking, illegitimacy was never a legal status at all: illegitimate children were those to whom the law denied the status of legitimacy. A child is legitimate at common law if his father and mother
were married to one another either at the time of his conception or at
the time of his birth (or probably at any time in between). The proportion of non-marital conceptions is far higher than the proportion
of non-marital births, although the trend is for fewer and fewer
couples to see a hasty marriage as the best solution. By "mother"
and "father" the law here means the woman and man genetically
responsible for the child's conception. However, the 1987 Act provides that a child born as a result of artificial insemination from a
donor other than the mother's husband should be treated as the husband's child unless it is proved in court that he did not consent to
the insemination (s.27). At present such couples should adopt, but
many may be tempted to avoid the issue by misinforming the registrar (which is a criminal offence) and relying on the presumption of
legitimacy. Even so, to "deem" the husband to be the father seems
to run counter to the general trend for children to know their origins.
It will also produce a peculiar result if a surrogate mother has her
husband's consent to conceive by A.I.D. and bear a child for

another couple (see *Re C. (a minor) (wardship: surrogacy)* [1985] F.L.R. 846). It is much more necessary to resolve whether the genetic or the "carrying" mother is the legal parent of a child born of ovum donation or embryo transfer (see *Warnock*, 1984).

The rules apply where the marriage is voidable (for example, because of inability or wilful refusal to consummate it) (Matrimonial Causes Act 1973, s.16). Logically they should not apply if the parents' marriage is wholly void (for example because one party was already married or was under 16); but if at the time of the act of intercourse or insemination leading to the conception, or at the time of the marriage if this was later, *either or both* of the parents *reasonably* believed that their marriage was valid, the child is legitimate (Legitimacy Act 1976, s.1; the father must have been domiciled in England and Wales at the date of birth); mistakes of law, for example as to the recognition of a foreign divorce decree, are included (1987 Act, s.28). There will obviously be problems for a person who is trying to establish his legitimacy on the basis of what his parents thought before he was born, particularly as this may well be for succession purposes after the parent in question has died. The section only applies to dispositions of property made after it was first introduced in 1959, but it *can* apply to succession to peerages and other titles, whereas legitimation cannot.

The common law insisted that the marriage take place before the birth: hence the need to get out the shot-gun. However, since 1926 a child has been regarded as legitimated if his parents marry after his birth, and since 1959 this has been so even though his parents could not have married when he was born because one was at the time still married to someone else (such cases were originally excluded because it was thought that to allow them would encourage adultery). The parents should then re-register the birth as though the child had been born legitimate, and unless the husband was originally registered as the father, some verification of his paternity will be required (Legitimacy Act 1976, ss.2 and 9). If the child has previously been adopted by his mother or father alone, he can still be legitimated and they may apply for the adoption order to be revoked (Adoption Act 1976, s.52).

On legitimation, the child acquires the same rights as a legitimate child, apart from those to peerages and other titles. For dispositions of property made before January 1, 1976, however, these rights only apply if the legitimation took place *before* the disposition; for later dispositions it does not matter when the legitimation took place, except that if the disposition itself depends upon the date of birth, then he is taken to have been born at the date of his legitimation rather than his actual birth, unless he was already entitled to the property as an illegitimate child (Legitimacy Act 1976, ss.5, 6 and Sched. 1).

It has been estimated that about 20 per cent. of the illegitimate children born between 1951 and 1968 will be legitimated by their parents' marriage (*Leete*, 1978). One of the main arguments advanced for allowing an "innocent" spouse to be divorced after five years of separation was the supposed existence of many children who might then be legitimated. But there seems to have been no dramatic increase in legitimations since this was introduced in 1971, and indeed the rate of legitimation now appears to be slipping down, to one in six of more recent birth cohorts. This could indicate that fewer children are being born into "stable illicit unions," but more probably that fewer couples are choosing to marry even if they are free to do so.

2. *Proving Parentage*

A child benefits from his parents' marriage in two ways. From the moment of his birth the identity of his father is known and he can enjoy an automatic legal relationship, involving both rights and responsibilities, with both his parents. A child born of unmarried parents will find it more difficult to establish the relationship as a fact, and if this is done it will have more limited consequences for them both, but particularly for the father. Every child born to a married woman is assumed to be her husband's child, until the contrary is shown. This applies even though the child must have been conceived before the marriage, or where the birth takes place within the normal period of gestation after the marriage has ended by death or divorce. Thus the presumptions can conflict if a woman who was widowed or divorced less than nine months before the birth has remarried while pregnant. A court would choose the most likely father (*Re Overbury* [1955] Ch. 122), but perhaps until then we should assume that she did *not* commit adultery? The presumption does not apply if at the time of conception the husband and wife were living apart under a decree of judicial separation (or under the now-discontinued magistrates' "non-cohabitation clause"), but these are rare. Mothers who are informally separated may well find that the court applies the presumption if they try to have the child adopted without telling their absent husbands.

The presumption has always been rebuttable, but the common law required very strong evidence before it would expose either the child or his mother to the horrible disabilities of "bastardy" or adultery. Nowadays the consequences of both are much less severe, and the Family Law Reform Act 1969 provides that the presumption may be rebutted by evidence which shows that it is "more probable than not" that the husband is not the father (s.26). Such evidence is of two types. One seeks to show that the husband and wife did not or could not have intercourse at the relevant time (and in the past the main difficulty was to identify the relevant time). The other seeks to show that even if they may have had intercourse, the child was not the product of it. The usual way of doing this is by blood tests. These now have up to a 99 per cent. chance of *excluding* a man from paternity. If he is not excluded, the fact that he is one in, say, 100,000 men who could be the father is not conclusive, but is certainly relevant alongside the other evidence that he is. Recently developed D.N.A. "fingerprinting", however, can now provide conclusive evidence (see *Webb*, 1986).

It is always possible for the parties and the person with parental rights over a young child to agree that blood tests shall be taken. Since 1969, a court has had power to direct that blood samples be taken from the child and all parties, in order to exclude a man from paternity; but under the 1987 Act it may direct that bodily samples be taken and scientific tests made simply to determine parentage (1969 Act, s.20; see 1987 Act, s.23). The court merely directs: the person concerned, or if he is a child under 16 (or is mentally incapable) the person who has care and control of him, may still object (1969 Act, s.21). If so, however, the court may draw such inferences from this as seem proper (s.23) and no doubt these will usually be unfavourable. Anyone who is seeking a remedy from a court in reliance on the presumption of legitimacy may be refused that remedy if he refuses to undergo a blood test, even though there is no other evidence to rebut the presumption.

The court has a discretion whether or not to direct a blood test, and may be tempted to refuse where the only result would be to "bastardise" a child who has no alternative father waiting to claim relationship. But the House of Lords has suggested that this is a matter of obtaining and disclosing evidence, rather than a matter of the child's upbringing, so that the welfare of the child is not necessarily the first and paramount consideration; in general it is now thought better that the truth be known (*S.* v. *S.*; *W.* v. *Official Solicitor* [1972] A.C. 24).

Where the parents are not married to one another, no presumptions apply. A finding of paternity in affiliation proceedings is evidence in any later civil proceedings and this is to be extended to findings in any proceedings in which it is necessary to establish that a person is the father before making orders about custody, access, property or maintenance (Civil Evidence Act 1968, s.12; see 1987

Act, s.29). The only other method of "official" recognition is
through registering the child's birth. It is possible to register, or re-
register, the birth so as to show the father's name in three circumstances: first, at the joint request of mother and father; second, at the
mother's request, if she declares he is the father and produces a
statutory declaration from him that this is so (following the 1987
Act, the father may do the same in reverse); and third, at the
mother's request, on production of an order naming him, and, if the
child is 16 or over, the child's written consent (following the 1987
Act, the range of orders is extended and the father may do the
same). (Births and Deaths Registration Act 1953, s.10; 1987 Act,
ss.24 and 25). Thus it will be possible to register the father without
the mother's co-operation, but only if there is a court order based on
a finding of his parentange. At present the father is named in
roughly 65 per cent. of registrations.

At present, the High Court has power to grant declarations of
legitimacy and legitimation which bind the whole world. Usually, of
course, this depends upon proving parentage, but there is no equivalent procedure for children of unmarried parents. Following the
1987 Act, however, anyone will be able to apply for a similar deter-
mination, not only as to his father's identity but also as to his
mother's (Family Law Act 1986, s.56; see 1987 Act s.22).

3. *Parental Rights and Duties*

The common law regarded the child born outside the legally
approved family unit as "nobody's child." Thus he scarcely enjoyed
a legal relationship with his mother, let alone his father. However,
case law gradually accorded her similar rights of custody and
upbringing to those of the father of a legitimate child. This is now
confirmed by statute, which provides that unless and until a court
order or local authority resolution deprives her, the mother has the
parental rights and duties exclusively (Children Act 1975, s.85(7)).
Whatever the family situation, the mother is the one with the right
to choose a name for her baby, to take him home from hospital (even
if he has been born as a result of a surrogacy arrangement; see *A*. v.
C. [1985] F.L.R. 445; but see the Surrogacy Arrangements Act 1985
in Chapter 11), to decide what discipline or medical treatment he
should be given, what education and religious upbringing he should
have, whether he may go abroad, and later on whether he may
marry before the age of 18; she alone can appoint a guardian for him
in her will. The father, even if he is living with them, has no rights in
these matters, although as a person with actual custody he may

incur criminal liability for neglect or ill-treatment, or for failing to educate the child properly.

(i) Orders for Parental Rights, Legal Custody or Access

Until 1959, the only thing that a father could do to try and obtain some voice in his child's upbringing was to make the child a ward of court. Since then he has been able to apply like any other parent for legal custody or access under the Guardianship of Minors Act 1971 (ss.9 and 14). The courts' procedure and powers have already been discussed in Chapter 3. But a right to apply to a court is very different from an automatic parental right. The father still has no powers unless the court chooses to give him some.

Perhaps more importantly, he cannot share custody with the mother even if they both want him to do so. Hence the Family Law Reform Act 1987 provides for him to apply for all the parental rights and duties, sharing these with the mother in the same way that married couples do (s.4). These orders will probably be made when the couple are cohabiting and want to co-operate in bringing up their child, but they could also be made where the father has in fact taken sole responsibility. Once made, disagreements between the parents would be settled by custody, access or other orders, just as they are between married couples. The only difference will be that parental rights orders in favour of fathers can be revoked, whereas there is no way, short of adoption, of taking away the parental status of a married man.

In deciding upon any order, whether for full parental rights and duties, legal custody or simply access, the welfare of the child is the first and paramount consideration. The mother's views will obviously be relevant in deciding whether they should share full parental rights. If the couple separate after long cohabitation, the considerations should be the same as between married parents (see Chapter 3). Where the mother is out of the picture, the court may take the benefits of blood relationship into account in deciding what is best for the child (see, for example, *Re C. (a minor) (wardship: surrogacy)* [1985] F.L.R. 846, where the commissioning parents were allowed to take the father's child born of a surrogacy arrangement); but few fathers will be able to offer a better home for the child than that provided or arranged by the mother. There is also an impression that the father has an uphill struggle even if he is only asking for access, which would be granted almost automatically to a married father (*Barber*, 1975). But the High Court has said that the child's right to maintain links with both sides of his family applies whether or not his parents are married to one another (*S. v. O.* (1977) 3

F.L.R. 15; *cf. M.* v. *J.* (1977) 3 F.L.R. 19; *B.* v. *A.* (1981) 3 F.L.R. 27.
The right of grandparents to apply for access to their grandchildren
(Domestic Proceedings and Magistrates' Courts Act 1978, s.14;
1971 Act, s.14A) includes their illegitimate grandchildren.

An order for full parental rights will bring with it the right to
decide upon the child's marriage, to appoint a guardian and also to
have any disagreement about a particular aspect of the child's
upbringing resolved by a court. An order for legal custody similarly
brings the right to appoint a guardian (along with the mother's
right), and confers the sole right to decide on marriage. The effects
upon children in care and adoption, which are very important in
practice, are mentioned below.

(ii) Children in Care

Many mothers who decide to keep their children have a great deal
of difficulty in doing so. The National Child Development Study
found that by the age of 11, 16 per cent. of the illegitimate children
who had stayed with their mothers had had to go into care at some
time, compared with only three per cent. of the legitimate (*Lambert
and Streather*, 1980). Ordinarily, the mother is sole "parent" for the
purposes of the Child Care Act 1980 (s.87(1)). The father has no
right to remove a child whom she has placed in care, although he is
included in the definition of "relative", so that the authority could
send the child "home on trial," or even discharge the child to him, if
it wished. However, if in future he obtains an order for full parental
rights and duties both he and the mother will count as parents (1987
Act, s.8(2)); even now, if he is granted custody, he becomes the
"parent" to the exclusion of the mother (1980 Act, s.8(2)). In *R.* v.
Oxford Justices, ex p. H. [1975] Q.B. 1, the mother had placed the
child in care and her rights had been assumed by resolution on
account of her mental illness. It was held that this did not affect the
father's right to apply to the court for custody, and that the magistrates should at least hear the case and decide what would be best
for the child.

Similarly, the father will not be a "parent" for the purposes of the
Children and Young Persons Acts; but if he has had charge or control of the child, he will be a "guardian" and may be able to apply
on the child's behalf for the discharge of a care or supervision order
and in future if he has an order for giving him actual custody, he will
count as a "parent" (1987 Act, s.8(1)).

The father was not originally amongst those who can complain to
the courts if access to a child in compulsory care is denied or withdrawn (Child Law Act 1980, Pt. IA, see Chapter 9). However, it has

been held that a court should at least hear his application for access under the Guardianship of Minors Act 1971 instead (*R.* v. *Oxford JJ. ex p.D.* [1986] 3 W.L.R. 447). However, it is not usually appropriate to use this Act to interfere in the local authority's discretion (*Re K. (an infant* [1972] 3 All E.R. 769), so that the court would be bound to reject his application (*Re M. (minors), The Times,* May 26, 1987). Following the Family Law Reform Act 1987 (s.2(1)), the father will be covered by the access provisions in the Child Care Act, as recommended by the Review of Child Care Law (1985).

(iii) Adoption

Perhaps the major limitation in the relationship between father and child arises when the mother wishes the child to be adopted. The father is not a "parent" and so his agreement to the adoption is not normally needed (*Re M. (an infant)* [1955] 2 Q.B. 479). In future, if he has full parental rights his agreement will of course be required, and it is at present if he has custody by court order (1987 Act, s.7). When a court frees a child for adoption, it must be satisfied either that he has no intention of applying for such orders or that he would probably fail (Adoption Act 1976, s.18(7)).

The courts' rules also provide that if he is liable by virtue of an order or agreement to maintain the child, he *must* be made a respondent to the application, so that his views can be heard. Adoption agencies and local authorities have, where appropriate, to make the same enquiries of these fathers as of other natural parents and report on these to the court. If appropriate, he may always be made a respondent. But this is not the same as a right to refuse consent; it will be of little use unless the father has a better alternative to offer the court. Thus some fathers opposing adoption also apply for custody (or try to make the child a ward of court; *F.* v. *S. (adoption: ward)* [1973] Fam. 203; but if the local authority is the adoption agency, the court may now be reluctant to allow him to use wardship; see *Re T.D. (a minor) (wardship: jurisdiction)* [1985] F.L.R. 1150). If so, the applications should be heard together, so that a proper choice between them can be made.

The issue arises in several different ways. If the mother has decided to place the baby with strangers for adoption at an early age, the father may not have been able to prevent her. The court's choice will be between the prospective adopters, who are no doubt suitable in every way and have been caring for the child almost since birth, and the father, who is related to the child by blood but has had no opportunity of forming an emotional bond with him, and is unlikely to have either such a good home or such a good mother-substitute to offer (*Re Adoption Application 41/61* [1963] Ch. 315; *Re O. (an infant)* [1965] Ch. 23). Exceptionally, however, the father may be able to convince the court that the child will be better with him. In *Re C. (M.A.)* [1966] 1 W.L.R. 646, the father had hoped to marry the mother but she had changed her mind and excluded him from all arrangements for the child. He was now reconciled with his wife, who made an excellent impression on the judge, and they could offer a good home. The judge took account of the risks of moving a toddler from the only home he had ever known, but he also took account of the help which the knowledge of blood relationship can give to the formation of attachment between father and child. The father succeeded.

It was estimated that about one-fifth of the illegitimate children born between 1951 and 1968 would be adopted by strangers (*Leete*, 1978) but few of those cases would be contested by the natural father. Contests are more likely over the 7 to 8 per cent. who might be adopted by the mother and the step-father she had since married. Section 37(1) of the Children Act 1975 now obliges the court to treat the case as an application for custodianship, if this would be appropriate and adoption would "not be better" for the child. To become the child of married parents still offers a child legal, social and psychological advantages of which the courts are well aware (*F.* v. *S.*, above). If the father is out of the picture, there can be no doubt of this. In some cases, however, his relationship with the mother was as stable as many marriages and his relationship with the child as good as any other father's. He may not want or be able to offer the child an alternative home, but his objections to the total severance of ties could be as valid as those of a divorced parent (see Chapter 8). In *Re E. (P.) (an infant)* [1968] 1 W.L.R. 1913, these were thought to be frivolous, compared with the advantages of wiping out the "stigma of bastardy" and enabling the child to become "so far as possible" a respectable member of society. Nowadays, the courts have modified their language, but the sentiment may still be there. Exceptionally, the courts might make access a condition of the adoption (*Re S. (a minor) (adoption order: access)* [1976] Fam. 1) but this should probably only be done if everyone agrees (*Re H. (a minor) (adoption)* [1985] F.L.R. 519). The alternative of custodianship has not yet been long enough in force to know what the courts will consider most "appropriate" in these cases.

Different again is adoption by the mother on her own. This deprives the child of a legal relationship with his father's family; at present it leads to slightly better succession rights from the mother's family but under the 1987 Act even this advantage will be lost (see later). Now that the short form birth certificate is in general use,

such adoptions will rarely serve any useful purpose (except sometimes for the acquisition of British Citizenship). Thus the courts are
now prohibited from granting an adoption on the sole application of
the child's mother or father, unless the other natural "parent" is
dead or cannot be found or there is some other special reason to
exclude him (Adoption Act 1976, s.15(3)). Although in 1975 the
word "parent" did not usually include these fathers, it was probably
intended to do so here.

Finally, other relatives may ask to adopt. There are obvious risks
of confusion and later disruption in, for example, grandparent adoptions and the courts must again consider custodianship if adoption
would "not be better" (Children Act 1925, s.37(1); and see p. 163,
below). Thus, if the balance is even, then the adoption should be
allowed (*Re S. (a minor)* [1987] 2 W.L.R. 977), where the mother's
parents were allowed to adopt; the balance may tip even further
where the father's parents wish to adopt, for they are less likely to
feel that the child will otherwise be a full member of their family (see
e.g. Re O. (a minor) (adoption by grandparents) [1985] F.L.R. 546).

4. *Financial Support*

Of all the problems facing the mother who decides to bring up her
baby on her own, money is probably the most serious. All one-
parent families are likely to be materially less well-off than their two-
parent counterparts, but unmarried mothers are the least well-off of
this already disadvantaged group (*Finer*, 1974; *Ferri*, 1976). Unlike
divorced or separated spouses, they cannot turn to the father for
support for themselves as well as the child. Unlike widows, they cannot turn to the state or their husbands' employers for a pension. Yet
they are more likely than either to be left unsupported at the very
time when they are unable to support themselves because the baby
is so young. Thus the main source of income, at least after any
maternity allowance has come to an end, is likely to be means-tested
supplementary benefit, or, if she can work for more than 24 hours a
week, family income supplement. Each of these will be reduced by
the full amount of any provision made by the father.

Before the 1987 Act, the father could only be made legally liable to
support his child by private agreement or by affiliation proceedings.
The mother was first given a private right of action against the
father in 1844, in fact before mothers of legitimate children had any
comparable right. But this was because the abolition, 10 years
earlier, of the power to take action against the father in order to
spare the poor law authorities' expenditure had unexpectedly led

to an increase rather than a decrease in illegitimate births (*Finer and McGregor*, 1974). The proceedings clearly revealed their ancestral connection with the poor law.

(i) Proceedings

Affiliation took the form of an *accusation* of paternity, brought before the predominantly criminal tribunal of the magistrates' court (albeit as domestic proceedings), with an appeal to the Crown Court. In most cases, the accusation had to be made by the mother (Affiliation Proceedings Act 1957, s.1), who could only apply if she was a "single woman" at the time of the application (1957 Act, s.1) or at the time of the birth (Legitimacy Act 1959, s.4). Although "single woman" was widely construed, it excluded a wife who could still claim maintenance from her husband; this does not seem a good reason to deprive the child of his father's support. The mother had to apply before the birth or within three years of it (1957 Act, s.2). However, if the "accused" paid money for the child's maintenance within three years of the birth, she could apply at any time; and if he ceased to live in England within three years of the birth, she could apply within 12 months of his return; and if they were married before the birth but that marriage, though consummated, was void because one of them was under 16, she could apply at any time. There was no excuse for these rigid rules, now that blood tests have up to a 99 per cent. chance of excluding someone wrongly accused of paternity, particularly as other applicants could apply even though the mother would be out of time.

Again, although it was not essential for the mother to give evidence, if she did so, her evidence had to be corroborated, not in full but at least in some "material particular by other evidence to the court's satisfaction" (1957 Act, s.4(1)). Her word, however credible the court in fact found it, was not enough. The case law on corroboration is extensive, but in these cases it usually took the form either of admissions or of circumstantial evidence of intercourse at the relevant time. Evidence of opportunity was not enough, for there must be some indication that they were likely to take advantage of it. Blood test evidence (see earlier) may exclude the "accused" but could also amount to corroboration if he is not excluded (*Turner* v. *Blunden* [1986] Fam. 120).

If the court did adjudge the defendant to be the putative father of the child, it could also order him to make periodical payments for the child's maintenance and education, or to pay a lump sum of up to £500, or both (1957 Act, s.4(2) and (5)). The court might use the lump sum to compensate for liabilities or expenses incurred before the order, including expenses in connection with the child's birth (such as the purchase of a layette, *Foy* v. *Brooks* [1977] 1 W.L.R. 160) or death (s.4(4)), but there is no power to award larger sums or make property settlements as there is on divorce.

It is not surprising, therefore, that affiliation proceedings were regarded as a major discrimination against both mother and child and few mothers were willing to bring them unless pressed to do so by D.H.S.S. officials. Under the Family Law Reform Act 1987, they are abolished. All civil courts will be able to order either parent to make periodical payments to the child or to the other parent for the benefit of the child, or to order limited lump sums, whether or not they also make a custody or access order; and the High Court and county courts will be able to order secured periodical payments, unlimited lump sums and the transfers and settlement of property as they can on divorce (Guardianship of Minors Act 1971, s.11B). For the first time, an unmarried mother may be ordered to provide for a child living with the father. The duration and age limits for period-ical payment order will be the same as in the other family jurisdic-tions apart from wardship (see Chapter 3).

The new provisions in the Guardianship of Minors Act 1971 also apply to children of married parents, so that orders may be made for all children whether or not there are matrimonial, custody or access proceedings on foot. Other provisions relating to financial relief will also apply to all parents, so that the ordinary procedures for recover-ing contributions from parents of children in care (Child Care Act 1980, ss.45 to 48; see Chapter 9) or residential accommodation (see National Assistance Act 1948, ss.42(1) and 43) or from "liable rela-tives" towards the cost of supplementary benefits (Social Security Act 1986, ss.24 and 26), or from parents of children in wardship (Family Law Reform Act 1969, s.6) or custodianship (Children Act 1975, ss.34, 34A, 34B and 35B; see Chapter 10), will apply irrespec-tive of whether or not the child's father and mother have ever been married to one another (1987 Act, s.2(1) and Sched. 2).

In one respect, however, the child of unmarried parents is always likely to be at a disadvantage, for there is no power to order the father to make provision for the mother as well as the child. If he is so young that his mother must give up work to care for him, that may be taken into account in deciding how much should be ordered for the child (*Haroutunian* v. *Jennings* (1977) 1 F.L.R. 62); but the £20 per week ordered in that case was still not enough to lift mother and child above supplementary benefit level. Most orders are extremely low, apparently lower than those for children of married parents (*McGregor, Blom-Cooper and Gibson*, 1970). No doubt the defendants are usually both younger and poorer and all are aware that the order will often benefit the D.H.S.S. rather than mother and child. If there is any property, however, it will be interesting to see whether the courts will be willing to use their new powers to make settlements for the child where on divorce they would make them for the custodial parent.

(ii) Agreements

The mother and father can enter into an agreement for the child's maintenance and this will be enforced by the courts (*Ward* v. *Byham* [1956] 1 W.L.R. 496). Provided that the terms are clear, no particular formality is required, although it is obviously sensible to have a properly drawn up document. Even if the mother agrees not to do so, the agreement does not prevent her bringing court proceedings later (*Follit* v. *Koetzow* (1860) 121 E.R. 274), although this could be a breach of contract.

Private arrangements may make provision which the court would not have power to order, and the courts have been increasingly prepared to given effect to those which are not embodied in formal documents, as long as a trust or the essential ingredients of a contract can be shown. Thus in *Tanner* v. *Tanner* [1975] 1 W.L.R. 1346 a man who bought a house for the mother and their twin daughters to live in was held to have granted her a contractual licence to stay there until the girls had finished school, in return for her agreeing to give up her own flat to look after the children and the house, some of which was let. The higher courts at least seem to have abandoned their moral condemnation of such arrangements.

5. *Property and Succession*

It is quite extraordinary that, while denying the relationship between father and child when the father was alive, the law was prepared to recognise it when he died. The rules which were developed for the dynastic purposes of the propertied classes were in fact abandoned before many of those which have to do with the welfare of the growing child.

It has always been possible to leave property to a *named* illegitimate child, but a general gift to "children" or "issue" was presumed to exclude the illegitimate unless the contrary was stated. Dispositions since 1969 are presumed to include not only them, but relationships traced through them, unless a contrary intention appears (1969 Act, s.15; replaced by 1987 Act, s.19). Succession to peerages and other titles is (of course?) excluded.

Before 1970, an illegitimate child could not claim anything if his father or his father's relatives died without leaving a will, and he could only claim from his mother if she had no legitimate children (this was one of the main reasons for her to adopt him if she got married). After 1969, he could participate in the intestacy of either parent, equally with any legitimate children (1969 Act, s.14). The parents might also participate in his, if he died without leaving a spouse or children of his own. This seems particularly unfair when the mother who has struggled to bring up the child alone is later deprived of half his estate, but there is a rebuttable presumption that the father died first. Under the 1987 Act, the rules of intestacy are to apply irrespective of whether any person's parents were married to one another (s.18). All are to be regarded as relatives and treated alike, but again there will be a rebuttable presumption that the father and his relatives died before the child.

Lastly, the courts' discretionary powers to adjust the dispositions made under a will or intestacy, if these do not make reasonable provision for the family of the deceased (see Chapter 7), have since 1970 applied to all his children. The courts can also award damages for the children if a parent is wrongfully killed (Fatal Accidents Act 1976, s.1(3) and (5)(a)).

Hence the only thing that the child of unmarried parents still cannot inherit from the father is his title or his nationality (British Nationality Act 1981, s.50(9)(b)). The latter is a serious discrimination, as British nationality now depends upon descent rather than birth here; the child of married parents can acquire it through mother or father, the child of unmarried parents only through his mother. Apart from this, the laws of both Scotland and England have now removed almost all the legal discrimination against him and done their best to remove the offensive labels as well. How much this will affect the attitudes of individuals and of society at large, only time will tell.

7 Guardians

The death of one or both parents is obviously a tragedy for a child, but it is a tragedy with far fewer unfavourable consequences for him than almost any other discussed in this book. There are almost always material disadvantages associated with growing up in a one-parent family, but the financial and housing situation of the bereaved is markedly better than that of the others (*Finer*, 1974; *Ferri*, 1976). Nor do children who have lost a parent show a significantly increased risk of delinquency (*Rutter*, 1971), or educational problems (*Ferri*, 1976), although some may be at greater risk of depressive illness in adult life (*Bowlby*, 1980). Bereavement is a quite different experience from other types of separation or loss (*Richards*, 1987). It is rarely accompanied by prolonged hostilities and bitterness between the parents, or by legal disputes about the children's future. It attracts only sympathy and compassion from society and none of the condemnation still attached to marital breakdown and unmarried parenthood.

1. *Caring for the Orphaned Child*

If a parent dies, the law rarely has to arbitrate a dispute between warring claimants for his children's custody; but it may regulate what is to happen to his parental rights and duties. This is normally determined by the law of guardianship. Some statutes give a specially extended definition to the terms "guardian" (as in the Children and Young Persons Acts or the Education Act 1944) or "guardianship" (as in the Mental Health Act 1983). Otherwise, *legal* guardianship is a relationship with a child which entitles the guardian to exercise parental rights and imposes parental responsibilities. It is quite different from custody, which is a selected bundle of those rights and duties, and may be conferred by guardianship itself or by court order in many different circumstances. Guardianship, for practical purposes, can only arise in three ways.

Natural guardians are the child's own parents. Although the old rule that the father was sole guardian has never been expressly abolished, married parents now have equal rights and authority over custody, upbringing and property. Where the parents are not married to one another, the mother alone has rights and authority unless the father is granted them by court order or is appointed guardian after her death. *Testamentary* guardians are those appointed by natural guardians to take their place in the event of death. *Court-appointed* guardians are those appointed by the courts under powers which arise on the death of one or both natural guardians. The court itself is technically the guardian of a child who is made a ward of court, but this is now more often done in circumstances other than the parents' death.

A guardian may be appointed for the child's person or simply for his "estate," but if there is no guardian of the estate, a guardian of the person has the powers of both (Guardianship Act 1973, s.7). His consent is necessary both to marriage and to adoption. He should, however, respect the parents' wishes about the education and religion of the child, unless these are overridden by the welfare principle. His criminal liability for neglect, ill-treatment or failure to educate is the same as that of a parent. But he cannot be ordered by a court to pay maintenance to anyone else for the child. An unrelated guardian who is caring for the child in his own home is not subject to the controls over private foster parents. However, the High Court (but no other) has power to remove any non-natural guardian, in the interests of the child's welfare, and, if it wishes, to appoint someone else to take his place (Guardianship of Minors Act 1971, s.6).

If there are joint guardians, each may exercise his powers without consulting the other(s), provided that another has not "signified disapproval" (Children Act 1975, s.85(3)). If they disagree, any may apply to a magistrates', county or the High Court, which can make whatever order it thinks proper (1971 Act, s.7; but magistrates cannot make any order relating to the child's property, s.15(2)(*b*)).

(i) Guardianship When One Parent Dies

(a) The surviving parent will normally be sole guardian. A non-marital father only becomes guardian if he has custody (or in future full parental rights) when the mother dies (1971 Act, s.3; Family Law Reform Act 1987, s.6(1)).

(b) The dead parent may have made a deed or a will appointing someone to be guardian after his or her death. An appointment made by a non-marital father is only effective if he had custody (or in future full parental rights) when he died (s.4; 1987 Act, s.6(2)). That person will act jointly with the surviving parent unless the latter objects, in which case the appointee will be excluded unless he applies to a court. On the other hand, the appointee may apply if he thinks that the surviving parent is unfit to have custody of the child. In either case, the court can choose between leaving the surviving parent as sole guardian; ordering them to act jointly; or excluding the surviving parent from guardianship.

(c) If no guardian has been appointed by the dead parent, or if he appointed someone who has died or refused to act, the courts have a curious power to appoint a guardian to act jointly with the survivor (s.3(1)); but in this case there is no power to exclude the surviving parent, which is even more curious as the court would presumably only consider such an appointment necessary if it had doubts about the fitness of the parent.

If any appointed guardian acts jointly with a surviving parent, the courts have express powers to make custody orders, grant access to the surviving parent (but not apparently to the guardian, which is a pity), and to order the surviving parent (but again not the guardian) to pay maintenance for the child (s.11; 1987 Act, s.13). Curiously again, they have the same powers even if the surviving parent has been excluded from guardianship (s.10). Thus in one case where a child's mother had died, a grown-up sister applied to the magistrates to be made joint guardian with the father, so that she could then apply for custody. But the High Court discouraged this: the court should first decide whether joint guardianship was in the child's best interests, ignoring the collateral purpose of applying for custody; and joint guardianship was unlikely to be beneficial where, as here, the potential joint guardians were at loggerheads with one another (*Re H. (an infant)* [1959] 1 W.L.R. 1163).

Disputes are most likely to arise if the parents were separated or divorced before the death, particularly if the custodial parent dies. The surviving parent will still be sole guardian, unless the deceased has made a will appointing someone; or the court can be persuaded to make an appointment (which is perhaps unlikely in view of *Re H.* above); or, but this is extremely rare, the court which granted a decree of divorce or judicial separation has made an order under section 42(3) of the Matrimonial Causes Act 1973 that the surviving parent was unfit to have custody of the children; the effect of this is to deprive him of his automatic right to custody and guardianship if the other parent dies (s.42(4)).

The problems which this can cause are amply illustrated by the case of *Re F. (a minor) (wardship: appeal)* [1976] Fam. 238. After a stormy marriage, including some violence by the father which was witnessed by the little girl, the parents separated when she was three and a half. The mother insisted that the father should leave when she discovered his affair with another woman. Some months later the father returned, forced his wife and child out of the house and installed the other woman. The wife went for some time to her parents and later got a flat near them. She was awarded custody at the divorce. The father had a child by the other woman and later married her. He sent presents and some money for his elder child, but saw little of her, principally because of the hostility of the mother and grandmother. The mother became ill and the grandmother and aunts looked after the child while she was in hospital. When the child was nearly eight, her mother died. Eleven days later, the father came and took her away to live with him and his new family.

This he had every right to do. The grandmother made the child a ward of court. But by the time the case came to be heard, a year later, the little girl was well settled with her new family and the Court of Appeal decided that she should remain there. The elderly grandparents were very close to the child, but extremely hostile to her father; he had now settled down with his new young family and was prepared to recognise and respect the child's fondness for her maternal relatives. The High Court or divorce court have always been able to grant access to grandparents who ask for it; and magistrates' or county courts now have power to do so if asked by the parents of a natural parent who has died (Guardianship of Minors Act 1971, s.14A(2): this applies also where the parents were not married to one another). Relatives of a deceased natural parent may also be given a hearing if there is an application to adopt the child (see Chapter 11).

The outcome in *Re F.* may have been the best in the long run. Had the child been settled with a much-loved step-father when her mother died, it might have been disastrous. The moral is obviously to plan ahead. If parent and step-parent have returned to the divorce court for joint custody, it is probable that that order survives the death of one of the divorced parties. But if the mother has appointed the step-father guardian in her will, he may apply to a local court for custody and the case should be heard far more quickly than a wardship application.

(ii) Guardianship When Both Parents Have Died

(a) If each parent has validly appointed a guardian, they will act jointly (s.4(5)). The court has power to resolve their differences (s.7), but it has no express powers to make custody orders as it has if one parent is still alive. If joint guardians cannot agree about where a child shall live, it may be desirable to make him a ward of court.

(b) If only one parent has appointed a guardian, he will have sole responsibility. The court cannot appoint a guardian where one parent has failed to do so (s.3), as it can where the other parent is still alive. But if it has already done so, and the surviving parent then dies, the court-appointed guardian will continue to act, either alone or jointly with any guardian appointed by the parent who was last to die (s.4(6)).

(c) If neither parent has appointed a guardian and there is no other person with parental rights over the child, any person can apply to the court to be appointed guardian (s.5(1)). This can be done at present even though a local authority has assumed parental rights by resolution (s.5(2)); the resolution will end automatically if an appointment is made (Child Care Act 1980, s.5(2)(c)).

(iii) Local Authority Care

One of the grounds for receiving a child into care under the Child Care Act 1980 is that he has neither parent nor guardian. Then, if there is also no custodian, the authority may at present assume parental rights by resolution. It is proposed that the authority should instead apply to the court to be appointed guardian, thus clearly distinguishing these cases from those where the child is at risk of harm from his family (R.C.C.L., 1985; D.H.S.S., 1987). The same procedure may also be adopted for children who have been "abandoned" in care by their parents.

(iv) Informal Arrangements

No doubt a great many orphaned children are cared for by relatives or friends without any formal appointment as guardians. There is no need to be appointed a legal guardian in order to claim social security "guardian's allowance": this is payable, without contribution conditions, to anyone who is caring for or maintaining a child if either (a) both parents are dead (usually only the mother if the parents were not married to one another); or (b) only one parent is dead, but all reasonable efforts have been made but failed to trace the other, or he is in prison (Social Security Act 1975, s.38); the allowance is not lost by adopting the child. Non-relatives who undertake the care of orphaned children without being appointed guardians are, however, subject to the controls over private foster parents (see Chapter 2). All people with actual custody or care of a child may incur criminal liability for neglect, ill-treatment or failure to educate him properly. But they will not have the non-delegable responsibility of parents or legal guardians; and they will not have any parental rights or authority, for example over such matters as marriage, and this could be to the child's disadvantage.

2. *Support*

Widows' families, though worse off than those with two parents or a sole male parent, tend to be better off than other fatherless families for two main reasons.

(i) Succession to Property

A parent who loses a partner through death can normally expect that whatever capital assets they had, including their home, will remain intact, whereas after divorce these will usually have to be shared in some way between two households.

If a person dies leaving children (whether or not they have grown up) but no will, his surviving spouse is entitled to personal chattels and the first £75,000 of the estate absolutely, and also to a life interest in half of the rest (Administration of Estates Act 1925, s.46). If the couple owned their home as joint tenants, the dead partner's half goes automatically to the survivor. If they owned it as tenants in common, or the dead partner was sole owner, the survivor is entitled to ask for his interest in it to be transferred to her as part of her £75,000; if it is worth more and she can afford it, she may make up the difference. If the home is rented under a protected or local authority secure tenancy, the survivor will normally be entitled to take it over whether the landlord likes it or not. These provisions only apply if the survivor was living there at the death; nor does a building society have to agree to transfer any mortgage; but provided that the income can be found to keep up the outgoings, the bereaved family should not lose its home.

The children (including the children of a child who has died before his parent) are entitled to the other half of the residue immediately and to succeed to the surviving spouse's life interest. If they are still under 18, the property is held on trust until they reach 18 or marry, but the income may be used for their maintenance and education before then. If there is no surviving spouse, the whole estate goes to them. (In turn, parents succeed to the estates of their children who die before them without leaving a spouse or children of their own.)

These rules only apply if the deceased left no will. If he did make a will, it will usually have been with the object of making proper provision for his family. Sometimes, however, a will or the rules of intestacy can produce unjust results. A man may leave a substantial legacy outside his family, perhaps not realising how small the residue will be; or a wife may abandon the family, but her husband never obtain a divorce or judicial separation (which prevents the usual rules operating) or think to make a will; or children who are self-supporting may claim shares which will leave dependent children without proper provision.

Under the Inheritance (Provision for Family and Dependants) Act 1975, therefore, a variety of people may apply to the courts for reasonable financial provision from the estate. These are the surviving spouse; any former spouse who has not remarried (unless at the divorce it was ordered that she should not be able to apply because their affairs were settled then); and any child of the deceased, of whatever age; any other child, again of any age, who was treated as a "child of the family" in relation to any marriage to which the deceased was ever a party (that is, any child, apart from one officially boarded-out by a local authority or voluntary organisation, who was treated by both spouses as a member of their family, whatever his parentage); and any other person who was being maintained by the deceased immediately before his death.

The court has power to award periodical payments, or lump sums, or order that property be transferred or settled upon them, or that property be bought out of the estate and transferred to or settled upon them. It has a wide discretion to take into account the needs and resources of all claimants and the beneficiaries under any will, and many other factors such as the education which was planned for the children and the conduct of the claimants towards the deceased. Provision for the surviving spouse should be full financial provision, at least as good as she might expect on divorce (and as the other principal claimant to the family's assets is now dead, it may well be better). Provision for children is not limited to those who are young, dependent or destitute, but it should only be what is reasonable for their maintenance (which could include a house). For other adult claimants, there must be dependency, and probably some indication that the deceased accepted a responsibility; the most successful claimants so far have been mothers of the deceased's extra-marital children.

(ii) Income

The family may have lost a breadwinner, but the various ways of compensating for this tend to be more reliable than periodical payments on divorce or separation. If the loss was caused by wrongdoing to the deceased, his spouse, a cohabitant of two years' standing and dependent children will have a claim against the wrongdoer under the Fatal Accidents Act 1976. There may be an occupational pension or private life assurance. Above all, and provided that her husband has paid the requisite contributions, a widow will usually be entitled to widowed mother's allowance if she has with her or is maintaining a child of the family under the age of 19; and if she is aged between 45 and 65 when her husband dies or she ceases to be entitled to widowed mother's allowance, there is a widow's pension; widows under pensionable age are also usually entitled to a widow's payment of £1,000 (Social Security Act 1975, ss.24 to 26; see Social Security Act 1986, s.36). These benefits are not, of course, available to divorced women, who do not become widows when their former husbands die, or to widowed or divorced men.

These benefits have the great advantage that they are not means-tested. Although, surprisingly perhaps, they are suspended during cohabitation, they are not lost or reduced because of private pensions, annuities or earnings. They are, however, taxable, which can be a very sore point. But the state is still kinder to widows and orphans that it is to other victims of family breakdown.

3. *Commentary*

Very little is known about the practice of guardianship and so few children are now orphaned that there must be much less need for it. It could be seen either as an anomaly, because it allows parents to confer their parental status on others without any court appointment or outside scrutiny, or as a sensible means of enabling responsible parents to provide for their children's care. If it is so sensible, however, should they not also be able to do so in other circumstances, for example while they are temporarily away or incapacitated, or so that a sole parent can share responsibility with another, such as the child's own father or a step-parent (see *Law Commission*, 1985)?

8 Step-Parents

Step-parenthood is obviously becoming more and more common. The National Child Development Study, of all children born in one week in 1958, found at each follow-up that about one-third of the parents who had lost the other parent had also found a new partner (*Ferri*, 1976). Remarriage has been most common amongst lone fathers, who seem to attract almost universal sympathy (*Marsden*, 1969). It is least common amongst widows, as might be expected, but it is becoming increasingly rare for children to lose a parent by death before they grow up. On the other hand, it is increasingly common for them to lose a parent by divorce, and the numbers of divorced people remarrying have naturally risen substantially (*Leete*, 1979); the proportion who remarry shortly after the divorce seems, however, to have fallen (*Haskey*, 1987; *cf. Leete and Anthony*, 1979). Most of the unmarried mothers who keep their children but who do not live with the natural father eventually provide them with a step-father (*Crellin, Kellmer Pringle and West*, 1971).

1. *The Legal Status of Step-Parents*

Whether the natural parent is widowed, divorced or unmarried, the status of the step-parent is initially the same. He will have the same responsibilities towards the children as does anyone with actual custody or care, but his marriage to the parent will give him no automatic parental rights over them (*Re N. (minors) (parental rights)* [1974] Fam. 40) or family relationship with them. The practical problems which this may cause, however, do differ somewhat according to the reason for the other parent's absence.

The most serious is likely to be the children's surname. If a widowed or unmarried mother has sole parental rights, there is nothing to prevent her changing it to that of their step-father if she so wishes. If she simply has custody after a divorce, she cannot change their name without her former husband's consent, unless the court gives leave. The court is governed by the first and paramount consideration of the children's welfare, but there has been some difference of opinion in the Court of Appeal about where their true welfare lies. Some cases (see *R. v. R. (child: surname)* [1977] 1 W.L.R.

1256; *D*. v. *B*. *(otherwise D.) (surname: birth registration)* [1979] Fam.
38) have suggested that a change of name is of relatively little
importance, as long as the children retain a knowledge of their true
identity. It may both spare them embarrassment and promote the
security of their new home. Others (most recently, *W*. v. *A*. [1981]
Fam. 14) have rejected the idea that it is a minor matter or that it
could ever be justified by the administrative convenience of mother
and school. Nor have they shown much sympathy for the children's
own wishes.

The surname problem, like the question of access by the divorced
parent, is part of a much wider debate about how far children should
be encouraged to maintain links with both sides of their genetic
inheritance. While the courts may *talk* of the rights of the child, it
sometimes seems that they *act* more in the interests of the absent
parent. The need to know one's origins must be set against the need
to feel comfortable and secure in the new family. Some step-families
obviously feel the need to appear "normal" more acutely than others
(*Burgoyne and Clark*, 1984).

The other legal difficulties of step-families tend to be associated
with the death of the step-parent or natural parent and can in theory
be solved by both of them making appropriate wills. If the step-
parent dies without making a will, his step-children have no right to
participate in his intestacy; but they can apply to the court for
reasonable financial provision from his estate (see Chapter 7), as
they have been treated by the deceased as members of his family.
The court will take into account the extent to which he assumed any
financial responsibility for them and the liability of anyone else
(such as a divorced or unmarried father) to maintain them. Children
who have become self-supporting have less chance of success. These
powers cannot be compared with automatic inheritance rights, and
of course the children will have no claims upon the estates of members of the step-parent's family unless expressly mentioned.

If the parent to whom the step-parent is married dies, there will
be guardianship problems unless she has appointed the step-father
guardian in her will. Otherwise he has no parental status and if she
was divorced, the father will be able to reclaim the children (see
Chapter 7). The case of *Re N. (minors) (parental rights)* [1974] Fam. 40
concerned two little girls born in 1962 and 1965. Their father died
shortly after the birth of the younger girl and their mother remarried
in 1966. She died in 1970. Shortly before this, the maternal grandmother moved in with the family and she had since looked after
them with the step-father. They began to disagree about the children's upbringing and in 1973 each applied to the magistrates to be
appointed guardian. The magistrates held that they had no power to

make an appointment, because the step-father already had parental rights. The High Court, however, held that he did *not*; but it also pointed out that if the magistrates went ahead and appointed either or both of them guardian, there might still be difficulties, because there is no power to make custody orders in that situation. If the mother had appointed the step-father guardian, however, the grand-mother could only have taken the matter to court by instituting wardship proceedings. Apparently, some solicitors now advise cus-todial parents to appoint guardians as part of the divorce "package" and some unmarried mothers are also doing so (*Law Commission*, 1985).

2. *Acquiring Some Status*

Even if the problems can be solved by both spouses making appro-priate wills, step-families often want more. They frequently wish to present a "normal" front to the world and for some legal recognition and security (*Burgoyne and Clark*, 1984). This is very natural, but if it stems from a desire to exclude the other natural parent, or from some insecurity in relationships within the new family, it is doubtful how far the law should go in satisfying it. They, and the law, may have to adjust their ideas of what is "normal," in view of the increas-ing phenomenon of successive marriages: the step-relation is not the same and perhaps we should not pretend that it is.

(i) Adoption

Adoption is obviously the most popular solution, because it solves all the new family's legal difficulties once and for all. It integrates the children, not only with the step-parent himself, but also with his whole family constellation. In 1971, nearly half the adoption orders made in England and Wales were in favour of a natural parent and step-parent, and more than half of those related to legitimate chil-dren.

There is usually little obstacle to adoption where the parents were not married to one another, for the father's agreement is not required unless he has a custody order, and the courts are generally sympathetic (see further in Chapter 6). There is equally little obstacle to the adoption of children where one parent has died, unless he has appointed a guardian, although the local authority's report to the court should mention any relative of a deceased parent who in the authority's opinion should be made a respondent (see Chapter 11). The merits of such adoptions are questionable: there are not the remaining legal disadvantages of birth outside marriage to be removed; the child will lose all relationship with the family of his dead parent; and this may add to the trauma and loss he has already sustained.

Any court hearing an adoption application from a step-parent, whether alone or jointly with the parent to whom he is married, now has a duty to treat the application as one for custodianship, if it is satisfied that the child's welfare would not be better safeguarded by the adoption and provided that any necessary agreements to adoption have been given or dispensed with (Children Act 1975, s.37(1)). This is, however, a weak duty, as it does not apply if the arguments are evenly balanced (*Re S. (a minor) (adoption or custodianship)* [1987] 2 W.L.R. 977). The usual qualifying periods of care are not required (see Chapter 10). This provision does not cover most step-parents of children involved in divorce, for they are already catered for elsewhere in the law.

Adoptions by step-parents of children whose natural parents are divorced raise more legal difficulties. The desire to adopt can be strongest here, for it will enable the child's name to be changed and exclude forever the possibly troublesome natural father. But his agreement is necessary unless it can be dispensed with; and even if he is only too willing to give it (perhaps because he will then be absolved from all financial responsibility), the court cannot grant the adoption if it is satisfied that the matter would be better dealt with by an order made in the divorce proceedings (Adoption Act 1976, s.14(3) for joint applications; s.15(4) for applications by step-parents alone). Magistrates should not make adoption orders which are inconsistent with custody or access orders made at the divorce without first referring the matter to the divorce court (*Re B. (a minor) (adoption by parent)* [1975] Fam. 127).

The Court of Appeal has pointed out that these adoptions need only be refused if the court is satisfied that the alternative would be *better (Re D. (minors) (adoption by step-parent)* (1980) 2 F.L.R. 102). The court should therefore be making a careful comparison of the advantages and disadvantages of the two solutions in each particular case (*Re S. (infants) (adoption by parents)* [1977] Fam. 173). Since 1979, this has become a little easier, because the couple may make their adoption application to the original divorce court, which may then choose the order most suited to their case.

The question of substance is still a difficult one, and courts have differed widely in their approach—some granting virtually no post-divorce adoption and some continuing much as before (*Masson, Norbury and Chatterton*, 1983). Inheritance and guardianship may be dealt with by making suitable wills, custodial rights may be secured by granting them joint custody, and the divorce court may also be prepared to authorise a change of surname or deny access to the other parent. The complete severance of the child's natural relationships, and their replacement with those which he knows to be artificial, may damage him both legally and emotionally (*Stockdale*, 1972); but so might a life of uncertainty and insecurity which he perceived as abnormal. There are other ways of satisfying a child's need to know his origins apart from maintaining a legal link which is of no other benefit to him. Much will therefore depend upon his age and understanding, and upon the quality of his relationships, not only with the absent parent but also with the absent parent's whole family. Thus the problem becomes most acute when that parent is opposed to the adoption.

The applicants may seek to argue that he has persistently failed, without reasonable cause, to discharge his parental obligations. But in *Re D. (minors) (adoption by parent)* [1973] Fam. 209, the court declared that some estrangement was only to be expected during the upset of a divorce; any failure must be so grave that the children will derive no benefit from maintaining the relationship. More difficult is the allegation that he is withholding his agreement unreasonably. A "reasonable parent" places great weight on what will be best for his children, and so the court must first ask itself whether the adoption would be best (*Re B. (a minor) (adoption by parent)* [1975] Fam. 127). That, as we have seen, is no easy question. However, if the parents' marriage broke up when the child was very young, if contact between them has since been minimal, and if the child thinks of the step-father as his "real" father, the court may conclude that the parent is being unreasonable (*Re D. (an infant) (adoption: parent's consent)* [1977] A.C. 602).

(ii) Custody, Access and Financial Provision

The step-parent of a child whose natural parents are divorced may intervene, without leave, in the divorce suit to ask for custody, perhaps jointly with his spouse. Other step-parents may apply for custodianship with the consent of the person having legal custody (who will, of course, be their own spouse) after the child has lived with them for three months. It is early days to say whether many will choose to do so, but it seems that few have sought custody from the divorce courts after being refused permission to adopt (*Masson, Norbury and Chatterton*, 1983).

Ironically, should the marriage between parent and step-parent come to an end, the courts can make orders about a step-child as if he were a child of their marriage. Courts dealing with any matrimonial dispute have power to make orders about the future of any "child of the family." Besides children of the marriage, these include any child, apart from one boarded-out by a local authority or voluntary organisation, who has been treated by both spouses as a member of their family (Matrimonial Causes Act 1973, s.52(1); Domestic Proceedings and Magistrates' Courts Act 1978, s.88(1)). This is not limited to step-children, but they are the most obvious example; and it is irrelevant to the definition that the step-father *thought* that he was the child's real father (*A. v. A. (family: unborn child)* [1974] Fam. 6).

However, that mistake is not irrelevant to whether he should be ordered to make any financial provision for the child. The court has to take into account whether, to what extent, on what basis, and for how long a spouse has assumed any responsibility for the maintenance of a child who is not his own; whether he did so knowing that the child was not his; and the liability of anyone else to maintain the child (1973 Act, s.25(3); 1978 Act, s.3(3)). A step-parent may also be ordered to make provision for a child for whom some-one also has been appointed custodian (Children Act 1975, s.34(1)(*b*) and (2)). At present, therefore, marrying the child's mother can lead to greater financial liability than being the child's natural father (although the Family Law Reform Act 1987 may redress the balance somewhat).

On the other hand, the concept of "child of the family" also means that, if the step-family breaks down, a step-parent can apply for custody or access to his step-children. And if that is granted, not only will he have obligations: he will also have some rights.

3. *Commentary*

Step-families throw into sharp relief the basic dilemma of custody law: should priority be given to disturbing the child's existing ties as little as possible or to cementing the new ones? Of course, it is better for the child if he can integrate all parents and step-parents into "his" family (*Wallerstein and Kelly*, 1980). But what is the law to do if this is not felt to be enough by the step-families themselves? The present flexible approach may be good enough, but it can easily lead to inconsistencies where like families are not treated alike. Do step-families need to have a new procedure to substitute for both adoption and custody, whereby they can easily agree to share parental responsibilities without depriving the other parent of whatever status he has? Perhaps private guardianship could supply it (*Masson*, 1984; *Law Commission*, 1985).

9 Local Authorities

On March 31, 1984, there were some 78,999 children in the care of local authorities in England and Wales, compared with 100,100 in 1979 (D.H.S.S., 1986a). There are many different routes along which they can arrive there: principally by reception into care under the Child Care Act 1980, possibly followed by a resolution assuming parental rights under that Act; or by care orders under the Children and Young Persons Act 1969; or by committal to care in wardship, divorce or other family proceedings. In practice, the children concerned can be divided into the "victims," the "villains," and the "volunteered," (see *Packman*, 1986) but these do not necessarily fit the legal categories. The main aims of the Review of Child Care Law (1985) were to simplify matters and to draw a much clearer distinction between the provision of voluntary services for families with children in need and compulsory measures to interfere with the legal rights of the child or his parents.

1. *Routes into Care*

(i) "Voluntary" Care under Section 2 of the Child Care Act 1980

Some 43 per cent. of the children in care on March 31, 1984 had been received under what is at present section 2 of the Child Care Act 1980, which accounted for 66.6 per cent. of the admissions during that year. Its purpose is to oblige local authorities to provide care for children whose parents are unable to look after them. The service is, however, expensive and can only be made available to those in genuine need. The proposals for regarding reception as part of a continuum of local authority services for all kinds of families have already been mentioned (see Chapter 2).

The present criteria are: (i) that the child is under 17; and (ii) either (a) that he has neither parent nor guardian or has been and remains abandoned by his parents or guardian or is lost, or (b) that his parents or guardian are, for the time being or permanently, prevented by reason of mental or bodily disease or infirmity or other incapacity or any other circumstances from providing for his proper accommodation, maintenance and upbringing; and (iii) that the intervention of the local authority under this section is necessary in the interests of the welfare of the child (s.2(1)). These conditions must "appear" to the local authority where the child happens to be: but responsibility can later be transferred to the authority where he usually lives (s.2(4) and (5)). It is now proposed to make it clear that the parents' difficulties can arise as much from their child's special needs as from their own problems and to allow authorities to provide residential services whenever this will promote the welfare of children in need, even if there is no specific duty to do so (R.C.C.L., 1985; D.H.S.S., 1987).

The section clearly leaves very great discretion to local authorities, to determine the level of provision and the types of case to be given priority, and to individual social workers, to apply those criteria to particular cases. In England, numbers received have dropped from well over 29,000 in 1976–77 to only 19,000 in 1983–84. Reasons for reception divide roughly into "service for the family" (often because of short term illness or other crises which can rapidly resolve); "rescue from the family" (because of unsatisfactory home conditions or a risk of harm); and the child's own behaviour (which can lead some parents to "volunteer" him) (see *Vernon and Fruin*, 1986; *Packman*, 1986). Whether the latter two categories are handled by care orders or voluntary reception seems to depend a great deal on local policies (see *Packman*, 1986).

The cardinal feature of this section is that it does *not* empower local authorities to remove children against their parents' wishes. Written parental consent is not a legal requirement, and in some cases, for example of orphaned or abandoned children, it will not be available. Sometimes parents may be advised to consider reception into care as a means of relieving stress which might result in child abuse and compulsory removal, so that the distinction between compulsion and volition can be blurred. Sometimes an older child may himself ask to be taken into care. But in all these cases, the section expressly states that it does *not* "authorise a local authority to keep a child in their care under this section if any parent or guardian desires to take over the care of the child . . . " (s.2(3)). Mere reception into care therefore gives the authority no parental rights other than those which must be associated with its statutory duties to provide accommodation and maintenance for him. These include a duty to keep the child in care as long as he is under 18 and still in need of it (s.2(2)); and the authority will have a better right to the actual custody of the child than anyone else apart from the "parent or guardian" (*Re A.B.* [1954] 2 Q.B. 385). But the authority does not have a better right than the parent or guardian once that person wishes to take it over.

"Parent" or "guardian" refers to any person with a legal right to the child, normally each of married parents, a non-marital mother (in future the father too if he has full parental rights by an order under the Family Law Reform Act 1987), or a legally appointed guardian. But if a court has awarded custody to any person, that person is "parent or guardian" to the exclusion of anyone else (s.8(2)). If, for example, a husband and wife have separated and the wife has been granted custody, the husband will not be entitled to discharge the child if his wife later gets into difficulties and has to put the child in care. The local authority could agree to discharge the child to him as a "relative or friend"; but if it refuses to do so, he will have to go back to the court and ask it to vary the custody order instead.

The fundamental "voluntary" principle was enacted partly so that parents could feel confident that in using the service they did not run more risk of losing their children than they would if they had made private arrangements. It reflects the increasing awareness of the dangers of separating children from their parents and our respect for the value and diversity of family life. Hence the section also aims at reuniting the family if at all possible. The authority has a positive duty to try and secure that the care of the child is taken over, either by a parent or guardian, or by a relative or friend (who must be of the same religion as the child or promise to bring him up in it) (s.2(3) again). This is not an absolute duty which arises in every case; it only applies where to do so is consistent with the child's welfare. Together, the authority's lack of parental rights and duty to arrange discharge have raised some tricky problems.

If a relative or friend wishes to have the child, and the authority considers this against his best interests, there is no problem about refusing, because the relative or friend has no right to the child. But if it would be best, there are three different ways of doing it. The child may either be boarded-out with the relative or friend as a foster parent; or allowed to be under his "charge or control"; or discharged from care entirely. But unless the parent is completely out of the picture, should the authority discharge his child without his consent? Might he not feel aggrieved if the authority to whom he had entrusted his child abdicated that responsibility to a member of his family without consulting him?

If on the other hand it is a parent or guardian who wishes to have the child, the problem is reversed. There is no difficulty if the authority considers this best, as it usually will. A great many admissions are for genuinely short term reasons, the most common being short-

term parental illness. Some of the other reasons suggest a more prolonged separation, for example where there is only one parent and
that parent is unwilling or unable to provide. Re-uniting the family
is not always in the child's best interests, perhaps because relationships within it were so negative that the separation was beneficial
rather than detrimental, or because the separation happened at such
an age or so long ago that new relationships have been established
which it would be more damaging to break. The authority, however,
has no parental rights. What then is it to do if it receives a request
for the return of a child which it firmly believes to be contrary to the
child's best interests?

Sometimes, it need do nothing, for the parents' claims to an older
child who wishes to remain in care are effectively unenforceable. In
Krishnan v. *Sutton London Borough Council* [1970] Ch. 181 the authority
had received a girl of 14 and boarded her out. Two years later her
father asked for her return. The authority tried unsuccessfully to
persuade her to go. An instruction to the foster parents similarly
produced no result. The father then tried to get her back by making
her a ward of court, but the judge refused to intervene. The father's
last step was to sue the local authority for breach of its statutory
duty to return her, seeking a mandatory injunction that it should do
so. This was refused; such orders are discretionary and the merits
did not justify one here; also the authority does not have a duty to
reunite the family unless this is in the child's interests. Thus if an
older child wishes to stay in care, the parent may be unable to
recover him either by self-help or by legal action. In *Re K. (a minor)*
(1978) 122 S.J. 626 a parent was refused habeas corpus to recover a
15-year-old girl who had placed herself in the authority's care.

But law-abiding local authorities cannot be expected to make a
practice of refusing to return children to the people who have a
legally enforceable right to them. They must look for ways of coun-
teracting that right. If the child is with foster parents who wish to
keep him, the authority may advise them of the possibilities of wardship, custodianship or adoption (see Chapter 10). If the authority
itself wishes to acquire the right to keep the child, it should not normally seek a place of safety order, followed by care proceedings
under the Children and Young Persons Act 1969, because the
grounds are designed for the removal of children whose present circumstances are unsatisfactory and not for keeping children whose
present circumstances are quite satisfactory but who may suffer
harm if they are changed (*Essex County Council* v. *T.L.R. and K.B.R.*,
(1978) 143 J.P. 309). Instead, it may be able to assume parental
rights by resolution under section 3 of the Act (see below), or seek
committal to care in wardship proceedings on the ground that there

are exceptional circumstances making it impracticable or undesirable to entrust the child to either parent or any other individual (see Chapter 5), or apply to free the child for adoption (see Chapter 11).

Once the child has been continuously in care for six months, the authority has a "breathing space" of 28 days. It is an offence for anyone to remove such a child, unless the local authority consents; and this applies equally to the parent or guardian, unless he has given the authority 28 days' notice of his intention (s.13(2)). It is not clear whether written notice is required. The object of this breathing space is not only, or even mainly, to allow the authority to take steps to keep the child. The circumstances in which this is either possible or appropriate are limited. The period may be used to counsel the parents, to provide them with help in re-establishing the home, and to smooth the transition for the child. However, after six months (*Rowe and Lambert*, 1973) or even less (*Millham et al*, 1986) the child's chances of returning home diminish rapidly. Six months therefore seemed both long enough to maintain parental confidence in the service and short enough to protect the child's own interests. An authority can assume parental rights before that time: but if faced with a firm demand for the child's immediate return, there will be no time to pass a resolution and the only possibility will be to make him a ward of court and seek an immediate order that he stays where he is for the time being. After the six months, it will be easier to pass a resolution.

But should local authorities allow this problem to arise at all? If they are offering a child care service to parents who are in temporary difficulties, should they break faith with their clients by changing the terms of their "contract" in mid-stream? Or, if they are in effect taking over responsibility for a child who has no, or no proper, parents, then should they not accept this from the start? In other words, should they not seek legal rights at an earlier stage and if possible after consultation with the parents, rather than as a hostile reaction to the emergency presented by their request for the child? The power to withhold children from their families without resort to court action seems incompatible with a truly voluntary service for both families and children and the Government now proposes to abolish it (D.H.S.S., 1987).

(ii) Resolutions Assuming Parental Rights under Section 3

Resolutions cover about two-fifths of the children in care under section 2. They may only be passed in respect of children who are already "in care" under that section. Technically the children remain in care under that section even after the resolution. Thus a resolution cannot be used to remove a child from an unsatisfactory home, but it may be passed even though the parent has already asked for the child's return (*Lewisham London Borough Council* v. *Lewisham Juvenile Court Justices* [1980] A.C. 273).

Before passing a resolution, the local authority's social services committee (or the smaller body to which the decision has been properly delegated) must consider whether the defined grounds exist and whether this is the right solution for the child. To do this, it should have full information to support the grounds, and about what will happen if the resolution is passed and what will happen if it is not (*Re D. (a minor)* (1978) 76 L.G.R. 653). The child's wishes and feelings should be considered and the authority may also want to consider the parents' views (D.H.S.S., 1984). Simply to rubber-stamp the recommendations of social workers may invalidate the resolution itself. The possible grounds are (s.3(1)):

(a) that the child's parents are dead and he has no guardian or custodian;

(b) that *a* parent, guardian or custodian of the child:

(i) has abandoned him; a person whose whereabouts have remained unknown for 12 months after the child has come into care is deemed to have abandoned him (s.3(8)); it is the parents' duty to keep in touch and not the other way about; *or*

(ii) suffers from some *permanent* disability rendering him *incapable* of caring for the child; *or*

(iii) while not within (ii), suffers from mental disorder within the meaning of the Mental Health Act 1983 which renders him *unfit* to have care of the child; mental handicap, being permanent, would fall within (ii); this condition does not require a compulsory admission to hospital, but it would obviously help in proof; the disorder need not be permanent and "unfit" is a broader term than "incapable"; *or*

(iv) is of such habits or mode of life as to be unfit to have the care of the child; there must clearly be an element of permanence or at least persistence here, but the words are vague enough to cover alcoholism, drug addiction, prostitution, habitual criminality, vagrancy, and much more besides; *or*

(v) has so *consistently* failed without reasonable cause to discharge the obligations of a parent as to be unfit to have the care of the child; the obligations of a parent are not merely financial, but include emotional commitment to the child (see*M.* v. *Wigan Metropolitan Borough Council* [1980] Fam. 114 where the parents repeatedly placed their children in care and rejected both them and all attempts to help improve relationships within the family); "consistent" is not quite the same as "persistent"—the failure need not have lasted all the child's life, or even for such a long time, but there must be some consistency in the failure alleged (*W.* v. *Sunderland Metropolitan Borough Council* [1980] 1 W.L.R. 1101, where neither the mother's failure to visit, nor her delay in getting her home ready for the child, were sufficiently consistent); the failure must be culpable (*O'D.* v. *South Glamorgan County Council* (1980) 78 L.G.R. 522), without an excuse such as lack of means, or plans for adoption, or the authority's own visiting policies; and it must be bad enough to suggest that the parent is unfit to care;

(c) that a resolution under ground (b) is in force in relation to one parent of the child, who is, or is likely to become, a member of the household comprising the child and his other parent. This was to meet the problem that a resolution under ground (b) only assumes the rights of the unfit parent, so that if there was another parent he could still discharge the child even though he might be living with the unfit one. The object was to allow the authority to ensure that the child would never live with the unfit parent, even though no criticism could be made of the other. But the wording is not good: a resolution can only be passed while the child is in care, in which case there is no household containing him and his fit parent;

(d) that throughout the three years preceding the passing of the resolution the child has been in the care of a local authority under section 2, or partly in the care of a local authority and partly in the care of a voluntary organisation. This was to meet the criticism that, unless the child was orphaned, resolutions could only be passed on the ground of fairly narrowly defined parental unfitness. Yet no matter how good the parent, there might come a point when the child had been in care for so long that removal would repeat and redouble the dangers of the initial separation (*Goldstein, Freud and Solnit*, 1973). The child's own welfare might then prevail over sympathy for his parents' misfortunes.

Each person who is deprived of parental rights by a resolution, unless the local authority does not know where he is, must immediately be given written notice of it, telling him of his right to object (s.3(2) and (3)). If he then, within a month of receiving this notice, serves a written counter-notice objecting to the resolution, it will automatically lapse 14 days later (s.3(4)), unless within that time the authority refers the case to the juvenile court (s.3(5)). It is then for the court to decide whether the resolution should lapse. To prevent this the local authority must prove three things: that the original ground on which it was passed was made out at the time; that there are still grounds on which a resolution could be founded, but these need not be the same as those on which it was originally passed (for example, where a mother now has a good reason for failing to visit, because the local authority has stopped her, but the child has been in care for three years; *W.* v. *Nottinghamshire County Council* [1982] Fam. 1); and that it is in the interests of the child (s.3(6)). Thus in the *Sunderland case* (above), the mother had been guilty of failing to take an interest in her baby when the resolution was passed; but then she had co-operated with visiting and rehabilitation plans until these had been stopped by the authority, so that at the time of the hearing there were no longer grounds for a resolution. Her appeal succeeded. Unlike care proceedings, the dispute is clearly between local authority and parents; the court has power to make the child a party and appoint a guardian *ad litem* for him if it thinks this necessary to safeguard the child's interests, or to call for an independent welfare officer's report (s.7). Either side may appeal to the Family Division of the High Court (s.6). However, in the *Glamorgan* case where the mother's appeal succeeded, the child remained in care as a ward of court.

The effect of a resolution is to vest parental rights and duties in the authority; but if it is passed only on account of one parent (as in ground (b)) and he had parental rights jointly with another parent, the authority will hold parental rights jointly with that parent (s.3(1)). There is no formal procedure for resolving disputes between them, but presumably that parent could discharge the child from care. "Parental rights and duties" means all rights and duties with respect to both the child and his property (Children Act 1975, s.85(1)). It does not however include the right to decide whether the child can be adopted, which remains with the natural parent (1980 Act, s.3(10)). Nor does it allow the authority to change the child's religion (s.4(3)). The parent is still under a duty to maintain the child (s.4(2)) and to keep the authority informed of his address (s.9). Nor is the resolution final.

It will normally continue in force until the child is 18 (s.5(1)). But it will automatically lapse if the child is adopted or freed for adoption or if a guardian is appointed under section 5 of the Guardianship of Minors Act 1971 (s.5(2)). The authority itself may rescind the resolution at any time if this would be for the child's benefit (s.5(3)). A parent who has been deprived of his rights under grounds (b), (c) or (d) may also apply to a juvenile court for the resolution to be ended. But he will have to prove either that there was no ground or making it (which will be impossible if the grounds were proved in court at the time, but not if there was no objection then) or that it should now be ended in the child's own interests. Thus the burden of proving that the child would now be better off without the resolution is firmly on the parent at this stage. If the resolution was passed on ground (a), any person who claims to be a parent, guardian or custodian can apply, presumably on the ground that it should never have been passed. Other interested people, such as relatives, have no right to apply to a court to end a resolution; but they may be able to persuade the authority to rescind it, and if the child is an orphan they could apply to a court to be made guardian.

A resolution does far more than guard against the possibility that a parent will seek to remove a child against the authority's advice. It has the more positive aim and effect of providing a child with a substitute legal parent to replace the natural parent which to most intents and purposes he does not have. It is, however, the only procedure whereby parents may lose most of their rights without any form of court order. Very few are contested; while some parents may feel relieved that their responsibilities have been lifted without a court finding against them, others could be deterred by the authority's "pre-emptive strike" and feel that any appeal would be useless. Other family members who might wish to look after the child have no rights in the proceedings, nor can they use wardship instead (*Re W. (a minor) (wardship: jurisdiction)* [1985] A.C. 791).

The Government (D.H.S.S., 1987; R.C.C.L., 1985) now proposes to amalgamate the resolution procedure with the new form of care proceedings. The new set of grounds will focus on the risk of harm to the child from leaving care (or staying in care under the threat of removal or damaging interference), rather than on the parents' own characteristics. If there is no such risk but the child needs a new family, then adoption or custodianship will usually be best. But if the child has no family and no substitute family can be found, the local authority may apply to become guardian instead (see Chapter 8). This might restore the procedure to something more like the original proposals of the Curtis Committee in 1946.

(iii) Care Orders under the Children and Young Persons Act 1969

Some 45 per cent. of the children in care on March 31, 1984 were subject to care orders under the 1969 Act, but these accounted for only 16 per cent. of the admissions during the year. Obviously they do not include any short term "service to family" admissions. Roughly a quarter of those in care under care orders were offenders; offenders were a rather higher proportion of these admissions during the year (about two-sevenths) but the care order is diminishing in popularity as a criminal disposal. The remainder were subject to care orders made in care proceedings or in place of a supervision order. The making, duration and discharge of orders have already been discussed in Chapters 4 and 5, for these depend upon the court and not upon the local authority.

The court may have had any one of a great many different objects in mind while making the order, but the legal effect is the same in each case. The local authority must take the child into its care and keep him there as long as the order is in force "notwithstanding any claim by his parent or guardian" (1980 Act, s.10(1)). While he is there, the authority has much the same responsibilities towards him as it has towards any of the other children in care. There is only one thing to distinguish the different types of care order children: where the order was originally imposed for a criminal offence and the child is found guilty of another imprisonable offence which the court thinks sufficiently serious, the court can restrict the authority's power to send the child "home on trial," either totally or limit it to a named individual for up to six months (1969 Act, s.20A; Criminal Justice Act 1982, s.22; see Chapter 4).

There are also only one or two legal rules which distinguish care order children from all the rest. The most important is that the authority has all "the same powers and duties" with respect to the child "as his parent or guardian would have" were it not for the order (s.10(2)). It is not clear how, if at all, these differ from the parental "rights and duties" which are assumed by a local authority resolution. Some care order children, particularly those removed from damaging homes at an early age, will need the authority to assume full responsibility for them. Others, particularly the offenders, will not. But the law makes no distinction between them and provides no definition of the authority's powers. They certainly do not include the right to change the child's religion (s.10(3)), although there seems nothing to prevent the authority bringing the child up in no religion at all (unless atheism or agnoticism are themselves religions?). Nor do they include the right to agree to the child's adoption (s.10(5)); this remains with the natural parents, but the care order may enable a suitable placement to be made and there may well be grounds for dispensing with the natural parents' agreement in some cases. It is not clear whether these powers include the right to decide whether the child may marry before 18, or any right to control his property as opposed to his person.

The local authority must appoint an independent person as a "visitor" for some care order children. These are children aged five or over, who are living in community homes which they have not been allowed to leave during the past three months in order to go to school or work, and who either have not lived with, visited or been visited by a parent or guardian during the past year, or have had only infrequent contact with them (s.11). The visitor's function is to visit, advise and befriend the child, and he is entitled to apply on the child's behalf for the discharge of the order. He may resign, or the authority may end his appointment, but if the child's circumstances are still the same, he must be replaced. These visitors reflect an obvious ambivalence in the local authority's relationship with care order children. On the one hand, the authority may be trying to do its best for the child, although it must also protect the public; and on the other hand, it may be doing so in circumstances and in a way which neither the child nor his parents want; it is thus part friend and part foe.

Equivalent orders can be made against civilian juveniles who commit offences against military discipline (e.g. Army Act 1955, Sched. 5A, paras. 6 and 7).

(iv) Interim Care Orders and Remands to Care

In the year ending March 31, 1984, some 2,300 children were admitted to care on remand, or following committal for trial or sentence, or after arrest in criminal cases (see Chapter 4). Another 2,200 were admitted on interim care orders (see Chapter 5). Together these made around 15 per cent. of all admissions, but only two and a half per cent. of all those in care on that date, reflecting again the short term character of these admissions. Their making and effect have already been discussed. The local authority's powers are usually the same as under a care order (1980 Act, s.10(1)), but may include the power to ask the court to transfer an "unruly" child to prison and may exclude the power to send a child "home on trial,"; and the grounds for using "secure accommodation" for children remanded to care charged with serious offences are wider than usual (see later).

(v) Committal to Care in Family Litigation

Nearly 10 per cent. of the children in care on March 31, 1984 had been committed to care as a result of private family litigation (see Chapter 3), including wardship and adoption. This may happen because the court can see no better alternative for a child from a broken home; but some orders are actively sought by local authorities who make children wards of court or intervene in divorce or similar proceedings in order to remove them from home or keep them in care. The effect is rather different from a care order under the 1969 Act or the assumption of rights by resolution. The authority must receive the child into its care as if under section 2 of the 1980 Act but must also keep him there despite his parents' claims. It does not, therefore, acquire any parental rights and duties above those which it always has when a child is in care. It is specifically prohibited from arranging for his emigration; and in wardship or divorce cases it is subject to any directions given by the court. Payment is ordered by the court, if at all, and the authority's after-care duties do not apply.

(vi) Other Cases

Children who have been removed from private foster homes (see Chapter 2), or from prospective adopters (see Chapter 11), or from voluntary homes which the D.H.S.S. is closing (see below), may be received into care under section 2 of the 1980 Act even though the normal grounds do not exist or they have reached 17.

Other children may be accommodated by local authorities even though they are not technically "in care" at all (and so most of what follows does not apply to them). These include: children who have been taken to local authority accommodation as a "place of safety"; mentally disordered children who may be placed in community homes without being taken into care (Mental Health Act 1959, s.9), so that their parents need not be made to pay; and people of 16 but under 21, who may be allowed to live in community homes which cater for their age group and are convenient for their work or education (1980 Act, s.72); and indeed community homes may be provided for any purpose connected with the welfare of children, whether in care or not (s.31(1)).

2. *Care in Care*

Whatever the legal route along which the child arrived in care, the law relating to his treatment while he is there is essentially the same (see Pt. III of the Child Care Act 1980). The general duty of local authorities to all these children is laid down in section 18(1):

> "In reaching any decision relating to a child in their care, a local authority shall give first consideration to the need to safeguard and promote the welfare of the child throughout his childhood; and shall so far as practicable ascertain the wishes and feelings of the child regarding the decision and give due consideration to them, having regard to his age and understanding."

While this duty is clearly most relevant to placement and other decisions relating to the child's stay in care, the section was drafted with positive planning for the child's long-term future in mind. Thus it is aimed at decisions about whether he should be allowed to leave care, whether to plan for eventual rehabilitation with his family, or whether to aim for a permanent substitute home. The duty to consider the welfare and wishes of each individual child can apply to decisions to close a children's home (*Liddle* v. *Sunderland Borough Council* (1983) 13 Fam. Law 250; *The Times* December 19, 1979) or at least to its timing (*R.* v. *Solihull Metropolitan Borough Council, ex p. C.* [1984] F.L.R. 363). The need to consult the child is most welcome, but it should also be good practice to consult his parents whenever possible. At present they do not even have the right to know where their child is.

The general duty is modified in two ways, mainly to take account of children who arrive in care because of criminal offences, but applicable to all. The authority is allowed to exercise its powers in a manner which may not be consistent with its duty to the child, if this seems necessary for the purpose of protecting members of the public (s.18(3)). Secondly, if the Secretary of State considers it necessary, for the same purpose, he may give directions to a local authority about how it should deal with a particular child in its care, even if these conflict with the child's welfare and wishes (s.19).

Section 18(2) reminds local authorities that in providing for children in care they must make such use of the facilities and services provided for children in the care of their own parents as seems reasonable in each case. Children in care have been deprived of so much that it is particularly important that they should not be deprived of services which children at home will take for granted, be they schools, play groups, youth clubs, hospitals, clinics, the youth employment service, or whatever.

(i) Placement

The advantages of local authority care, at least in an ideal world, are that it has a wide range of child care facilities open to it and expert staff to select the placement which is most appropriate for each individual child; to handle it with sensitivity to the needs and feelings of all involved; and to make constructive long-term plans based on regular reviews. The placement alternatives are set out in section 21 and the authority must now (subject to the welfare principle) choose one as close as practicable to the child's home.

(a) *Boarding-out*

Before the Children and Young Persons Act 1969, local authorities had a positive duty to board-out all children in their care, unless this was impracticable or undesirable. This legal preference for foster care was removed, partly because the initial enthusiasm for it was not always borne out by results, for so many long-term placements broke down (*Dinnage and Kellmer Pringle*, 1967), and partly because it was not suitable for many of the juvenile offenders then coming into care. Nevertheless, 48 per cent. of the children in care on March 31, 1984 were boarded-out, compared with 36 per cent. in 1979. Boarding-out is subject to the detailed provisions of the Boarding-Out of Children Regulations 1955 (made under section 22 of the 1980 Act). These make an interesting comparison with the law on private fostering (discussed in Chapter 2) and with supervision orders over children living at home (see Chapter 5). They apply whenever a child is boarded-out, either by a local authority or a voluntary organisation, with foster parents "to live in their dwelling as a member of their family," unless this is merely for a holiday of not more than 21 days or the child has been placed with a view to adoption (reg. 1).

Short and long-term fostering. The Regulations distinguish in various ways between short-term placements for less than eight weeks (reg. 24) and long-term placements for more than eight weeks (reg. 16). If a placement which was originally intended to be short continues beyond eight weeks, the long-term regulations come into force. Anything required by them which has not in fact already been done must be done immediately, unless the extension is not expected to last more than four weeks, in which case the long-term regulations do not apply unless and until it goes on longer than that (reg. 30).

Selection of foster parents. There are now no restrictions upon the people who may become local authority foster parents. Fostering with members of the child's own family seems to be particularly successful (*Rowe et al*, 1984). However, a child cannot be boarded-out unless a social worker has first visited the foster parents and their home and reported in writing that they will be suitable to the child's needs. In short-term placements this is all that is required (reg. 25); indeed, it need not be repeated if a child receiving full-time education has already been boarded-out there within the past four months and is returning, for example during holidays from boarding school (reg. 29). On long-term placements, however, the social worker must be personally acquainted with the child and his needs, or at least fully informed of them, and must report that the foster home is likely to suit those particular needs. He must also report specifically upon the foster parents' reputation and religion and their suitability in age, character, temperament and health to have charge of the child, upon whether any member of the household is suffering from a physical or mental illness which might adversely affect the child, or has been convicted of an offence making it undesirable for the child to associate with him, and upon the number, sex and approximate age of the people in the household. The authority has a positive duty not to board-out the child unless his history and the reports indicate that placing him in that household would be in his best interests (reg. 17). All this should involve both the careful selection of foster parents in the first place and the equally careful matching of individual children and families, very different from the situation when parents are forced into the private market.

Medical examination. Except in an emergency, a child must not be boarded-out unless he has been examined by a doctor within the three months beforehand, and the doctor has made a written report on his physical health and mental condition (reg. 6). Thereafter children under two must be examined within a month after placement and then at least every six months; and children over two must be examined within a month if they were not seen beforehand, and then at least every year (reg. 7). In addition, adequate arrangements must be made for medical and dental attention as required (reg. 8). But regulations 6 and 7 do not apply to short-term placements of school-children who have already been with the same foster parents within the past four months (reg. 29).

Religion. Long-term foster parents must if possible be of the same religion as the child and must in any event give an undertaking to bring him up in, and encourage him to practise, his own religion (reg. 19 and Sched.). Short-term foster parents must either give the same undertaking or be told by letter of the child's religion and the obligations they would have under the undertaking (reg. 27). Again, this need not be repeated if they have already had the same school-child within the past four months (reg. 29).

The foster parents' undertaking. Long-term foster parents must sign the statutory undertaking (reg. 20), unless the child is 16 or over when he first goes to them, in which case they need only sign the parts which seem to fit (reg. 23(2)). Short-term foster parents taking a child under 16 must either sign the undertaking or be told by letter of the obligations it contains (reg. 27). Again, this need not be repeated if they have had the same school-child within the past four months (reg. 29).

The undertaking itself is quite extraordinary (Sched.). Apart from religious upbringing, the foster parents must look after the child's health, consult a doctor if he is ill, allow him to be medically examined when the authority requires it, allow the D.H.S.S. or local authority social worker to visit the home and see the child at any time, notify changes of address in advance, and tell the authority immediately of any "serious occurrence" affecting the child. But it also has two promises which some people think are mutually contradictory: to care for the child and bring him up as they would a child of their own and to allow him to be taken away from them whenever the authority asks. This illustrates the difficulty and ambivalence of the foster parents' task, as well as a potentially yawning gap between the popular and professional views of long-term fostering. Incidentally, the undertaking says nothing about education, but as people with actual custody of the child, the foster parents will have the same rights and duties under the Education Acts as have the parents.

Visits. In long-term placements of children under 16, a social worker must usually visit the home and see the child within a month of the placement, and thereafter as often as the child's welfare requires, but not less than once every six weeks for children under five and once every two months for children over five; if one child is placed with one foster parent, the first visit must be within two weeks and thereafter every six weeks; once any child has been in a foster home for more than two years, however, he need only be visited every three months (reg. 21). Children who reach 16 must be visited within three months and thereafter every three months. Children who are first boarded-out over that age must be visited within a month and thereafter every three months (reg. 23(3)(a) and (b)). In addition, a social worker must always visit within a month of the foster parents' moving house (reg. 21(1)(c) and (2)(c) and 23(3)(c)) and immediately if there is any complaint by or about the child, unless action on it seems unnecessary (reg. 21(1)(d) and (2)(d) and 23(3)(d)).

In short-term placements of children under 16, a social worker must visit the home and see the child within two weeks and thereafter every four weeks (reg. 28(1)). If the child is over 16, the social worker must see him, but not necessarily the home, within a month (reg. 28(2)). If a school-child has already been boarded-out with the same foster parents within the past four months, he and the home need only be visited within a month (reg. 29). In all cases, the social worker must visit immediately if there is any complaint by or about the child, unless action on it seems unnecessary.

Every time a social worker sees a child who is boarded-out, he must consider the child's welfare, health, conduct and progress, and then make a written report. Every time he sees the foster home, he must make a written report about its condition (reg. 9). If social workers were not spending all this time visiting and reporting on foster homes, could it be more usefully employed?

Boarding-out in another area. Children must not be placed outside England and Wales unless special circumstances make this desirable (reg. 3), but they may be sent to foster parents who live in the area of another authority. In long-term cases, the care authority must (unless it is urgent or they have had another child in the same household within the past three months) first ask the area authority whether anything is known which might make the proposed placement detrimental to the child (reg. 17(1)(c)). In all cases, the care authority must give particulars of the placement to the area authority (regs. 18 and 26); and inform the area authority when and why the placement ends and whether it is intended to place another child in that household (reg. 21(1)). In turn, the area authority must tell the care authority if it learns of any reason to think that the placement may no longer be in the child's best interests (reg. 12(2)). The care authority may if it wishes arrange for the area authority to carry out any or all of its supervisory duties over any or all of the children it has boarded-out there, and to report back as arranged (reg. 13). Last, if the supervisor, whichever authority he is from, removes a child because he seems to be at risk, the other authority must be told (reg. 5(2)).

Boarding-out by a voluntary organisation. All these rules apply to children boarded-out by voluntary organisations in just the same way. The relationship between the organisation and the local authority for the area is the same as that between a care authority and an area authority described above. However, the area authority does have the additional responsibility of ensuring that the organisation is able to supervise properly, and if it is not, the authority must take over. It can only do this with the organisation's consent or after a month's notice, during which the organisation can appeal to the D.H.S.S.; it may also apply to be allowed to resume supervision after a year (reg. 14). It is also possible for a voluntary organisation to board-out a child in its charge who is in fact in the care of a local authority (reg. 15). The care authority must be told of the placement and why it ends; and if the area authority takes over the supervision, the care authority must be told and the regulations will for the time being apply as if the care authority had done the boarding out.

Records and registers. Authorities must keep up-to-date case records of all children boarded-out by them, whether in their own area or elsewhere, or whom they are supervising (reg. 10). Voluntary organisations must keep similar records for all children they board-out. The records are confidential (*Re D. (infants)* [1970] 1 W.L.R. 599, *Gaskin* v. *Liverpool City Council* [1980] 1 W.L.R. 1549). They must be kept for at least three years after the child reaches 18 (or dies younger) and be open to inspection by the D.H.S.S.

Local authorities must also keep registers of all children boarded-out in their area by any agency, whether or not they are supervising (reg. 11). Certain particulars are required. The registers must be kept for at least five years after the child has or would have reached 18 and be open to inspection by the D.H.S.S.

Removal. The agency cannot allow a child in its care to remain with any foster parents if it appears that this is no longer in his best interests (reg. 4). Furthermore, if the supervising social worker thinks that the conditions endanger the child's health, safety or morals, he may remove the child immediately (reg. 5(1)). If the foster parents are, for good or bad reasons, unco-operative, the authority might seek to enforce the undertaking by bringing habeas corpus (*Re A.B.*, [1954] 2 Q.B. 385). If there are serious fears for the child, a search warrant under section 40 of the Children and Young Persons Act 1933 could be obtained (see Chapter 5), although refusal to allow visiting or removal of the child is not automatically grounds for doing so. There are restrictions on removing certain children from foster homes pending the hearing of custodianship or adoption proceedings. The relationship between the foster parents and the child, including the ways in which they may try to keep him, is discussed in Chapter 10. Yet despite all this careful selection and regulation, foster parents are not agents of the social authority for the purpose of holding the authority liable if the child is injured as a result of their negligence (*S.* v. *Walsall Metropolitan Borough Council* [1986] 1 F.L.R. 397).

(b) *Community homes*

The proportion of children placed in community homes continues to decrease. Local authorities must arrange for places to be available for children in their care, or for the welfare of others who are not in care, in a suitable variety of homes, whether residential nurseries, ordinary children's homes, or those which approximate to the old remand homes and approved schools (1980 Act, s.31). Some are provided by local authorities; some are provided by voluntary organisations, with either an authority or the organisation responsible for running and equipping them and employing staff; these are exempted from the usual controls over voluntary homes.

All community homes are subject to the Community Homes Regulations 1972. These give the child the right to practise his religion as far as practicable (reg. 8), and his parents the right to be told of his death, serious injury or serious illness (reg. 6). Facilities for visiting must be provided, but it is up to the managers how they are used (reg. 9). Discipline is to be kept by "good personal and professional relationships." Anything more must be given general approval in advance by the responsible local authority, which must take into account the purpose and character of the home and the sort of children for whom it is provided. The approved measures must be reviewed every year and full particulars of their use must be kept by the person in charge (reg. 10). Corporal punishment in homes must therefore keep within the limits set by the authority, as well as the general limits on "lawful chastisement" discussed in Chapter 1.

(c) *Voluntary homes*

Children in care may also be placed in voluntary homes which are not community homes, if the managers agree. A voluntary home is "any home or other institution for the boarding, care and maintenance of poor children" supported wholly or partly by voluntary contributions or endowments, apart from a school, mental nursing home or residential home for the mentally disordered (1980 Act, s.56). They are registered and controlled by the D.H.S.S., and subject to the Administration of Children's Homes Regulations 1951. These are similar to the Community Homes Regulations 1972, but they are more precise about corporal punishment (reg. 11). This may only be imposed upon girls under 10 and boys under 16; children under 10 may only be smacked on their hands with the bare hand of the person in charge (or his deputy if he is ill or away); boys between 10 and 16 may only receive up to six strokes of the cane upon their clothed posteriors.

If the D.H.S.S. refuses or cancels a home's registration, it may require the local authority to remove the children and receive them into care (1980 Act, s.57(6)). Local authorities also have a vague duty to visit children in voluntary homes from time to time in the interests of their well-being, and a right of entry both for that purpose and to visit their own children accommodated there (s.68). Some children, of course, are in the care of the voluntary organisation itself, which is now in much the same position as a local authority (see Chapter 2).

(d) *Homes provided by the D.H.S.S.*

The D.H.S.S. provides homes, known as youth treatment centres, for children in care who are in need of particular facilities and services which are unlikely to be readily available in community homes (1980 Act, s.80). They are mainly designed for the most disturbed young offenders.

(e) *Other arrangements*

There is a compendious power to make such other arrangements for the child's accommodation and maintenance as seem appropriate to the authority. Obvious examples are hostels, residential employment, boarding schools, and bed and breakfast houses. If the child is under 16, the authority may "volunteer" him for admission to a psychiatric hospital, where it must visit him if it has parental rights (Mental Health Act 1983, s.116).

(f) *"Home on trial"*

The authority may allow any child in its care, either for a fixed period or until it decides otherwise, to be under the "charge and control" of a parent, guardian, relative or friend (s.21(2)). This applies to all children in care, whether or not the authority has parental rights, apart from those offenders whom a court has said cannot be sent home at all, or only to a specified person, for up to six months (see Chapter 4). But there is no way of recovering a child in voluntary care who is allowed to return to his parents. Children who are subject to care orders or resolutions may be recovered by the normal absconding procedures (below) and there is a specific crime of harbouring or concealing a resolution child who has been recalled from home trial (s.14). If a child is allowed to go to relatives it should be made clear whether this is a boarding-out, or a home trial, or a complete discharge from voluntary care: for once the child has been in care for six months, the relatives will commit a crime if they keep him away from the authority which still has him in care (s.13). Home trial was used for nearly 14 per cent. of all children in care on March 31, 1984, compared with 18.7 per cent. in 1979; it is still particularly common in education cases, where the object is to enforce school attendance rather than to remove the child from home. It is obviously an essential means of trying to bring about a controlled return in cases of child abuse; but as the case of Jasmine Beckford showed all too clearly (*Blom-Cooper*, 1984), it is easy to lose sight of the authority's parental responsibilities once the child has gone home. The D.H.S.S. has been given power to make regulations to govern these placements (Children and Young Persons (Amendment) Act 1986, s.1) but this has not yet been implemented.

(g) *Secure accommodation*

Secure accommodation means any place provided for locking up children ("restricting their liberty"), whether in a community home, youth treatment centre, behaviour modification unit in a psychiatric hospital (see *R.* v. *Northampton Juvenile Court, ex p. London Borough of Hammersmith and Fulham* [1985] F.L.R. 193), or elsewhere. Most children in care, whether voluntarily or compulsorily, or detained under the various place of safety powers, can only be locked up in certain circumstances: either where they have a history of absconding and are likely to abscond from any other accommodation, thereby putting at risk their physical, mental or moral welfare; or where they are otherwise likely to injure themselves or others (1980 Act, s.21A(1)). Children remanded to care charged with violent or serious offences, or having a history of violence, may be locked up if they are otherwise likely to abscond (Secure Accommodation (No. 2) Regulations 1983, reg. 7). However, these restrictions do not apply at all to children detained under section 53 of the Children and Young Persons Act 1933 or to those detained or arrested by a police officer under sections 28(4) and 38(6) of the Police and Criminal Evidence Act 1984 (reg. 6).

Even if the required grounds exist, the required procedures must be followed. Children under 10 cannot be locked up in a community home without prior approval from the D.H.S.S. (reg. 4). No child can be locked up for more than 72 hours in any 28 day period without the authority of a juvenile court (reg. 10; there is leeway for children detained during weekends and public holidays, see reg. 11). The court may authorise up to three months more (reg. 12) and then further periods of up to six months at a time (reg. 13); remanded children may be authorised for the duration of the remand but no longer (reg. 14). The child must be given legal aid unless he is too well off or has refused it (1980 Act, s.21A(6)) and the parents must be informed (reg. 15). Appeals lie to the Crown Court (s.21A(5)). Wards of court can only be locked up by direction of the judge (Secure Accommodation (No. 2) (Amendment) Regulations 1986) and should usually be separately represented.

In addition, local authorities must appoint review panels to consider, at least every three months, children in secure accommodation in community homes for whom they are responsible (reg. 16). They have to consider the views of all concerned and take into account the child's welfare in deciding whether it is still appropriate for him to be there (reg. 17).

(ii) Reviews

The authority's general duty indicates that greater emphasis should now be placed upon long term planning for the future of children in care. Children who need permanent homes should not be kept waiting, but neither should children who need to be reunited with their own families as soon as possible. Long-term foster placements must be reviewed within three months and thereafter at least every six months (1955 Regulations, reg. 22); this should be done, as far as practicable, by people other than the visiting social worker, but modern practice would encourage case conferences in which social worker, foster parents, parents and the child himself were involved, as well as senior staff (D.H.S.S., 1976). More important, there is a general duty to review the case of *each* child in care every six months, and if he is subject to a care order to consider whether to apply for its discharge (1969 Act, s.27(4)). This duty was thought inadequate and imprecise, and eventually authorities will be required to conduct reviews in accordance with regulations covering their manner and frequency, and the matters to be taken into account (1980 Act, s.20). The child already has a right to have his views considered (s.18(1)), although his parents do not. As with case conferences about suspected child abuse, reviews may make decisions which can vitally affect the interests of the whole family, yet it is difficult to see how far they can or should go in trying to observe the rules of natural justice. Perhaps worse is the evidence that statutory reviews play little part in positive planning for children in care (*Sinclair*, 1984), and indeed that purposeful forward planning is still all too rare, despite more than a decade of consciousness of the "children who wait" (see *e.g. Vernon and Fruin*, 1986).

(iii) Parental Contact

Part of that depressing picture is the lack of positive effort to keep family and child in touch, particularly in the early days after an admission, even though the chances of leaving care depend so much upon what happens to the family in the meantime (*Milham et al*, 1986). For a while attention was focussed on the decision to sever links with the family with a view to planning a permanent substitute to home (see *Adcock and White*, 1980b). Concern about this led to the present procedure under Part IA of the 1980 Act.

If a local authority wishes to refuse or terminate parental access to a child in compulsory care (s.12A), it must serve formal notice on the parent, guardian or custodian concerned (s.12B). Local authorities should not delay responding to requests for access for more than two to three weeks (*R. v. Bolton Metropolitan Borough, ex p. B.* [1985] F.L.R. 343). If access is denied or ended, the parent may apply to the juvenile court within six months (s.12C). Clearly, this causes difficulties if there are also adoption proceedings in another court (see *Southwark London Borough Council* v. *H.* [1985] 1 W.L.R. 861, where it was decided that the access case should be heard first). The court may grant an access order, which should specify when, where, how often and the like (s.12C(3); *Devon County Council* v. *C.* [1985] F.L.R. 1159). The child's welfare is the "first and paramount" consideration no matter what the reason for his being in care (s.12F(1)). The rules about separate representation of the child (s.12F(2)–(4)) and appeals (s.12C(5)) are the same as for parental rights resolutions. Either the parent or the local authority can later apply to vary or discharge the order (s.12D). A single magistrate may suspend the order for seven days in an emergency where he is satisfied that continued access will put the child's welfare seriously at risk (s.12E).

Thus the parent can only go to court after all access has ended and often there is a considerable delay before the case can be heard. It is now planned to give parents a statutory right to reasonable access unless this is denied or withdrawn by a court, which may decide the matter at the outset or later (D.H.S.S., 1987; R.C.C.L., 1985). But are legal procedures or even Codes of Practice (see s.12G and D.H.S.S., 1983) going to bring about the massive change in practice needed?

(iv) Contributions

If a child is in care under section 2 (or 3) of the 1980 Act or a care order (but not an interim order) under the 1969 Act, his parents are liable to maintain him (1980 Act, s.45(1)(i)) except while he is home on trial (s.45(3)) or after notice has been given of intention to adopt him (see Adoption Act 1976, s.31(3)). Under the Family Law Reform Act 1987, this will also apply to extra-marital fathers. No parent is liable for any time while he is receiving supplementary benefit or family income supplement (1980 Act, s.45(1A)). Once the child reaches 16, only he is liable (s.45(1)(ii)).

Contributions are normally "agreed" between the authority and contributor (s.46). The authority cannot go to court unless it has first proposed an amount and either this has not been agreed within a month or there has been a default in the agreed payments (s.47(1). The amount proposed must not be more than the authority would normally pay for boarding-out, but may either be a standard charge or what the authority thinks reasonable in the circumstances (s.46(2)). The authority need not seek any charge if it would be unreasonable in the particular case to do so (s.46(4)). If the authority goes to the magistrates' court for a contribution order (s.47), the amount cannot be more than the sum proposed but may be less. The same procedure must be gone through for a variation (s.48). It does not apply to children committed to care in family proceedings, but that court may order periodical payments to the authority.

(v) Absconding

Not all children in care are prisoners. If a child in "voluntary" care runs or is taken away, there is little the authority can do to recover him unless it is prepared to institute care or wardship proceedings, although some absconders may later be placed in secure accommodation (see above). But once he has been in care for six months, anyone who helps or takes him without the authority's consent will be guilty of a criminal offence, and this includes a parent unless he has given 28 days' notice of his intention (1980 Act, s.13).

If a resolution has vested parental rights in the authority, the same offence is committed by anyone who helps him run away, or takes him away, or prevents his returning, and there is an additional offence of failing to return him when asked from a period of home trial (s.14). This does not apply to a parent whose rights have not been assumed, but the six months rule does. In addition, a magistrate may order someone believed to have the child to produce him in court, or issue a warrant authorising a social worker to search specified premises and remove the child (s.15).

Children who are remanded or committed to care under the 1969 Act can always be arrested without warrant by a policeman, if they absent themselves from wherever the authority requires them to live. A magistrates' court also has power to order someone believed to have the child to produce him in court, and to issue a warrant to a policeman to search specified premises and arrest the child. It is also an offence to harbour or assist such an absconder (s.16).

3. *After Care*

When a child is in care as a result of a court order, the authority must keep him until the order lapses at 18 or 19 or is earlier discharged by the court (in which case it could be replaced by a supervision order). When a child is in "voluntary" care, he must be kept until 18, unless the local authority concludes that his welfare no longer requires it, or he is discharged to a parent, guardian, relative or friend. The rights assumed by a resolution will last until 18 or the resolution ends, but a child might remain in voluntary care after that, or the rights may be suspended while a custodianship order is in force. Resolutions end automatically if a guardian is appointed for the child (1980 Act, s.5(2)(c)) and both resolutions (s.5(2)(a) and (b)) and care orders (1969 Act, s.21A) end automatically if the child is adopted or freed for adoption.

Children who leave care when they grow up often do not have a family to fall back on; nor, as single people will they have any prior-

ity for local authority housing. But the authority does have some
responsibilities. If a child leaves care at or after 16, for example on
starting work, the local authority where he is must "advise and
befriend" him until he is 18, unless he clearly does not need it (s.28).
If a child leaves care at or after 17, the care authority has power, if
he requests it, to visit, advise and befriend him up to the age of 21,
and in exceptional cases it may give him financial help (s.29). There
is also a more general power to contribute to the cost of accommodation and maintenance for a child who has left care after reaching
16 and is now 17 but under 21; or to pay an educational grant to a
child who left care after reaching 17 and is under 21; and if the
course continues after 21, these contributions or grants may continue until it is finished (s.27). Most of these have now been super-
seded by the social security and educational grants systems, so that
the housing problem is perhaps the most serious. Local authorities
should no doubt encourage independence as "their" children grow
up (and they can arrange emigration, s.24, or apprenticeships, s.23)
but special consideration is due to people who have been deprived of
the permanent family backing which so many take for granted; these
powers may therefore be clarified and expanded (D.H.S.S., 1987).

4. *Local Authorities and the Courts*

One of the most complex and difficult areas of family law is the relationship between the powers of courts and local authorities, and
between the courts themselves, in deciding the future of children
who may need care away from home.

Apart from care orders made in criminal cases, there are three
main schemes for compulsorily admitting or detaining children in
care: care proceedings, resolutions and committal in wardship or
other family proceedings. If a local authority feels that its powers
under the 1969 or 1980 Acts are insufficient or inappropriate, there
is nothing to prevent it making the child a ward of court. This could
be because the grounds for care orders or resolutions are too narrow
(see the *Sunderland* and *Glamorgan* cases mentioned in section 1(ii)
earlier or *Re C.B. (a minor)* [1981] 1 W.L.R. 379); or because the
authority has failed in care proceedings in the juvenile court and
cannot at present appeal (see *Re D. (a minor) (justices' decision: review)*
[1977] Fam. 158; *Re C. (a minor) (justices' decision: review)* (1979) 2
F.L.R. 62); or even in access proceedings where it can (*Re L.H. (a
minor) (wardship: jurisdiction)* [1986] 2 F.L.R. 306); or because a high
status court with wider powers and more flexible rules of evidence
and procedure is preferred to a lay bench with more limited powers

and more rigid rules of evidence and procedure; or because the authority would prefer to have the guidance of the High Court (or perhaps a county court) in solving a particularly complex or delicate case (for example, the proposed abortion, *Re P. (a minor)* [1986] 1 F.L.R. 272 or sterilisation, *Re B. (a minor) (wardship: sterilisation)* [1987] 2 W.L.R. 1213 of a care order child). Parents themselves might well prefer this to being told that the authority wishes to take away their rights because they are unfit (see, for example, the "heroin baby" case, *Re D. (a minor)* [1986] 3 W.L.R. 1080).

But while it is clear that the authority can invoke the wardship jurisdiction in these cases, it is now equally clear that the family can not. Thus a mother could not use wardship to seek access to a child removed under a care order (*A.* v. *Liverpool City Council* [1982] A.C. 363) or even to forestall care proceedings which had not yet been started (*W.* v. *Shropshire County Council* [1986] 1 F.L.R. 359; *W.* v. *Nottinghamshire County Council* [1986] 1 F.L.R. 565). In the past, parents might be allowed to use it in effect to appeal against an unfavourable result in care proceedings (*Re H. (a minor) (wardship: jurisdiction)* [1978] Fam. 68) but now it seems that they can not. Similarly, relatives or foster parents who have no claims under the statutory schemes cannot fill the gap with wardship instead (*Re W. (a minor) (wardship: jurisdiction)* [1985] A.C. 791; see Chapter 10).

The reasoning is that the courts must not use a non-statutory jurisdiction which stems from the royal prerogative to interfere or conflict with decisions which Parliament has said are the province of local authorities. Thus if the authority has power to decide the matter in question (be it access or discharge to relatives) the court cannot do so unless the authority wishes it to. If, however, Parliament has left gaps in the authority's powers, there is no conflict and the court can help. Where, on the other hand, it is alleged that the authority has broken its statutory duties, abused its powers or taken a decision which no reasonable authority could have taken, the decision should be challenged by judicial review and not by wardship (*Re D.M. (a minor) (wardship: jurisdiction)* [1986] 2 F.L.R. 122).

The end result is widely felt to be unjust. If the court can fill the gaps left by Parliament in the authority's powers to protect children, why can it not fill the gaps left in the court's powers to hear claims by parents or relatives? The underlying reason is that it would then become virtually impossible to prevent parents and others from invoking wardship whenever they felt unhappy or aggrieved by an authority's decision about anything important. It was thought that this would "open the floodgates" to huge numbers of cases which would swamp the courts (see *A.* v. *Liverpool City Council*, above). The official view is also that local authorities should be allowed to concentrate their resources on doing the best job they can for children and families alike and that courts are not the best places for reviewing the details of how they go about it (*House of Commons*, 1984; R.C.C.L., 1985). Others, not surprisingly, feel differently (see, for example, *Family Rights Group*, 1982 and 1985).

If the gaps left by Parliament in the family's rights are thought to be deliberate, why are not the gaps left in the authority's powers? The Review of Child Care Law (1985) has for the first time considered all the statutory schemes in an effort to unify their principles and procedures; in particular it has proposed grounds upon which the state should be able to intervene compulsorily in family life. Although the wardship jurisdiction was not affected, would it any longer be justifiable to use it once Parliament had approved such a unified and would-be comprehensive scheme (see *Law Commission*, 1987b)?

Rather different questions arise where two statutes conflict or overlap. For example, non-marital fathers who have not yet been granted any parental rights have no place in either the resolution or, at present, the access procedures under the 1980 Act. A domestic court may hear an application for access (*R. v. Oxford JJ., ex p. D.* [1986] 3 W.L.R. 447) or custody (*R. v. Oxford JJ., ex p. H.* [1975] Q.B. 1) under the Guardianship of Minors Act instead; but the *A. v. Liverpool* principle has now been held to apply to such access applications (*Re M. (minors), The Times* May 26, 1987). Courts may also make custody orders about care order children. These will usually do no more than define who is to have the child should the care order be discharged (*M. v. Humberside County Council* [1979] Fam. 114) but a divorce court may occasionally make an order which supersedes the care order (*E. v. E. and Cheshire County Council (No. 2)* (1979) 1 F.L.R. 73).

It would all be a great deal easier if all the people who can at present seek custody or access under other legislation could also apply in care proceedings in the juvenile court (see R.C.C.L., 1985; D.H.S.S. 1987). It would be even easier if there were machinery for ensuring that all the claims and questions relating to a single child could be dealt with at the same time (see R.C.C.L., 1985). The worst example is that a foster parent's claim for adoption or custodianship goes to a domestic or county court, while the parent's claim for access goes to a juvenile court. It is hardly surprising that many people want a unified family court which could deal with everything together. But in such a court, would there be any justification for the wardship jurisdiction at all?

10 Relatives and Foster Parents

"Care-giving" is a convenient term where a child is being looked after by someone other than his natural parents or legal guardian but has not been legally adopted. It obviously includes a wide variety of arrangements, with relatives or with non-relatives, for short or long periods, with or without payment, and with or without the intervention of a child care agency. Each situation, however, presents the law with the same two problems. The first—how far the law either can or should impose some control upon the making and conduct of these arrangements—has already been discussed in Chapter 2. The second—the legal relationship between care-giver and child and how far it should be given any security—is the subject of this chapter.

Relatives or well-wishers of a child may occasionally resort to the courts even though they neither have, nor wish to have, actual care of him. Any interested person may make the child a ward of the High Court with a view to challenging some particular aspect of his upbringing, such as his proposed education or medical treatment; interested people may also be given leave to intervene in divorce proceedings which involve a child, perhaps to ask for access; grandparents have a statutory right to apply to magistrates who are making custody orders in matrimonial proceedings, or to any court making custody orders under the Guardianship of Minors Act 1971, in order to seek access to their grandchildren; they must usually wait for a spouse or parent to make the first move, but if the parent who is their own child has died, they may themselves take the initiative in taking the matter to court; the Children and Young Persons (Amendment) Act 1986, s.3(2) will also give the courts power to make grandparents parties to care proceedings. These powers are very little used, but they do recognise that families extend far beyond the household group of man, woman and child; and that this may be just as important for the child as it is for the adults involved.

1. *Insecurity*

One of the main justifications for social work involvement in arrangements for the care of children away from home is the extreme difficulty of the care-giver's task. She must be able to supply both the physical and psychological needs of a child who has experienced the stress, either of separation from his most-loved adult, or of previous negative relationships with the adults around him. She must try to do this, not as total substitute for the absent parents, but as someone who shares the responsibility with both the agency (if there is one) and the parents. And, save in cases where the placement breaks down at the foster parents' request, it is the parents or the agency who decide how long the child may stay.

If the child is privately placed with relatives or foster parents, the natural parents retain the right to remove him at will. This is so whatever they may have agreed with the care-givers, for it is not possible to surrender or transfer parental rights by agreement (Children Act 1975, s.85(2)). If the child has been boarded-out by a local authority or voluntary organisation, the foster parents must undertake to return the child when asked by the agency (Boarding-out of Children Regulations 1955, see Sched.). The agency may be asking for the child because it has itself decided to end the placement; or because it has no legal right to refuse the parents' request for the child's return—but this is a matter for the agency to decide and so foster parents should not return the child to the parents on their own initiative; or because although the agency had parental rights, a court has decided to return them to the parents—but foster parents who have been looking after the child for at least six weeks, ending within the past six months, now have a right to be notified of an application for the discharge of a care order made in care proceedings and to be given a hearing (see Chapter 5).

The law may be right to draw some distinction between official foster parents and others. The others will usually have some connection with the child apart from the simple fact of care; they may be acting out of kindness or family feeling; and they may receive little or no payment. Official foster parents form part of the agency's child care service; they are professionally chosen and advised; they may be relatives, but usually have no connection with the child apart from the fact of care; that care is often undertaken during temporary breaks from home, for example while the mother is ill or having another baby; and they are paid. However, until recently, the boarding-out allowance was expected to do no more than cover the costs of keeping the child, and sometimes not even that; foster parents who would only act for some profit, however small, were regarded with

suspicion. The truly professional foster parent, who receives inten-
sive training and social work support, in return for taking particularly difficult children at a realistic fee, is a relatively recent
development.

In the days when children came into public care because they
had been orphaned, abandoned or removed from extremely
damaging homes, it was easier to see foster care as a completely
"fresh start." When the service was extended to children from
quite ordinary homes whose need for substitute care arose from illness or other misfortunes and was often purely temporary, the
emphasis changed (*Packman*, 1981). The parents had to feel that
they did not run the risk of losing their children forever if they used
the service. This coincided with a growing understanding of the
dangers of separating children from their most-loved parent-
figures, and of the confusion and self-doubt experienced by many
children who are brought up away from their natural parents. The
aim became to reunite the natural family if at all possible. The
emphasis was upon an "inclusive" model of fostering in which
links with the family were maintained and encouraged, and both
families and agency worked together toward the common good
(*Holman*, 1975).

In practice, this is extremely difficult to achieve. There are many
purely short term placements where the child soon goes home or
leaves for something more permanent. There are many long term
placements which break down. But there are also a good many
which go on for a very long time and gradually develop into the
child's permanent "home." Only a few of these appear to fit the preferred "inclusive" model, although the favourable results of many
placements with relatives suggests that this would indeed be the best
if it could be achieved (*Rowe et al.*, 1984). Inevitably, however, as
time goes on the child puts down roots, yet both he and his foster
family must experience the ambiguities and insecurities of the fostering relationships (see e.g. *Triseliotis*, 1980 and 1983).

This has inevitably led to debates about whether permanence and
security can only be achieved by expanding the use of adoption or
whether there is a need for a "half-way" house, in which the child
cannot readily be moved but remains a member of his natural family
and can retain his links with them (e.g. *Tizard*, 1977). These debates
are often coloured by the knowledge that much more could be done
to preserve and foster those links at the outset (*Triseliotis*, 1980; *Rowe
et al.*, 1984; *Milham et al.*, 1986); legal procedures are of little importance compared with the practice which has led up to them. The
ways in which any care-giver might seek to acquire some legal security are listed below, followed by a discussion of the principles upon

which a court would operate if called upon to adjudicate a custody dispute between such care-givers and the child's natural parents.

2. *Procedures for Keeping the Child*

(i) Adoption

Adoption is the ultimate solution, for it involves a complete and irrevocable transfer of the child from one family to another. The outcome for the child is usually far more favourable than in any other form of substitute care-giving (*Seglow, Kellmer Pringle and Wedge,* 1972). Part of the reason for this may be the high degree of security and commitment which it involves. Another reason could be that it tries to reproduce, as closely as possible, the "normal" family. For that reason, among others, it is not always the right solution, particularly where the child can expect to retain some contact with his natural parents.

In any event, it will not usually be available. It can only happen by order of a court, and the court must be satisfied on three basic points: first, that the adoption will safeguard and promote the welfare of the child throughout his childhood; secondly, that any necessary parental agreement has either been given or can be dispensed with on defined grounds; and thirdly, that the child has been continuously in the actual custody of the applicants throughout the three (or in some cases 12) months immediately before the order. The procedure for freeing the child for adoption enables the second to be dealt with before the other two and prevents a child in care from being removed while the application is pending. The rule that a child cannot be removed from prospective adopters if they have had him for five years makes it easier for them to fulfil the third criterion. The introduction of adoption allowances has also made it financially possible for some (see further in Chapter 11). For a while, after the Children Act 1975, it seemed that adoption was developing into a more flexible institution which could also cover children who retained links with their natural families. Now that an alternative has been made available, adoption may be reverting to its more traditional role.

(ii) Wardship

Any of the parties involved, whether relatives, foster parents, the agency or the child's own parents, may seek to resolve the problem by making the child a ward of court.

However, if the child is in the care of the local authority, the position is complicated by the High Court's reluctance to interfere in the authority's statutory responsibilities (*A.* v. *Liverpool City Council* [1982] A.C. 363). This means that the court will not allow foster parents to use the procedure to challenge the local authority's decision to remove a child from their care (*Re M.* [1961] Ch. 328; *Re T. (A.J.J.) (an infant)* [1970] Ch. 688). Nor can relatives use it to try and obtain the child's discharge from care. In *Re W. (a minor) (wardship: jurisdiction)* [1985] A.C. 791, the parents had rejected their four year old daughter and consented to care proceedings with a view to freeing her for adoption. Her uncle and aunt and grandparents knew nothing of this and wanted her to remain in the family, cared for by uncle and aunt. The House of Lords held that although the child care scheme did not give the relatives a right to be heard in court, the local authority had ample power to consider whether it would be better for the child to "be brought up within her natural family and have the comfort and support of a loving relationship with her uncle and aunt," even though "there may be dangers in bringing [her] up in a family which includes the parents who had rejected her" (Lord Scarman). As the decision clearly lay within the authority's statutory powers, the court should not interfere.

Thus despite its apparently broad scope, wardship is not an ideal method of granting some security to a deserving care-giver. Even if the case is one in which the court is prepared to hear the merits, proceedings take place in the Family Division of the High Court. Although the court sits in large cities as well as London, these are often geographically inconvenient. The procedure is careful, complicated and slow. Legal representation is virtually essential and unless legal aid is available the expense will be considerable. If the care-givers succeed, the child must remain a ward of court, so that any alteration in the status quo, or major decision affecting his upbringing, must be referred to the court at further expense and delay. The remedy is therefore limited to local authorities and a small number of comparatively well-off or unusually determined litigants (*Law Commission*, 1987b). Indeed the court would be unable to cope with large numbers. But its existence and scope does put the new custodianship jurisdiction into some perspective.

(iii) Custody and Custodianship

Until December 1985, when Part II of the Children Act 1975 came into force, wardship was almost the only way short of adoption of establishing a claim to someone else's child. Third parties may be granted custody in proceedings between husband and wife or mother and father (see Chapter 3), but this depends upon a spouse or parent taking the first step. A court hearing a matrimonial dispute between the care-givers themselves may also make custody orders about any child whom they have treated as a member of their family, apart from one officially boarded-out by a local authority or voluntary organisation; but this will not always affect the rights of a parent who is not a party to the marriage. The limitations of this choice were thought to lead, on the one hand, to many adoption applications which would distort rather than replace the child's natural family, and on the other hand, where adoption was impossible, to difficulties in establishing the child in a secure and committed substitute home (*Stockdale*, 1972).

The solution could simply have been to allow anyone to apply for custody, and to trust the courts to make orders only where this was genuinely best for the child. The courts would then have had to abandon their reluctance to interfere in cases where the child was in care, for otherwise the problem of the long-term local authority foster parent would have remained, while relatives and private foster parents acquired much better rights. But to do this would not only have given the courts unprecedented powers to review the merits of social workers' decisions, but would also have had dramatic implications for the nature of fostering and the confidence of parents in the child care service.

The result was a compromise. The new procedure allows certain people to apply (although of course they may not succeed) to the local magistrates' or county court, or to the High Court, for an order giving them legal custody, but only if they have been looking after the child for some time. In keeping with the Act's principal objective, of finding an alternative to unsuitable family adoptions, these periods can differ as between relatives and other applicants, and even more significantly according to whether a person already having legal custody (usually of course a parent) agrees to the application being made.

(a) *The applicants*

The applicant or applicants must be "qualified" in one of three ways (s.33(3)): (i) a relative or step-parent with whom the child has had his home for at least the three months before the application is made is qualified to apply if he has the consent of "a person having legal custody" of the child; (ii) for anyone else applying with similar consent, the qualifying period is a total of 12 months, which may be in separate periods provided that it includes the past three months; (iii) if there is no such consent, the qualifying period for all applicants is a total of three years, including the past three months.

Joint applications are possible, but there is no requirement, as there is in adoption or the boarding-out regulations, for applicants to be married to one another. Step-parents of children involved in divorce are expressly excluded, unless the parent other than the one they married has died or disappeared, or it has since turned out that the child should not have been named as a "child of the family" in the divorce proceedings at all (s.33(5) and (8)); otherwise a step-parent can and should apply to the divorce court for custody. Where natural parents were not married to one another or one has died, however, step-parents must use custodianship.

Only the consent of "a" person having legal custody is required for the shorter periods to apply; thus if both parents have custody only one need consent. A local authority with parental rights under a care order or resolution is presumably a "person having legal custody". However, if no-one has legal custody, or if the applicant himself has it, or the person with it cannot be found, the shorter periods apply without the need for consent (s.33(6)). Consent is to the *application* and not as in adoption to the order. There is no way of dispensing with it, save by the roundabout way of applying to adopt.

(b) *Custodianship as an alternative*

The court can direct that certain other applications be treated as if they were for custodianship. Provided that any necessary agreements have been given or dispensed with, the court hearing an adoption application can direct that it be treated as one for custodianship if it thinks that this would be more appropriate (s.37(2)). In the case of adoption applications by relatives or step-parents (again excluding step-parents of children involved in divorce), this is obligatory if the court is satisfied that the child's welfare would not be better safeguarded by adoption than custodianship (s.37(1)). Extraordinarily, therefore, the court has no power to direct custodianship where it has been unable to dispense with parental agreement to adoption precisely because custodianship would be better (*Re M., (a minor) (custodianship : jurisdiction)* [1987] 1 W.L.R. 162). Where the arguments are evenly balanced, moreover, there is no need to consider custodianship (*Re S. (a minor) (adoption or custodianship)* [1987] 2 W.L.R. 977). Lastly, a court hearing a magistrates' matrimonial dispute or a Guardianship of Minors Act custody dispute, and which thinks that custody should be granted to a third party, may treat the application as if the third party had applied for custodianship (s.37(3); Domestic Proceedings and Magistrates' Courts Act 1978, s.8(3)). In all these cases, it does not matter that the applicant would not have been "qualified" to apply for custodianship in the first place (s.37(4)).

(c) *Interim protection*

Removal of the child is prohibited while an application is pending, but only if the child has had his home with the applicant for a total of at least three years (s.41(1)). In most other cases, the person having legal custody will have consented and is thus unlikely to remove the child; but a change of mind is always possible and occasionally there will be someone else who has the right to remove the child and who has not consented. If removal is feared, the applicant may be able to get an interim custody order, as in Guardianship of Minors Act cases (s.34(5) and Guardianship Act 1973, s.2(4)). If the automatic prohibition applies, removal is only possible if the applicant agrees or with leave of a court, or by way of arrest, or under some statutory authority; a local authority cannot remove a child who was in its care before going to the applicant and is still in its care, unless the applicant consents or a court gives leave (s.41(2)).

Contravention is a criminal offence (s.41(3)). The courts may also direct a particular person not to remove the child if there is reasonable ground to think that he intends it (s.42(2)). If the child is unlawfully removed, the courts may order his return (s.42(1)), and if this is not done, the High Court or county court may authorise a court officer, and a magistrates' court may authorise a policeman, to search specified premises for the child and return him (s.42(3) and (4)).

(d) *Reports*

Notice must be given to the local authority by the applicant within seven days of making the application (s.40(1)), unless it is a case which the court itself has directed shall be treated as custodianship (s.37(4); Domestic Proceedings and Magistrate Courts Act 1978, s.8(5)). The authority must then investigate and produce a report (1975 Act, s.40(2) and (3)). The section mentions matters such as the wishes and feelings of the child, the means and suitability of the applicants, information about the applicants' household, and the wishes and means of the natural parents. The Custodianship (Reports) Regulations 1985, however, require very similar details to those expected of local authorities or adoption agencies on adoption. The court also has the usual power to call for a welfare officer's report from either the local authority or a probation officer (s.39). Both types of report are covered by the usual rules as to disclosure (see Chapter 3).

It is hard to see why it was thought necessary to provide for both, although section 40 ensures that there will be some investigation of every case, no matter how uncontested or straightforward. If the object was to provide an equivalent to the agency's report in adoption cases, then the reporter should be independent of any authority which has the child in its care. If the object was to recognise the interest of the local authority in such cases, then it was unnecessary to insist that they be involved in others.

(e) *Effect of the order*

The order, if made, will vest "legal custody" of the child in the applicant, or one or more of them (s.33(1)). The right of anyone else to legal custody will be suspended for the time being (s.44(1)), unless the custodian is married to the person who already has it, in which case they will share it (s.44(2)). There is therefore no way of splitting custody up between the applicant and the natural parent. "Legal custody" means all those parental rights and duties which relate to the child's person as opposed to his property (s.86). It will include the right to decide whether the child may marry under the age of 18 (Marriage Act 1949, s.3) and to be treated as "parent" for the purposes of the Child Care Act 1980 (s.8(2)), including the access provisions. The custodian will thus have almost complete control over the child's upbringing (and any dispute between joint custodians can be referred to a court as can disputes between parents, 1975 Act s.38). But there are important differences from adoption: the custodian cannot automatically emigrate with the child (s.86); he cannot appoint a testamentary guardian for the child or change the child's surname; and the child remains in his natural family for such purposes as inheritance. The natural parents retain the right to decide whether the child may be adopted, and the link with them is preserved through the possibilities of ancillary orders and later revocation.

(f) *Ancillary orders*

The court may grant access to the child's mother, father, grandparents, or anyone in relation to whose marriage he has been treated as a "child of the family" (s.34(1)(a) and (2)). This may later be varied or discharged at the request of the person granted access or the custodian (s.35(3) and (4)). The court may order the child's mother or father, or person who has treated him as a "child of the family," to make periodical payments, or to pay a lump sum of up to £500, to or for the benefit of the child (s.34(1)(b) and (c)). It can also revoke maintenance orders made by other courts, or vary them for the benefit of the custodian (s.34(1)(d) and (e)). Under the Family Law Reform Act 1987, these orders will be available against unmarried parents, whereas previously the custodian could only make a separate application for an affiliation order against the father (s.45) and a step-father could not even do that. The duration of periodical payment orders, and the considerations to be taken into account by the court, have been harmonised with those in the other custody jurisdictions (ss.34A and 34B and Chapter 3). Orders may be revoked or varied at the request of the person paying or the custodian (s.35(3) and (4)). Lump sum orders may not be varied, but may be made payable in instalments, and further lump sums may be ordered on variation applications (s.35A). Finally, the court has the same power to make supervision orders, or commit the child to the care of a local authority, as it has in ordinary custody cases (s.34(5)).

(g) *Custodianship over children in care*

If the child is in "voluntary" care, the custodian becomes his "parent" and may discharge him. If the local authority has parental rights under a care order or a resolution, its right to legal custody will be suspended but presumably its other rights remain. The local authority, the child or (presumably) the custodian could apply for discharge of a care order and the authority could rescind a resolution (Child Care Act 1980, s.5(4)). However, it might wish to remain the person whose rights would revive if the custodianship ended. Whether or not the child was in care before the order, the local authority is able (but not obliged) to pay contributions to a custodian towards the cost of keeping the child, unless the custodian is a step-parent (1975 Act, s.34(6)).

(h) *Revocation*

A custodianship order may be revoked on the application of the child's custodian, mother, father, guardian or *any* local authority (s.35(1)). A person who has previously applied unsuccessfully for revocation cannot apply again unless either the previous court directed that he should be able to do so or there has been a change in the circumstances or some other good reason for considering revocation again (s.35(2)). This is no doubt designed to spare custodians the anguish of repeated applications from parents who have changed their minds or never wanted the order in the first place, but the essential point about custodianship is that it does not sever their relationship completely. On the other hand, custodians will not be making the final commitment which adoptive parents make, for they will be able to apply for revocation themselves. This is the main reason why the court considering any revocation application must discover who will have legal custody if the order is revoked (s.36(1)).

If there is no-one, the court must make a care order (s.36(2)). Normally, however, it will be the person whose rights were suspended by the order; if the court has misgivings about him, it may either allow him to regain custody subject to a supervision order or instead make a care order (s.36(3)). The court will have a duty to call for a local authority or probation officer's report on the desirability of returning the child, unless it already has sufficient information (s.36(4)).

3. *Principles*

Both the wardship and custodianship jurisdictions are governed by the familiar principle in section 1 of the Guardianship of Minors Act 1971: "Where in any proceedings before any court . . . the legal custody or upbringing of a minor . . . is in question, the court, in deciding that question, shall regard the welfare of the minor as the first and paramount consideration . . . " (see also 1975 Act, ss.33(9)). But what is the relative weight to be given to the wishes and claims of the natural parents if these conflict with the welfare of the child? And how do the courts interpret the welfare of the child in such cases? These questions were authoritatively decided by the House of Lords in the leading case of *J.* v. *C.* [1970] A.C. 668.

In 1958 a little boy was born to Spanish parents who were working in England. The mother suffered from tuberculosis and so the baby was cared for by an English couple for some 10 months, until she was well enough to look after him. Later, the parents took him back to Spain, but the family lived in very poor circumstances in Madrid, where the climate did not suit the little boy and his health deteriorated. In 1961, through the former foster parents' Spanish maid, who visited the family while on holiday in Madrid, it was arranged that the boy should come back to them. Nobody contemplated that this would be permanent, but no time limit was agreed. The boy was formally received into the care of the local authority and boarded-out with the foster parents. There he settled down and his health improved. A proposal that the parents should return to work in England did not bear fruit, and the mother did not take up an offer to pay for her to visit the boy. In 1963 he started school, and the foster mother wrote a "tactless" letter to the mother, remarking how English he was becoming. The mother became worried, and after a request for him to spend a holiday in Span had been refused by the foster parents, formally asked the local authority for his return. The foster parents countered with notice of their intention to apply to adopt. In December 1963, the local authority, feeling caught between the child care and adoption legislation, made the child a ward of court. It took until July 1965 for the case to be heard and the parents, having been assured that the authority would look after their interests, were not there. The judge ordered that care and control should remain with the foster parents, but that the boy should be brought up a Roman Catholic and with knowledge of his Spanish origins and the Spanish language. In 1967, the foster parents applied to change his religion so that he could be sent to an Anglican choir school; the parents countered with a renewed application for his return. By this time both their material circumstances and the mother's health were very much better, but the boy was now nine, and had been with the foster family since he was three, was very close to his foster brother, had learned to play cricket and spoke only "pidgin" Spanish. The case was heard by the judge in 1967, then by the Court of Appeal, and finally by the House of Lords in 1968. All decided that he should stay where he was but remain a Roman Catholic.

The case raised very neatly the precise application of the "welfare principle" in such disputes. It could be argued that the Act (originally passed in 1925) applied only to disputes between mother and father and had done nothing to affect the common law's presumption in favour of natural parents, whose rights could only be overriden if the child's welfare was clearly in danger. If that were so, the natural parents might have succeeded, for apart perhaps from not taking up the offer to visit, they could hardly be criticised for letting the boy go to England and now had a satisfactory home to offer. If, on the other hand, the child's welfare was the first as well as an overriding consideration, he should surely remain where he was happy and settled, whatever the rights and wrongs between the parents and foster parents.

The House of Lords decided that the section applied just as much to disputes between parents and "strangers" as it did between mother and father. It meant just what it said: the welfare of the child was always the first and paramount consideration. But where does that leave the natural parents? Is the child's welfare in fact the *sole* consideration?

On the one hand, we have Lord MacDermott's words, that the section connotes "a process whereby, when all the relevant facts, relationships, claims and wishes of parents, risks, choices and other circumstances are taken into account and weighed, the course to be followed will be that which is most in the interests of the child's welfare. . . . " This suggests that the claims of natural parenthood are only relevant in so far as they indicate what will be best for the child. On the other hand, we have Lord Upjohn, who said this: "The natural parents have a strong claim to have their wishes considered, first and principally, no doubt, because it is normally part of the paramount consideration of the welfare of the infant that he should be with them; but also because natural parents may themselves have strong claims to have their wishes considered as normally the proper persons to have the upbringing of the child they have brought into the world." This suggests that where the welfare considerations are more evenly balanced, the parents' claims can be taken into account in their own right. The majority agreed with Lord MacDermott, but in practice there may be little difference between the two.

In disputes between parents and "strangers" there is often a conflict between two important welfare factors. One is the danger of disturbing a situation which has been working well for some time. The other is the possible risk to the child's sense of identity and personal worth if he is brought up by people who are not his "own," particularly if he is cut off from other links with his family and background or given a negative picture to them.

In 1926, a judge was able to discount the dangers of disruption: " . . . at her tender age [six] one knows from experience how mercifully transient are the effects of partings and other sorrows, and how soon the novelty of fresh surroundings and new associations effaces the recollection of former days and kind friends . . . " (*Re Thain* [1926] Ch. 676). A modern judge would certainly not dismiss as "transient" the effects of "partings and other sorrows." It is usually thought that he would not now order that a little girl who had been brought up by her uncle and aunt since she was a baby should be returned to her father and step-mother. However, it is worth recalling that a juvenile court, in care proceedings, ordered that Maria Colwell should be returned to her natural mother after six years with an uncle and aunt and that this course was unopposed by the social workers concerned. No doubt the social workers' case was partly coloured by their view of what the court's decision was likely to be (this was only shortly after the decision in *J.* v. *C.*), but it was also coloured by what they saw as her long-term interests—rehabilitation with her natural family. That cannot be questioned as an ideal, but perhaps both courts and social workers should ask themselves *why* it is usually better for children to be brought up by their natural parents. Truly "natural" parents love their children and feel responsible for them, and the child will benefit both from this and from the sense of normality and identity which it will bring. If other people have developed the same love and commitment towards the child, so that the child feels normal and secure with them, their relationship cannot lightly be put at risk for the sake of more dubious advantages to the child's later sense of his place in the world.

4. *Commentary*

It is far too simple to see these cases as a conflict between the "rights of parents" and the "welfare of the child." The welfare of the child in itself demands that very careful consideration be given to the natural parents' claims. Should they be entitled to anything more? Procedurally, they already have much more, because non-parents have such limited rights to apply to the courts. This produces many complications and anomalies, particularly for step-parents, and there is little reason to believe that non-parents would abuse a much wider right to apply. Local authority foster parents may be a special case, because parents must be able to feel confidence in using the child care service and local authorities must be able to provide and plan for each child in the way they think best. But if official foster parents could only apply with consent or after a period of caring for the child (perhaps less than the current three years), should other people be able to apply without any restrictions at all (see *Law Commission*, 1986)?

If the restrictions on making applications were lifted, is there any need to reconsider the principles applicable? To reintroduce a preference in favour of natural parents might put the welfare of some children seriously at risk. Also, if a child has made his home with another family for some time, and especially from an early age, it is impossible to say whether his "birth" or his "psychological" parents should have the preference. The welfare principle allows the court to give preference to the true psychological parent (e.g. *B.R.* v. *Ealing London Borough Council* [1985] F.L.R. 999). It is not a question of choosing between the family and the institutions of the state but between two families, both of which could well be called "natural."

Part IV
New Families

11 Adoption

Adoption is the virtually complete and irrevocable transfer of a child from one legal family to another. It was first introduced into English law by statute in 1926; in other legal systems its purpose has been to provide an heir to carry on the family's name and property, but in England its principal object has always been to provide permanent and secure family care for a child whose natural parents are unable or unwilling to keep him. The typical adoption is therefore seen as the placement of a baby by an unmarried mother through an adoption society with a childless couple who are complete strangers to the natural family. In practice, many adoptions take place in quite different circumstances; but the stereotype has had an important influence upon the law and its practice.

1. *The Court*

Adoption cannot take place without a court order, but the court is not always called upon to adjudicate a dispute between contesting parties. Usually, it acts as a check upon the decisions already made by other people and as a formal recognition of the vital change in the child's status. But with the decreasing supply of young babies offered for adoption has come an increasing emphasis on adoption as a way of providing a permanent new home for older and often "hard to place" children. Disputes and difficulties are perhaps more likely to arise with these than with the conventional adoption case. Applications may be made either to the High Court or to the applicants' local county or magistrates' court. The High Court must deal with cases where neither applicant is domiciled in this country, but in practice it deals with only a handful of cases. Most go to county courts, where they are dealt with by a judge, usually in his private room in a building where no criminal cases are tried.

2. *Qualifications to Adopt and be Adopted*

The qualifications to adopt and be adopted make some attempt to reproduce a normal family structure. A person can only be adopted while still a child under 18, and only then if he has never been married (Adoption Act 1976, ss.72(1) and 12(5)). Every applicant for adoption, whether related to the child or not, must be at least 21 years old (ss.14(1) and 15(1)). The law lays down no maximum age, but agencies and courts may be reluctant to accept applicants who will be elderly while the child is still a teenager.

Applications may be made by one person or by two people together, but joint applicants must be married to one another (s.14(1)) and the stability of their marriage will be an important factor for the agency and the court. A sole applicant must either be unmarried (that is, single, widowed or divorced) or, if married, must satisfy the court that his or her spouse cannot be found or is incapable because of physical or mental ill-health of making an application or that they are living apart and the separation is likely to be permanent (s.15(1)). Applicants must attach medical reports to their application to the court, unless one is the child's parent or it is an agency placement, where the agency must do so, for their health is obviously an important factor in safeguarding the welfare of the child throughout his childhood.

There is no difficulty if the applicant, or one of joint applicants, is domiciled in any part of the United Kingdom, Channel Islands or Isle of Man (ss.14(2)(a) and 15(2)(a)). If this is not the case, it may be possible to obtain a convention adoption order (s.17) from the High Court, or an order from the High Court or a county court, allowing the applicant to take the child abroad to be adopted (s.55). These will need specialist legal advice and are outside the scope of this book.

Provisions which aim to discourage adoption by step-parents (Chapter 8), by one natural parent (Chapter 6) and by other relatives such as grandparents (Chapter 10) have already been mentioned. All stem from the Houghton Committee's view (*Stockdale*, 1972) that adoption should replace, rather than distort, the natural family. Another provision which reflects that hope is the procedure for concealing the applicants' identity under a serial number (Adoption Rules 1984, rr. 14 and 23(3)). This may protect them and the child from the problems which might arise should the mother regret her decision and try to trace them, but the mother does not have a similar privilege.

3. *Arranging Adoptions*

The law puts certain general limitations on arranging adoptions and also makes detailed rules about how individual placements are to be carried out.

(i) Prevention of "trafficking"

The first object is to avoid the risk of children being bought and sold. It is an offence to give or receive any payment or reward either for giving or for receiving a child for adoption or for making the arrangements (s.57). Courts are prohibited from making adoption orders in favour of people who have contravened this rule (s.24(2)). Contributions towards the expenses of an adoption agency are excepted, and so are payments specifically permitted by the court. The court may approve these retrospectively at the time of the hearing (see *Re Adoption Application: Surrogacy, AA212/86, The Times,* March 12, 1987, although there the judge held that payments made to a surrogate mother who had not acted for profit were not in fact " payment or reward" under this section). The D.H.S.S. may also approve schemes submitted by agencies for payment *by the agency* of allowances to actual and prospective adopters: the object is to encourage adoptions of whole families, handicapped children or long-term foster children, where applicants might be deterred by the expense or the loss of the boarding-out allowance. Similarly, it is an offence either for parents or for prospective adopters to advertise their desire for adoption, or for anyone other than an adoption agency to advertise their willingness to make adoption arrangements (s.58). Under the Surrogacy Arrangements Act 1985, it is an offence to negotiate, on a commercial basis, arrangements for a woman to bear a child in order to hand him over to someone else, or to advertise for such people, or to advertise willingness to take part. Once born, the mother may decide to keep the child (see *A. v. C.* [1985] F.L.R. 445) or the commissioning parents may take him (see *Re C. (a minor) (wardship: surrogacy)* [1985] F.L.R. 846): any proceedings will be governed by the child's best interests.

(ii) Agency Placement

The law also makes some attempt to ensure that the vital placement decisions are handled by qualified and experienced people who are not acting for personal profit. No "body of persons" is allowed to arrange adoptions apart from a local social services authority or approved adoption society (1976 Act, s.11). Adoption societies must be approved by the Secretary of State who may refuse or withdraw his approval, provided that he gives his reasons and an opportunity to make representations beforehand (ss.3, 4, 5, 8 and 9). At present, all local social services authorities have power to act as adoption agencies (Adoption Act 1958, s.28), but not quite all of them do so. Under the 1976 Act, all will eventually have a duty to provide a comprehensive adoption service to meet the needs of children, parents and prospective adopters in their area, whether directly or through approved adoption societies (ss.1 and 2).

All agency placements are subject to the Adoption Agencies Regulations 1983, which should mean that they are superior to placements arranged by private individuals. For example, natural parents should have a clearer idea of what they are doing from the first, because the agency must explain the legal implications and procedures and provide a counselling service for them, including non-marital fathers where this is practicable and in the child's interests (reg .7(1) and (3)). It must also discover a long list of particulars about them all and obtain a medical report upon the child (reg. 7(2) and (3) and Sched.). The prospective adopters should be most carefully chosen, for before accepting them as suitable, the agency must provide them with similar information and services, obtain another long list of particulars and a medical report, and also obtain reports on their home and on interviews with two referees, and from their local authority (reg. 8 and Sched.). The risk that placements might turn out badly, whether sooner or later, should be reduced because the decision that a child should be adopted or freed for adoption, that prospective adopters are suitable to adopt, and that particular adopters are suitable for a particular child can only be taken after considering the view of an expert adoption panel (regs. 11(1), 10, 9 and 5). When proposing the particular placement to the adopters, the agency must give them written information about the child, his health, history and background. If they accept, it must follow up the placement with visits, advice and help (reg. 12).

The law requires an agency to take three considerations into account when making its decisions. It must give *first* consideration to the need to safeguard and promote the welfare of the child throughout his childhood (1976 Act, s.6). In recent years, the emphasis of adoption practice has shifted, away from providing the prospective adopters with the perfect babies they wanted to match the ones they were unable to have themselves, towards providing children of all shapes, colours, abilities and sizes with parents whose prime aim is to give a loving and stable home to a child in need. The child, rather than the prospective adopters, must be the first consideration. The second consideration is the need to discover, so far as this is practicable, the child's own wishes and feelings in the matter and to give them appropriate weight having regard to his age and understanding (s.6 again; see also reg. 7). Finally, the agency must have regard so far as is practicable to any wishes of the natural parents about the child's religious upbringing (s.7).

After placement, an adoption order cannot be made unless the child is at least 19 weeks old and at all times during the previous 13 weeks has had his home with the applicants or one of them (s.13(1)). The court must also be satisfied that the agency has had sufficient opportunity to see the child with the applicant, or both applicants together, "in the home environment" (s.13(3)). Hence the agency is now responsible for what used to be called "welfare supervision" and must make its own report to the court (Adoption Rules 1984, r. 22(1) and Sched. 2).

(iii) Private Placements

The agency regulations obviously do not apply to private adoption placements, whether by third parties, such as doctors, lawyers or matrons of nursing homes, or by the family itself. Much concern has been expressed about the quality of these placements (*Stockdale*, 1972). It is thought that there may be little choice between applicants or children; that applicants may have been rejected by the agencies; that the rules against payments are harder to enforce; that there may be inadequate counselling and supervision, and potentially damaging contact between natural and adoptive families. On the other hand, the National Child Development Study found no evidence that the children did any worse than those who had been placed by supposedly more expert agencies (*Seglow, Kellmer Pringle and Wedge*, 1972). Nevertheless, it is now an offence for *anyone* other than an adoption agency to make arrangements or place a child for adoption, except with a relative or under an order of the High Court. It is also an offence to receive a child for adoption in such circumstances (1976 Act, s.11).

If a child has not been placed for adoption by an agency, the 13-week probationary period still applies if the applicant or one of them is a parent, step-parent or relative of the child, or if the child was placed by order of the High Court (s.13(1)). In any other case, an adoption order cannot be made unless the child is at least 12 months old and has had his home with one or both applicants throughout the preceeding 12 months (s.13(2)).

Also, unless the child was placed by an adoption agency, all applicants (whether or not they are parents, step-parents or relatives) must give notice to the local authority for their home area at least three months before the order (s.22(1)). The child then becomes a "protected child" (s.32) and the authority must visit, in order to satisfy itself about the child's well-being and offer any necessary advice to the prospective adopters (s.33(1)). Social workers have power to inspect the premises (s.33(2)); refusal to let them in is not only a criminal offence (s.36(1)(*b*) but is automatically grounds for obtaining a warrant for a policeman to search for and remove the child (s.37(1) and Children and Young Persons Act 1933, s.40). The authority may also apply to a juvenile court to remove the child from unfit people or detrimental premises (1976 Act, s.34); the grounds and effects are the same as for private foster children (see Chapter 2).

More importantly, the authority must investigate the proposed adoption and report to the court (ss.22(2) and (3); Adoption Rules 1984 r. 22(2)). The court must be satisfied that the authority has been able to see the child and applicants together "in the home environment"(s.13(3)). The authority must investigate whether the child's placement was illegal; if it was the court is not expressly prohibited from making an adoption order, as it is where illegal payments have been made, but it has been held that only the High Court may do so (*Re S. (arrangements for adoption)* [1985] F.L.R. 579).

4. *Parental Agreement*

(i) Whose Agreement is Required?

No adoption order can be made unless the child is "freed" for adoption (see below) or the court is satisfied that each parent or guardian of the child, freely and with full understanding of what is involved, agrees unconditionally to the making of that order, unless that agreement can be dispensed with (1976 Act, s.16(1)). Agreement is given in writing to a reporting officer appointed by the court, whose task is to witness it and ensure that it is genuine (s.65(1)(*b*) and Adoption Rules 1984, rr. 5 and 17).

A mother cannot give effective agreement until she has had at least six weeks to get over the birth, but this does not prevent the child being placed before then if she has already made up her mind (s.16(4)). The agreement of each parent or guardian is required, but this does not include a non-marital father (*Re M. (an infant)* [1955] 2 Q.B. 479) unless he has custodial rights by court order in which case he counts as a "guardian" (s.72(1); see further in Chapter 6).

Where the mother is a married woman, her husband also presents a problem. She may wish to conceal the birth from him, but the law presumes that her child is his until it is proved to the contrary. Courts vary in their willingness to accept the mother's word about her child's parentage so that her husband may not have to be approached at all. To keep him in ignorance on her word alone is to deprive both him and the child of the possible benefit of the law's presumption, but in some cases the evidence may be so clear that the court is prepared to do so.

Otherwise, "guardian" means a person legally appointed to take the place of a parent who has died (see Chapter 7). It does not include a local authority which has parental rights under a care order or resolution, although an agency cannot place such a child without its consent and it must always be made a respondent to the application (r. 15(2)). The parent's agreement is still required, although in these cases it may sometimes be easier to find grounds for dispensing with it.

(ii) Dispensing with Agreement

The majority of adoptions have parental agreement, but an increasing proportion of them do not, and one of the most difficult legal problems is how far it is proper to deprive parents of their right to decide. Adoption means the complete and final severance of all ties with the child they have brought into the world, yet the child's future well-being, happiness and security may sometimes be much better safeguarded by adoption than by any other arrangement. The child's welfare is now the *first* consideration for the court (1976 Act, s.6), but it is not the *paramount* consideration: if it were, the court might be able to override parental objections simply because the adoption would be better for the child. Given the general evidence of the comparative success rates of children adopted by strangers, children brought up by their mothers alone, and children who are fostered for a long time, the mother's right to withhold her agreement might virtually disappear once she had allowed others to take care of him (see e.g. *Tizard*, 1977). Instead, the law allows the court to dispense with parental agreement on one or more of six grounds (s.16(2)).

(a) That the parent or guardian cannot be found or is incapable of giving agreement.

"Cannot be found" usually means that all reasonable steps have been taken to find the parent, but without success. In *Re F.(R.) (an infant)* [1970] 1 Q.B. 385 the applicants wrote to the mother's last known address, advertised in the press, and tried to trace her through the post office, all without success, and so the trial court dispensed with her consent and made the order. When the mother found out about it, she alleged that the applicants knew her father's address and that he was in touch with her, yet never approached him. The Court of Appeal allowed her to appeal, even though five months had now elapsed since the order, because all reasonable steps had not been taken to find her.

Exceptionally, a parent "cannot be found" if there are no practicable means of communicating with him to obtain his agreement, as where the child had illegally escaped to this country from a totalitarian regime and any attempt to communicate with his parents there would be very dangerous for them (*Re R. (adoption)* [1967] 1 W.L.R. 34). In that case, the parents were also "incapable" of consenting, but this will usually refer to mental incapacity.

(b) That the parent or guardian is withholding his consent unreasonably.

It is this ground which has caused the most legal difficulty, but is also most frequently used. Instead of focussing on the parent's incapacities or behaviour towards the child, it asks the court to evaluate the reasonableness of her state of mind; the courts' views on the weight to be given to the child's best interests in making that evaluation have undergone a considerable change. The early cases suggested that it was always prima facie reasonable for a parent to withhold consent to such a drastic step; the fact that adoption would be better for the child did not in itself make this unreasonable, although it might be so if the parent had vacillated to an unusual degree or been in some way culpable in her behaviour.

But in the leading case of *Re W. (an infant)* [1971] A.C. 682 Lord Hailsham rejected the idea that the parent had necessarily to be culpable, callous, indifferent or neglectful of her duties. The court must not simply substitute its own decision for that of the parent; the question is whether a reasonable parent in the circumstances of this particular case *could* withhold her agreement. A reasonable parent is entitled to take her own feelings into account, but she will also consider very carefully what is best for her child's long term welfare, including the advantages of adoption and the disadvantages of disrupting a young child in a settled home. As Lord Denning said in *Re L. (an infant)* (1962) 106 Sol.J. 611:

> "A reasonable mother surely gives great weight to what is better for the child. Her anguish of mind is quite understandable; but it may still be unreasonable for her to withhold her consent. We must look and see whether it is reasonable or unreasonable according to what a reasonable woman in her place would do in all the circumstances of the case."

Thus the child's welfare may not be the sole or the paramount consideration for the parent, but it certainly plays a great part. The court's duty to give first consideration to the need to safeguard and promote the welfare of the child throughout his childhood has not affected this (*Re P. (an infant) (adoption: parental consent)* [1977] Fam. 25), but in practice it would have made little difference if it had.

The application of this test will vary according to the context.

Many cases might better be termed unreasonable "withdrawal" of agreement, because the parents have decided to place their children for adoption and then changed their minds. A mother may have received inadequate counselling from her social worker and been subject to great pressure from family and friends. Her circumstances may now have improved. She can scarcely be blamed for what has happened, but the child may have been with the applicants from an early age and be just at the point where a disruption in the normal process of forming relationships is most dangerous. These were the essential facts in *Re W.* (above); in *O'Connor* v. *A. and B.* [1971] 1 W.L.R. 1227 the mother had since married the father, but there was some doubt about the stability of their relationship and the child had been with the applicants for two and a half years. In both, the House of Lords dispensed with agreement. In *Re H. (infants) (adoption: parental consent)* [1977] 1 W.L.R. 471, Ormrod L.J. observed that: " . . . it ought to be recognised by all concerned with adoption cases that once formal consent has been given or perhaps once the child has been placed with the adopters, time begins to run against the mother and, as time goes on, it gets progressively more and more difficult for her to show that the withdrawal of her consent is reasonable."

Where the parent has never indicated any willingness to have the child adopted, the attitude may be different. This is particularly so with applications by one parent and a step-parent (discussed in Chapter 8) or by long-term foster parents of children in compulsory care, for in each case the court is not usually choosing between the two *homes*. The child is likely to stay where he is, whether or not he is adopted. The question is whether he should become a fully intergrated member of the new family or whether he should retain some links with the family of his birth. In judging the reasonableness of the parent's attitude towards that question, the courts have tended to look at the quality of those links and the sincerity of the parent who wishes to keep them, as well as at the benefits of increased security and commitment in the new family.

Applications by foster-parents of children removed from unsatisfactory homes have generally turned on whether any access by the natural parents is likely to be beneficial. If it would, then refusing agreement is not unreasonable and custodianship is now the preferable alternative (*Re M. (minors) (adoption: parent's agreement)* [1985] F.L.R. 921; see also *Re H.; Re W. (adoption: parental agreement)* (1983) 4 F.L.R. 614). If the child's future security depends upon cementing his ties with the foster parents or the possibility of access is remote, then it may be unreasonable to refuse (*Re F. (a minor) (adoption: parental consent)* [1982] 1 W.L.R. 102, *Re V. (a minor) (adoption: consent)*

[1986] 3 W.L.R. 927). Access should not be made a condition of adoption unless all agree both to the adoption and to the condition (*Re H. (a minor) (adoption)* [1985] F.L.R. 519).

(c) That the parent or guardian has persistently failed without reasonable cause to discharge the parental duties.

This is most likely to be suggested in applications by step-parents or foster parents, for a parent who has placed her child for a conventional adoption has every excuse not to discharge her parental duties. These include the natural and moral obligation to show an affectionate interest in one's children, as well as the legal duty to maintain them financially (*Re P. (infants)* [1962] 1 W.L.R. 1296). A "persistent" failure must be longstanding and virtually permanent, so that the child will derive no benefit from maintaining the relationship (*Re D. (minors) (adoption by parent)* [1973] Fam. 209). This is perhaps more likely to be so where parents have lost touch with their fostered children than it is when the mother and father have been estranged after a divorce (see Chapter 8). But parents may have an excuse if their lack of contact is the result of the local authority's own conduct.

(d) That the parent or guardian has abandoned or neglected the child; or (e) has persistently ill-treated the child; or (f) has seriously ill-treated the child, but in this case the rehabilitation of the child within that household must, for whatever reason, be unlikely.

These will rarely apply to a conventional placement for adoption, which is not abandonment in the technical sense. Occasionally, they may apply to a divorced father. More importantly, however, they would justify plans for adoption in serious cases of child abuse. Once the child has been removed from home, and provided that each parent was involved, there is no legal obstacle to adoption. For many such children the best solution may be a completely fresh start with a carefully chosen new family, but of course the court would also have to be persuaded of that.

(iii) Freeing for Adoption

This new procedure is designed for two rather different purposes. One is to allow the mother to agree to adoption in general before any specific application is ready; the object here is to spare both her and the prospective adopters the agony of prolonged uncertainty with the ever present possibility of a change of mind. The other is to enable an agency which already has a child in its care to have the parents' agreement dispensed with, either before the child is placed at all, or at least without involving the prospective adopters in a contested hearing.

An application to free a child for adoption is made to court by an adoption agency; at least one parent must consent to this, or the child must already be in the agency's care and the agency wants the court to dispense with each parent's agreement (1976 Act, s.18(2)). The court must be satisfied that the agreement of each parent to an adoption has either been given or can be dispensed with on any of the usual grounds (s.18(1)); but it cannot dispense with any agreement unless the child has already been placed or placement is likely (s.18(3)); parents should not be unwillingly deprived of their rights unless an eventual adoption is clear. The court must also be satisfied that an extra-marital father either has no intention of applying for custody or would be unlikely to succeed if he did (s.18(7)). The order, if made, will extinguish all parental rights and vest them in the agency (s.18(5)).

Each parent may declare, either when the child is freed or later (ss.18(6) and 19(4)) that she wants no further involvement in the child's future. If a parent does not do this, she must be told after a year whether her child has been adopted or placed (s.19(2)) and if he has not been adopted by then, she must be notified whenever a placement begins or ends or he is eventually adopted (s.19(3)). If he has not been adopted or placed, she can apply for the order to be revoked on the ground that she wishes to resume her parental rights and duties (s.20(1)), but the court must give first consideration to the child's welfare (s.6). If the order is revoked, parental rights will return to her, even if they were in a local authority before the order was made (s.20(3)). If her application fails, she will not be able to try again without the court's leave, and the agency will no longer have to keep her informed (s.20(4) and (5)). Agencies who use this procedure therefore have to have facilities for caring for children whom they cannot place immediately.

5. *Return or Removal before the Hearing*

(i) By the Prospective Adopters

The prospective adopters may decide that they no longer wish to proceed. If the child was placed with them for adoption by an agency they should give written notice of their decision to the agency, and then return the child within seven days of this (1976 Act, s.30(1)(*a*) and (3)). They should also return the child within seven days of withdrawing an application which is already pending before a court. If the child is and remains in the care of a local authority, there is no reason why the authority should not board-out the child in the same home instead. If a child in care was not originally placed with a view to adoption, the same procedure applies, but it is expressly stated that the child need not be returned unless the authority asks (s.31(1)). In private and family cases, the child may well stay where he is even though an adoption plan is abandoned.

(ii) By the Agency or Local Authority

The agency itself may decide that it wishes to end the placement. Provided that the application has not yet been made to the court, the agency may serve written notice upon the prospective adopters, who must then return the child within seven days (s.30(1)(*b*) and (3)). Once the application has been made, the agency can only serve such a notice with leave of the court (s.30(2)).

If a child in local authority care was not originally placed with a view to adoption, but the foster parents have given notice of their intention to apply to adopt, the local authority can no longer recover the child by the usual means. It must use the same procedure as in ordinary agency placements (s.31(1)), and this means that it will require the court's leave once the application has been made. Thus if one local authority receives notice in respect of a child who is in the care of another authority, the former must inform the latter. Parental contributions are no longer payable.

The supervising local authority may of course seek a place of safety order in order to remove a "protected child" (see above).

(iii) By the Natural Parents

The natural parent may wish to recover the child. If she still has parental rights, she may usually come and take him, but there are three exceptions.

First, if an application is made to free for adoption a child who is in the care of the applying agency, a parent who did not consent to that application being made must not remove the child from the person with whom he has his home without the court's leave (s.27(2)).

Secondly, once an adoption application has been made to the court, a parent who has signified her agreement cannot remove the child from the applicants against their will, except with the court's leave (s.27(1)). Once the application is made, therefore, the prospective adopters will usually be able to keep the child if they wish to allege unreasonable "withdrawal" of agreement. This provision applies not only to formal agreements witnessed by the reporting officer but also to preliminary agreement before placement (*Re T. (a minor) (adoption: validity of order)* [1986] Fam. 160).

Thirdly, if the child has had his home with the prospective adopters for a *continuous* period of five years, the child cannot be removed against their will, except with the court's leave, not only once an actual adoption application has been made (s.28(1)), but also once they have given notice to the local authority of their intention to apply (s.28(2)). In the second case, they cannot "freeze" the situation for ever; the prohibition will lapse after three months unless an application is made before then, and once lapsed it cannot be renewed by giving a fresh notice for the next 28 days, which would give plenty of time to remove the child if this were appropriate. These prohibitions, however, apply not only to the natural parents, but also to anyone else who might otherwise remove the child, the only exceptions being the child's arrest or some statutory provision. But a local authority can only remove a child who is in its care in accordance with the procedure set out in (ii) above.

The purpose of this rule is to make it easier for long-term foster parents to apply to adopt without parental agreement. They will still have to persuade the court to dispense with this but at least they can prevent the parent's removing the child before they try to do so. Contrary to popular belief, however, it has made no difference to their position with any local authority which has the child in its care: after they have given notice, the authority can still serve notice upon them to return the child within seven days, but once they have applied to the court, this can only be done with the court's leave.

It is a criminal offence to contravene either of these prohibitions (ss.27(3) and 28(7)). A court may also prohibit a suspected removal in advance (s.29(2)). Then the High Court or a county court may authorise a court officer, and a single magistrate may authorise a policeman, to search specified premises and return the child (s.29(3) and (4)).

6. *Reports to the Court*

It used to be necessary in every adoption case for the court to appoint a guardian *ad litem* to safeguard the child's interests. This meant that three different social workers might be involved: one from the agency which made the placement, one from the local authority responsible for "welfare supervision," and the guardian chosen by the court. This was thought unnecessary, wasteful and confusing to natural and adoptive parents alike (*Stockdale*, 1972). Since 1984, therefore, their responsibilities have been arranged differently; essentially the same rules apply to applications both to adopt and to free for adoption.

An agency must now follow up its own placements and report to the court. In non-agency placements, the local authority must supervise, investigate and report to the court. Both reports must give extensive particulars about the child, his parents, the prospective adoptors and the actions of the agency or local authority involved. They must indicate whether any respondent is under 18 or mentally disabled and also whether they think that anyone else should be made a respondent, such as a non-marital father, the mother's husband, or a deceased parent's relative. They must conclude with their own views on whether the adoption is in the child's best long-term interests, what effect it will have on the natural parents, whether the child will be fully integrated into adopters' household, family and community, and what effect it is likely to have on them. Where appropriate, the relative merits of adoption and custody should be discussed. The report should end with a recommendation for or against adoption and, if against, with alternative proposals. Similar reports are required from an agency which applies to free a child for adoption (Adoption Rules 1984, rr. 22(1) and (2) and 4(4)(*b*); report-writers should consult schedule 2 for the full details).

In addition, parental agreement to adoption must be witnessed and verified by a reporting officer appointed by the court. Reporting officers must be members of the panels (set up under section 103, Children Act 1975) and independent of any agency which has the child in its voluntary or compulsory care or has been involved in making the adoption arrangements. Thus there is always an independent check upon the reality of parental agreement; in freeing cases, the reporting officer must also investigate whether an extra-marital father intends to apply for custody or would be likely to succeed, and whether the parent has been able to renounce further involvement with the adoption. The officer must report on all this to the court, and also inform the court if any parent or guardian is unwilling to agree (Adoption Rules 1984 rr. 5 and 17).

If a parent is unwilling to agree, the court *must* appoint a guardian *ad litem* for the child. In the High Court, the guardian will be the Official Solicitor if he consents and the applicant does not ask for someone else to be appointed. Otherwise, the guardian will again come from the panel and must again be independent of all the agencies involved. There is no objection, however, to the same person acting as reporting officer and guardian.

Thus the independent investigator in adoption cases is now mainly concerned with parental agreement or whether it should be dispensed with. The court may, however, appoint a guardian *ad litem* in any other case where there are "special circumstances" and the welfare of the child requires it. Whatever the reason for his appointment, the guardian must investigate (so far as he thinks necessary) the agency or local authority reports and the statement of facts relied upon to dispense with parental agreement. His object is always to safeguard the interests of the child and he should advise whether the child should attend the hearing. He must make a report to the court and also (unless the court excuses him) be present at the hearing (Adoption Rules 1984, rr. 6 and 18).

All these reports are confidential to the court. The court will send copies of the agency or local authority reports to the guardian *ad litem* or reporting officer, but not the other way about. The parties have no right to see any of them.

7. *The Hearing*

The hearing will be in private. The applicants must always attend (exceptionally only one joint applicant need be there but the other must verify the application by affidavit). The child must also be there unless the court thinks that special circumstances make this unnecessary. The respondents are the parents (unless the child is free for adoption), any agency having the child in its care or involved in the adoption arrangements, anyone liable by order or agreement to maintain the child, the spouse of a married sole applicant, and anyone else the court thinks should be joined. In the High Court, the child is always a party, in the other courts never. Any respondent may attend and be heard, although this will obviously be unusual unless there is any dispute. If the natural mother does attend, and the applicants have chosen to conceal their identity behind a serial number, the hearing must be conducted in such a way that she does not see them or learn their names without their consent (Adoption Rules 1984, rr. 23 and 15).

(i) Granting the Adoption Order

The court cannot do this unless it is satisfied that the child is free for adoption or that all the necessary parental agreements have been given or can be dispensed with; that the child has been with the applicants for the required time; that where necessary, the proper notice has been given to the local authority; and that the applicants have not made or received any unlawful payment for the adoption. Provided that all this is clear and the report is favourable, the adoption is likely to go through without difficulty, but the final decision always rests with the court. The court itself must give first consideration to the need to safeguard and promote the welfare of the child throughout his childhood; and it must also give whatever consideration to the child's own wishes and feelings is "due" in the light of his age and understanding (1976 Act, s.6). Some courts may have quite decided views on certain sorts of case. For example, some judges have been reluctant to allow baptised Christian children to be brought up by non-Christian adopters; have had doubts about racial differences between adopters and child, or about the suit-ability of older applicants to care for a young child, and so on. Agencies will probably want to discover their local courts' views, so that they can either take them into account or choose their court accordingly.

(ii) Interim Orders

Provided that the necessary agreements have been given or dis-pensed with, and where necessary notice was given to the local auth-ority, a court which is still not sure that the adoption is the right solution may make an interim order (s.25). This leaves the child with the applicants, but instead of the full transfer of adoption, they will only have custody, and the court may make ancillary orders about the child's supervision and maintainance if it wishes. The order lasts for a specified period of up to two years (and if originally fixed for less may be extended up to a maximum of two years). The object is usually to resolve any lingering doubts about the suitability of the adopters and it is rarely right to put off the decision in this way (*Re O. (a minor) (adoption by grandparents)* [1985] F.L.R. 546). Excep-tionally, the order may be made where the court thinks that adop-tion is not the right solution but wishes to leave the child where he is while the possibility of return to a natural parent is explored (see *S.* v. *Huddersfield Borough Council* [1975] Fam. 113). Nowadays custo-dianship would usually be a better way of doing this.

(iii) Custody and Custodianship

Custody and custodianship are in a sense always alternatives to adoption, provided that the applicants are able to apply and in fact do so. Thus in theory a step-parent's application to adopt a child whose parents are divorced should be made to the same divorce court, so that an application for joint custody may be made if the court refuses adoption because the matter would be "better dealt with" under the Matrimonial Causes Act 1973 (1976 Act, ss.14(3) and 15(4)). Others may be qualified and willing to apply for custo-dianship. Otherwise, provided that the necessary agreements to adoption have been given or dispensed with (see *Re M. (a minor) (custodianship: jurisdiction)* [1987] 1 W.L.R. 162; *Re A. (a minor) (adoption: parental consent)* [1987] 1 W.L.R. 153), the court may treat the case as if the applicants had applied and been qualified to apply for custodianship. This is mandatory in relative or step-parent applications where adoption would "not be better" for the child than custodianship (1975 Act, s.37(1)) and possible in other cases where custodianship would be "more appropriate" (s.37(2)). The intention is plain but the drafting is not: and surely it should always be possible to grant custodianship where parental agreement cannot be dispensed with precisely because custodianship would be better?

(iv) Refusing the Order

If an adoption application is refused in an ordinary agency placement, this is likely to be either because of doubts about the applicants' suitability or because the mother has withdrawn her agreement. The child must therefore be returned to the agency within seven days, unless the court extends this up to six weeks (1976 Act, s.30(3) and (6)). This is to give the agency extra time to make new arrangements for a child who is not to go back to his natural parents.

In other cases, the refusal is just as likely to result from doubts about the suitability of an adoption order as it is from doubts about the suitability of the adopters. They are much more likely to keep the child. If he is in the care of a local authority, the authority may well decide to leave him where he is, particularly if long-term foster parents have been unsuccessful in an attempt to dispense with the natural parents' agreement. In unsuccessful step-parent applications, the parent to whom he is married will still have custody. Even in other private or family cases, the parent may be happy to leave the child where he is.

But whether the child stays where he is or returns to his natural parent, the court may not be happy. In "exceptional circumstances," it now has power to order that the child be under the supervision of a local authority or probation officer, or even to commit the child to care (s.26); these have the same effect as orders made in family litigation (see Chapter 3).

However, no court may hear another application by the same adopters for the same child, unless the first court exempted them from this rule, or the second court finds that there has been a change in the circumstances or some other reason for letting them try again (s.24(1)). They may, of course, appeal against the refusal, but they should not make the child a ward of court as a disguised way of doing so.

8. *Effect of Adoption*

Adoption effects a virtually complete and irrevocable transfer of the child from one family to another, with one or two exceptions and qualifications.

(i) The Transfer

There are three aspects to the transfer itself. First, from the moment the order is made, all parental rights and duties relating to the child vest in the adoptive parents (1976 Act, s.12(1)). The court has power to impose such terms and conditions as it sees fit (s.12(6)), but as these are difficult to enforce and likely to detract from the main purpose of adoption, they are rare. A condition of access to the natural parents should only be imposed in exceptional cases where all consent (*Re H. (a minor) (adoption)* [1985] F.L.R. 519; *Re M. (a minor) (adoption order: access)* [1986] 1 F.L.R. 51), nor should adopters have to report back to a deeply concerned natural father (*Re C. (a minor) (adoption order: condition)* [1986] 1 F.L.R. 315). Thus the adoptive parents will normally have an unfettered right to bring the child up, decide his education and religion, and whether he should emigrate, marry under the age of 18, or even be adopted again (which may be more likely, now that so many more marriages, including those of adoptive parents, are breaking down). They will also have full responsibility for looking after him properly, educating and maintaining him.

Secondly, although the order has no effect on parental rights and duties so far as they relate to the time before it is made (s.12(2)), once made it extinguishes the rights and duties of anyone other than the adopters, whether these arose naturally or by court order (s.12(3)(*a*)). Care orders and resolutions cease. The natural parents will have no right to keep in touch with the child and no duty to maintain him. Although arrears under a maintenance order or agreement may be recovered, no further liability can accrue (s.12(3)(*b*); there are two minor exceptions, for maintenance agreements which either constitute a trust or expressly provide for continuing despite adoption, so that a natural parent may deliberately set out to provide for a child who is to be adopted, s.12(4)). No new orders can be made.

However, adoption does more than simply transfer and extinguish parental rights and duties, for this would only be a drastic form of custody order. For almost every legal purpose, adoption removes the child from one family and places him in another. Thus as regards anything which happens after the adoption, the child is to be treated as the child of the adoptive parents' marriage (or, if there is only one adopter, as his legitimate child, but not the child of any particular marriage); and he is not to be treated as the child of anyone else (s.39(2)). The Act somewhat unnecessarily declares that this prevents an adopted child from being illegitimate. The main effect, however, is that any reference to a child, or issue, or any other family relationship in any statute or legal document now automatically includes an adopted child or a relationship traced through adoption, unless the contrary intention is expressed.

This only affects dispositions of property, which took effect on or after January 1, 1976. Before then, an adopted child could only claim property under a general disposition (for example, "to all my grandchildren") if he had been adopted before it. The person who had died or disposed of his property was presumed only to want to benefit those about whom he had a chance of knowing and whom he could exclude if he wished. Under the new rule, the person who is making such a disposition (which includes dying without making a will, so that the rules of intestacy apply) is presumed to want to benefit any future adopted children just as much as any future natural children; if he wishes to exclude them, he must say so. The only difference now is for dispositions which depend upon the child's date of birth (for example, "to all my grandchildren living at my death"); an adopted child is taken to have been born on the date of the order, so that he is not "living at my death" if the order came later, even if he had in fact already been born. If, on the other hand, the grandfather had left his property to be divided between all his grandchildren when they reached 21, the adopted child will take on his real birthday.

(ii) Exceptions

The most important exceptions to the general principle relate to marriage, nationality and peerages. There are certain people to whom one is so closely related either by blood (or sometimes by marriage) that one is not allowed to marry them. An adopted child remains in his natural family for this purpose. Thus he cannot marry his natural mother, grandmother, sister, aunt or niece. This raises the problem that an adopted child will normally have no way of knowing who his natural relatives are, but he can trace his original birth certificate in order to find out, for this purpose even if he is under 18. An adopted person is also forbidden to marry his adoptive parent, for this might indeed introduce a damaging ambiguity into the relationship, but he is not prevented from marrying his other adoptive relatives. There is no eugenic reason why he should be, but the possibility of marriage between adoptive brother and sister might do some damage to normal family relations.

An adopted person is not automatically his adoptive parents' child for any purpose connected with British citizenship, or immigration control. This is to prevent evasion by adoption abroad, for the general principle applies to all recognised adoptions, wherever they took place. However, a child who is adopted *here* either by a married couple either of whom is a British citizen, or by a sole adopter who is a citizen, will automatically gain citizenship if he does not already have it (British Nationality Act 1981, s.1(5)).

Adoption does not affect succession to peerages and other titles, or to any attached property, for these still depend upon the blood line. Nor need it affect entitlement to social security death benefit, to a pension already being paid for a child when he is adopted, or to an insurance policy against the child's funeral expenses (but nothing more) which is transferred to adoptive parents.

(iii) Irrevocability

With two exceptions, an adoption order is irrevocable. If a child has been adopted by one parent alone and subsequently legitimated by his or her marriage to the other parent, the court may on their application revoke the adoption order, so that the child becomes the legitimated child of both, instead of the adopted child of one and the step-child of the other (1976 Act, s.52). Convention adoption orders may occasionally be annulled (s.53).

Adoption orders may sometimes be appealed to a higher court, High Court and county court orders to the Court of Appeal, magistrates' orders to the Family Division of the High Court. There are normally only six weeks in which to appeal, after which the order can certainly be considered final, although the appeal court could in an exceptional case grant leave to appeal out of time. An appeal is more likely where an adoption has been refused rather than granted, except where the court has dispensed with a parent's agreement. Neither side should use wardship as a disguised form of appeal (*Re O. (a minor) (wardship: adopted child*) [1978] Fam. 196).

(iv) Discovering Origins

The Children Act 1975 gave all adopted people who have reached 18 the right to obtain a copy of their original birth certificate (1976 Act, s.51), and someone under 18 who is intending to marry is entitled to ask whether the marriage is prohibited.

However, a counselling service must be offered to all people who wish to trace their origins in this way, from the Registrar-General's Department itself, or from the local authority for the area where the person is, or from the authority for the area where the adoption order was made, or from an approved adoption society which arranged it. People who were adopted before the 1975 Act was passed are obliged to take advantage of this counselling and the counsellor will usually be able to reveal far more about their origins and the circumstances of their adoption than they will learn from the simple birth certificate to which they have a right. People who have been adopted since the Act was passed will not be obliged to have counselling and may have less need of the extra information, because agencies now advise adoptive parents about how to tell the child of his origins and supply them with information to help them do so.

Nevertheless, an earlier study in Scotland suggested that relatively few adopted children embark upon this search, and even fewer do so in the hope of actually meeting their natural parents. Many of these were unhappy and lonely people, who had learned of their adoption in a distressing or negative way, or whose experiences in the adoptive family had not been entirely satisfactory, and who desperately needed to discover "who they were" (*Triseliotis*, 1973). The counsellor will be able to explore the searcher's motivation and may be able to satisfy his needs without encouraging a search for the natural parent which could be distressing and damaging to both. The natural parent has no right to object to a disclosure which could reopen a deeply upsetting experience which she had thought closed. Present experience suggests that the possibility of a damaging meeting causes concern to counsellors in only a tiny proportion of cases: most inquirers, however deep their own needs, appeared to be equally considerate towards those of both their natural and their adoptive parents (*Day and Leeding*, 1980; *Triseliotis*, 1984). But the needs of the traditional adopted child may be rather different from those of an older child adopted from care, perhaps after a history of serious abuse or against his parents' will (*Harmes and Timms*, 1985).

9. *Commentary*

Adoption law and practice have come a long way since 1926. Then the stereotype of the unmarried mother giving up her baby to childless strangers may have applied. Certainly much of the law's development has reflected it—in the increasing professionalisation of the task of arranging adoptions, culminating in the prohibition of private placements in 1984; in the increasingly wholesale legal effects of an order, culminating in the 1975 Act provisions; and in the developing suspicion of step-parent and intra-family adoptions which might confuse the child by distorting rather than replacing family relationships. Yet at the same time, while the supply of babies for conventional placement decreased, the demand remained or even increased; adoption came to be considered for the previously "unadoptable"— older or handicapped children, children of mixed race, large families, victims of child abuse where rehabilitation in the natural family would not work. Inevitably, the adoption of children with their own life stories cannot wholly conform to stereotype. Until custodianship was brought into force in December 1985, a rather different view of adoption seemed to be emerging, in which links might well be preserved between past and present or future and the real question was who should control these. Now that there is an alternative, it will be necessary to think more carefully and precisely about what both have to offer, in terms of membership of either family, severing or preserving links, confusing or falsifying identities and so on. It is unfortunate that the law itself on this choice is so confusing.

REFERENCES AND FURTHER READING

Adamson, G. (1973) *The Care-Takers* (Bristol: Bookstall Publications)

Adcock, M. and White R. (1980a) "Care Orders or the Assumption of Parental Rights—The Long Term Effects" [1980] *Journal of Social Welfare Law* 257

Adcock, M. and White, R. (eds.) (1980b) *Terminating Parental Contact: An Exploration of the Issues relating to Children in Care* (London: Association of British Adoption and Fostering Agencies)

Adcock, M., White, R. and Rowlands, O. (1983) *The Administrative Parent—A study of the assumption of parental rights and duties* (London: Bristish Agencies for Adoption and Fostering)

Adler, R. (1985) *Taking Juvenile Justice Seriously* (Edinburgh: Scottish Academic Press)

Anderson, R. (1978) *Representation in the Juvenile Court* (London: Routledge)

Bagley, C. (1980) "Adjustment, Achievement and Social Circumstances of Adopted Children in a National Survey" (1980) *102 Adoption and Fostering* 47

Bainham, A. (1986) "The Balance of Power in Family Decisions" [1986] *Cambridge Law Journal* 262

Barker, D. (1975) *Unmarried Fathers* (London: Hutchinson)

Bean, P. (ed.) (1984) *Adoption—Essays in Social Policy, Law and Sociology* (London: Tavistock)

Berridge, D. (1985) *Children's Homes* (Oxford: Blackwell)

Black, Sir H. (1979) *Legislation and Services for Children and Young Persons in Northern Ireland—Report of the Children and Young Persons Review Group* (Chairman: Sir H. Black) (Belfast: H.M.S.O.)

Blom-Cooper, L. (1985) *A Child in Trust—The Report of the Panel of Inquiry into the Circumstances surrounding the Death of Jasmine Beckford* (London: London Borough of Brent)

Bowlby, J. (1971) *Attachment and Loss Vol. 1: Attachment* (Harmondsworth: Penguin)

Bowlby, J. (1975) *Attachment and Loss Vol. 2: Separation: Anxiety and Anger* (Harmondsworth: Penguin)

Bowlby, J. (1980) *Attachment and Loss. Vol. 3: Loss, sadness and depression* (London: Hogarth Press)

Brandon, J. and Warner, J. (1977) "A.I.D. and Adoption: Some Comparisons" (1977) 7 *British Journal of Social Work* 235

Bromley, P.M. (1984) "Aided conception: the alternative to adoption" in Bean, P. (ed.), *op. cit.*

Brophy, J. (1985) "Child Care and the Growth of Power: the status of mothers in custody disputes" in Brophy, J. and Smart, C. (eds.) *Women in Law* (London: Routledge)

Brown, A. (1986) "Family circumstances of young children (1983) 43 *Population Trends* 18

Burgoyne, J. (1984) *Breaking Even: Divorce, Your Children and You* (Harmondsworth: Penguin)

Burgoyne, J., Ormrod, R., and Richards, M. (1987) *Divorce Matters* (Harmondsworth: Penguin)

Burgoyne, J. and Clark, D. (1984) *Making A Go of It: A Study of Stepfamilies in Sheffield* (London: Routledge)

Central Policy Review Staff (1978) *Services for Young Children with Working Mothers* (London: H.M.S.O.)

Central Statistical Office, (1977) *Social Trends 17* (London: H.M.S.O.)

Clarke Hall and Morrison (1985) *Law relating to Children and Young Persons* 10th (loose-leaf) edn. by Booth, Dawe M., Harris, B. and White, R.H. (London: Butterworths)

Council of Europe (1981) *European Convention on the Legal Status of Children born out of Wedlock* (Strasbourg: Council of Europe)

Crellin, E., Kellmer Pringle, M.L. and West, P. (1971) *Born Illegitimate: Social and Educational Implications* (Windsor: National Foundation for Educational Research)

Cretney, S.M. (1984) *Principles of Family Law* 4th edn. (London: Sweet and Maxwell)

Cretney, S.M. (1987) *Elements of Family Law* (London: Sweet and Maxwell)

Crown Prosecution Service (1985) *Code for Crown Prosecutors* (London: H.M.S.O)

Curtis, M. (1946) *Report of the Care of Children Committee* (Chairman: Miss M. Curtis) Cmd. 6922 (London: H.M.S.O.)

Davis, G., Macleod, A., and Murch, M. (1983) "Undefended Divorce: Should Section 41 of the Matrimonial Causes Act 1973 be repealed?" (1983) 46 *Modern Law Review* 121

Day, C. and Leeding, A. (1980) *Access to birth records: the impact of section 26 of the Children Act 1975*, A.B.A.F.A. Research Series No. 1 (London: Association of British Adoption and Fostering Agencies)

Derrick, D. (ed.) (1986) *Illegitimate—the experience of people born outside marriage* (London: National Council for One-Parent Families)

D.H.S.S. (1974) *Memorandum on Non-Accidental injury to Children* L.A.S.S.L. (74) 30; C.M.O. (74) (London: D.H.S.S.)

D.H.S.S. (1974) *The Family in Society: Dimensions of Parenthood* (London: H.M.S.O.)

D.H.S.S. (1976) *Guide to Fostering Practice* (London: H.M.S.O.)

D.H.S.S. (1977) Local Authority Circular L.A.C. (77) 1, *Children and Young Persons Act 1969—Intermediate Treatment* (London: D.H.S.S)

D.H.S.S. (1980) *Child Abuse: Central Register Systems* L.A.S.S.L. (80) 4; H.N. (80) 20 (London: D.H.S.S.)

D.H.S.S. (1982) *Child Abuse: A Study of Inquiry Reports, 1973–81* (London: H.M.S.O)

D.H.S.S. (1983) *Code of Practice: Access to Children in Care* (London: H.M.S.O.)

D.H.S.S. (1984) Local Authority Circular L.A.C. (84) 5, *Parental Rights Resolutions* (London: D.H.S.S.)

D.H.S.S. (1985) *Consultative Paper on Revision of the Nurseries and Child Minders Regulation Act 1948* (London: D.H.S.S.)

D.H.S.S. (1985) *Social Work Decisions in Child Care—Recent Research Findings and their Implications* (London: H.M.S.O.)

D.H.S.S. (1986a) *Children in Care in England and Wales, March 1984* (London: D.H.S.S.)

D.H.S.S. (1986) Health Circular HC (86) 1 *Family Planning Services for Young People* (London: D.H.S.S.)

D.H.S.S. (1986) *Legislation on Human Infertility Services and Embryo Research: A Consultation Paper* Cm 46 (London: H.M.S.O.)

D.H.S.S. (1986) *Child Abuse—Working Together: A draft guide to arrangements for inter agency co-operation for the protection of children* (London: D.H.S.S.)

D.H.S.S. (1987) *The Law on Child Care and Family Services* Cm 62 (London: H.M.S.O.)

Dickens, B.M. (1981) "The Modern Function and Limits of Parental Rights (1981) 97 *Law Quarterly Review* 462

Dingwall, R., Eekelaar, J.M. and Murray, T. (1983) *The Protection of Children—State Intervention and Family Life* (Oxford: Blackwell)

Dingwall, R. (1986) "The Jasmine Beckford Affair" (1986) 49 *Modern Law Review* 489

Dinnage, R. and Kellmer-Pringle, M.L. (1967) *Foster Home Care: Facts and Fallacies* (London: Longman)

Dodds, M. (1983) "Children and Divorce" [1983] *Journal of Social Welfare Law* 228

Dunlop, A.B. (1980) *Junior Attendance Centres* Home Office Research Studies No. 60 (London: H.M.S.O.)

Eekelaar, J.M. (1973) "What are Parental Rights?" (1973) 89 *Law Quarterly Review* 210

Eekelaar, J.M. and Clive, E. (1977) *Custody after Divorce* (Oxford: Centre for Socio-legal Studies)

Eekelaar, J.M. and Katz, S. (eds.) (1978) *Family Violence: An International and Interdisciplinary Study* (Toronto: Butterworth)

Eekelaar, J.M. (1982) "Children in Divorce: Some Further Data" (1982) 2 *Oxford Journal of Legal Studies* 62

Eekelaar J.M., Dingwall, R. and Murray, T. (1982) "Victims or Threats? Children in Care Proceedings" [1982] *Journal of Social Welfare Law* 68

Eekelaar, J.M. (1984) *Family Law and Social Policy* 2nd edn. (London: Weidenfeld and Nicolson)

Eekelaar, J.M. (1986) "Gillick in the Divorce Court" (1986) 136 *New Law Journal* 184

Eekelaar, J.M. (1986) "The Emergence of Children's Rights" (1986) 6 *Oxford Journal of Legal Studies* 161

Eekelaar, J.M. and Maclean, M. (1986) *Maintenance after Divorce* (Oxford: Clarendon)

Family Rights Group (1982) *Accountability in Child Care—Which Way Forward?* (London: Family Rights Group)

Family Rights Group (1985) *Response to Discussion Papers 1–12 of the Child Care Law Working Party* (London: Family Rights Group)

Family Rights Group (1986) *Promoting links: keeping families and children in touch* (London: Family Rights Group)

Farmer, E. and Parker, R. (1985a) *A Study of Interim Care Orders* (Bristol: University of Bristol)

Farmer, E. and Parker, R. (1985b) *A Study of the Discharge of Care Orders* (Bristol: University of Bristol)

Farson, R. (1978) *Birthrights* (Harmondsworth: Penguin)

Ferri, E. (1976) *Growing Up in a One-Parent Family* (Windsor: N.F.E.R. Publishing)

Finer, M. and McGregor, O.R. (1974) "The History of the Obligation to Maintain" *Appendix 5 to the Report of the Committee on One-Parent Families* (Chairman: The Hon. Mr. Justice Finer) Cmnd. 5629–I (London: H.M.S.O.)

Finer, Sir M. (1974) *Report of the Committee on One-Parent Families* (Chairman: The Hon. Mr. Justice Finer) Cmnd. 5629 (London: H.M.S.O.)

Field-Fisher, T.G. (1974) *Report of the Committee of Inquiry into the Care and Supervision provided in relation to Maria Colwell* (Chairman: T. G. Field-Fisher Q.C.) (London: H.M.S.O.)

Fisher, M., Marsh, P. and Phillips, D. with Sainsbury, E. (1986) *In and Out of Care—The Experiences of Children, Parents and Social Workers* (London: Batsford/B.A.A.F.)

Fletcher, R. (1973) *The Family and Marriage in Britain*, 3rd edn. (Harmondsworth: Penguin)

Franklin, B. (ed.) (1986) *The Rights of Children* (Oxford: Blackwell)

Freeman, M.D.A. (1979) *Violence in the Home* (Farnborough: Saxon House)

Freeman, M.D.A. (1983) *The Rights and Wrongs of Children* (London: Frances Pinter)

Freeman, M.D.A. (1984) "Subsidised adoption" in Bean, P. (ed.), *op. cit.*

Freeman, M.D.A. and Lyon, C.M. (1984) *The Law of Residential Homes and Day-Care Establishments* (London: Sweet and Maxwell)

Geach, H. and Szwed, E. (eds.) (1983) *Providing Civil Justice for Children* (London: Edward Arnold)

George, V. (1970) *Foster Care: Theory and Practice* (London: Routledge)

George, V. and Wilding, P. (1972) *Motherless Families* (London: Routledge)

Gill, D. (1977) *Illegitimacy, Sexuality and the Status of Women* (Oxford: Blackwell)

Goldstein, J., Freud, A. and Solnit, S. (1973) *Beyond the Best Interests of the Child* (New York: Free Press)

Goldstein, J., Freud, A. and Solnit, S. (1980) *Before the Best Interests of the Child* (London: Burnett Books)

Graham, J. and Moxon, D. (1986) "Some trends in juvenile justice" (1986) 22 *Home Office Research Bulletin* 10

Haimes, E. and Timms, N. (1985) *Adoption, identity and social policy: the search for distant relatives* (Aldershot: Gower)

Hall, J.C. (1968) *Arrangements for the Care and Upbringing of Children (section 33 of the Matrimonial Causes Act 1965)* Law Commission Published Working Paper No. 15 (London: Law Commission)

Hall, J.C. (1972) "The Waning of Parental Rights" [1972] *Cambridge Law Journal* 248

Hallett, C. and Stevenson, O. (1980) *Child Abuse: Aspects of Inter-Professional Cooperation* (London: George Allen and Unwin)

Harding, L.M. (1987) "The Debate on Surrogate Motherhood: the Current Situation, Some Arguments and Issues: Questions facing Law and Policy" [1987] *Journal of Social Welfare Law* 37

Haskey, J. (1982) "Widowhood, widowerhood and remarriage" (1982) 30 *Population Trends* 15

Haskey, J. (1987) "Social class differentials in remarriage after divorce: results from a forward linkage study" (1987) 47 *Population Trends* 34

Hayes, M. (1979) "Supplementary Benefit and Financial Provision Orders" [1978–79] *Journal of Social Welfare Law* 216

Heywood, J.S. (1978) *Children in Care: the development of the service for the deprived child*, 3rd edn. (London: Routledge)

Hilgendorf, L. (1981) *Social Workers and Solicitors in Child Care Cases* (London: H.M.S.O.)

Hillingdon Council Area Review Committee on Child Abuse (1986) *Report of the Review Panel into the death of Heidi Koseda* (London: London Borough Council of Hillingdon)

Holman, R. (1973) *Trading in Children—A Study of Private Fostering* (London: Routledge)

Holman, R. (1975) "The Place of Fostering in Social Work" (1975) 5 *British Journal of Social Work* 3

Home Office (1965) *The Child, the Family and the Young Offender* Cmnd. 2742 (London: H.M.S.O.)

Home Office (1968) *Children in Trouble* Cmnd. 3601 (London: H.M.S.O.)

Home Office (1970) *Part I of the Children and Young Persons Act 1969—A Guide for Courts and Practitioners* (London: H.M.S.O.)

Home Office (1976) *Observations on the 11th Report of the House of Commons Expenditure Committee* Cmnd. 6494 (London: H.M.S.O.)

Home Office, Welsh Office, D.H.S.S. (1980) *Young Offenders* Cmnd. 8045 (London: H.M.S.O.)

Home Office (1983) Home Office Circular No. 42/1983, *Criminal Justice Act 1982: Implementation of Part I (Young Offenders)* (London: Home Office)

Home Office (1985a) Home Office Circular No. 14/1985, *The Cautioning of Offenders* (London: Home Office)

Home Office (1985b) Home Office Circular No. 9/1985, *Regimes in Detention Centres* (London: Home Office)

Home Office (1986) *Police and Criminal Evidence Act 1984: Codes of Practice* (London: H.M.S.O.)

Home Office (1986a) Statistical Bulletin 14/86, *The Sentencing of Young Offenders under the Criminal Justice Act 1982: July 1983–June 1985* (London: Home Office)

Home Office (1986b) *Custodial Sentences for Young Offenders* (London: H.M.S.O.)

House of Commons (1975), 11th Report of the Expenditure Committee, Session 1974–75, *The Children and Young Persons Act 1969*, H.C. 534 (London: H.M.S.O.)

House of Commons (1977), Select Committee on Violence in the Family *Violence to Children* Session 1976–77, H.C. 329 (London: H.M.S.O.)

House of Commons (1984), Second Report from the Social Services Committee, Session 1983–84, *Children in Care* H.C. 360 (London: H.M.S.O.)

Jackson, B. and Jackson, S. (1979) *Childminder—A Study in Action Research* (London: Routledge)

James, A. and Wilson, K. (1984) "Reports for the Court: The Work of the Divorce Court Welfare Officer" [1984] *Journal of Social Welfare Law* 89

Justice (1975) *Report on Parental Rights and Duties and Custody Suits* (London: Stevens)

Kahan, B. (1979) *Growing Up in Care* (Oxford: Blackwell)

Kellmer Pringle, M.L. (1974) *The Needs of Children* (London: Hutchinson)

King, M. (ed.) (1981) *Childhood, Welfare and Justice* (London: Batsford)

Lambert, L. and Streather, J. (1980) *Children in Changing Families: A Study of Adoption and Illegitimacy* (London: Macmillan)

Law Commission (1968) *Report on Blood Tests and the Proof of Paternity in Civil Proceedings* Law Com. No. 16 (London: H.M.S.O.)

Law Commission (1976) *Report on Matrimonial Proceedings in Magistrates' Courts*, Law Com. No. 77 (London: H.M.S.O.)

Law Commission (1979) Working Paper No. 74, *Illegitimacy* (London: H.M.S.O.)

Law Commission (1982) *Report on Illegitimacy* Law Com. No. 118 (London: H.M.S.O.)

Law Commission (1985) Working Paper No. 91, *Review of Child Law: Guardianship* (London: H.M.S.O.)

Law Commission (1986) *Illegitimacy: Second Report* Law Com. No. 157 (London: H.M.S.O.)

Law Commission (1986) Working Paper No. 96, *Review of Child Law: Custody* (London: H.M.S.O.)

Law Commission (1987a), Working Paper No. 100, *Care, Supervision and Interim Orders in Custody Proceedings* (London: H.M.S.O.)

Law Commission (1987b) Working Paper No. 101, *Wards of Court* (London: H.M.S.O.)

Lawson, A. (1980) "Taking the Decision to Remove the Child from the Family" [1980] *Journal of Social Welfare Law* 141

Leete, R. (1978) "Adoption Trends and Illegitimate Births" (1978) 14 *Population Trends* 9

Leete, R. (1979) *Changing Patterns of Family Formation and Dissolution in England and Wales 1964–76*, O.P.C.S. Studies on Medical and Population Subjects No. 39 (London: H.M.S.O.)

Leete, R. and Anthony, S. (1979) "Divorce and Remarriage: A Record Linkage Study" (1979) 16 *Population Trends* 5

Lewis, C. (1986) *Becoming a Father* (Milton Keynes: Open University Press)

Lowe, N.V. (1982) "The legal status of fathers: past and present" in McKee, L. and O'Brien, M. (eds.), *The Father Figure* (London: Tavistock)

Lowe, N. and White, R. (1986) *Wards of Court*, 2nd edn. (London: Barry Rose)

Luepnitz, D.A. (1982) *Child Custody* (Lexington: Lexington Books)

Lyon, C.M. (1985) "Safeguarding Children's Interests?—Some Problematic Issues surrounding Separate Representation in Care and Associates Proceedings" in Freeman, M.D.A. (ed.) *Essays in Family Law* (London: Stevens)

Macleod A. and Malos, E. (1984) *Representation of Children and Parents in Child Care Proceedings* (Bristol: University of Bristol Family Law Research Unit)

Macleod, A. with Borkowski, M. (1985) *Access after Divorce: The Follow-Up to the Special Procedure in Divorce Project* (Bristol: University of Bristol)

Maddox, B. (1980) *Step-parenting: How to Live with other People's Children* (London: Unwin)

Maidment, S. (1975) "Access Conditions in Custody Orders" (1975) 2 *British Journal of Law and Society* 182

Maidment, S. (1976) "A Study in Child Custody" (1976) 6 *Family Law* 195 and 236

Maidment, S. (1978) "Some Legal Problems Arising out of the Reporting of Child Abuse" [1978] *Current Legal Problems* 149

Maidment, S. (1980) "The Relevance of the Criminal Law to Domestic Violence" [1980] *Journal of Social Welfare Law* 26

Maidment, S. (1981) "The Fragmentation of Parental Rights" [1981] *Cambridge Law Journal* 135

Maidment, S. (1981) *Child Custody: What Chance for Fathers?* Forward from Finer No. 7 (London: One Parent Families)

Maidment, S. (1984a) *Child Custody and Divorce* (London: Croom Helm)

Maidment, S. (1984b) "The Matrimonial Causes Act, s. 41 and the children of divorce: theoretical and empirical considerations" in Freeman, M.D.A. (ed.) *State, Law and the Family: Critical Perspectives* (London: Tavistock)

Mair, L. (1971) *Marriage* (Harmondsworth: Pelican)

Marsden, D. (1967) *Mothers Alone: Poverty and the Fatherless Family* (Harmondsworth: Penguin)

Marsh, P. (1986) "Natural families and children in care: an agenda for practice development (1986) 10 (4) *Adoption and Fostering* 20

Martin, J.P. (ed.) (1978) *Violence and the Family* (Chichester: Wiley)

Masson, J., Norbury, D. and Chatterton, S.G. (1983) *Mine, Yours or Ours? a study of step-parent adoption* (London: H.M.S.O.)

Mayall, B. and Petrie, P. (1977) *Minder, Mother and Child* (London: University of London Institute of Education)

McGregor, O.R., Blom-Cooper, L. and Gibson, C., (1970) *Separated Spouses* (London: Duckworth)

Millham, S., Bullock, R., Hosic, K. and Haak., M. (1986) *Lost in Care—The Problems of Maintaining Links between Children in care and their Families* (Aldershot: Gower)

Ministry of Health (1968) *Nurseries and Child-Minders Regulation Act 1948 (as amended by section 60 of the Health Services and Public Health Act 1968)—Memorandum of Guidance for Local Health Authorities*, Circular 36/68 (London: Ministry of Health)

Mitchell, A. (1985) *Children in the Middle* (London: Tavistock)

Mnookin, R. (1975) "Child Custody Adjudication: Judicial Functions in the Face of Indeterminacy" (1975) 39 *Law and Contemporary Problems* 226

Morgan, P. (1975) *Child Care: Sense and Fable* (London: Temple Smith)

Morris, A., Giller, H., Szwed, E. and Geach H. (1980) *Justice for Children* (London: Macmillan)

Morris A. and Giller, H. (eds.) (1983) *Providing Criminal Justice for Children* (London: Edward Arnold)

Mortlock, B. (1972) *The Inside of Divorce* (London: Constable)

Murch, M. (1980) *Justice and Welfare in Divorce* (London: Sweet and Maxwell)

Murch, M. and Bader, K. (1984) *Separate Representation for Parents and Children* (Bristol: University of Bristol Family Law Research Unit)

Norris, T.L. and Parton, N. (1987) "The Administration of Place of Safety Orders" [1987] *Journal of Social Welfare Law* 1

One Parent Families (1980) *An Accident of Birth—A Response to the Law Commission's Working Paper on Illegitimacy* (London: National Council for One Parent Families)

One Parent Families (1982) *Against Natural Justice: A Study of the Procedures used by Local Authorities in Taking Parental Rights Resolutions over Children in Voluntary Care* (London: National Council for One-Parent Families)

Owen, D. *et al.* (1986) *A review of the Children Act 10 years on—its effect on foster care policy and practice* (London: National Foster Care Association)

Packman, J. (1981) *The Child's Generation—Child Care Policy in Britain*, (Oxford: Blackwell)

Packman, J. (1986) *Who Needs Care? Social-work Decisions about Children* (Oxford: Blackwell)

Parker, D. (1982) "Legal Aspects of Artificial Insemination and Embryo Transfer" (1982) 12 *Family Law* 103

Parker, H. (ed.) (1979) *Social Work and the Courts* (London: Edward Arnold)

Parker, R.A. (1966) *Decision in Child Care: a Study of Prediction in Fostering* (London: George Allen and Unwin)

Parker, R.A. (ed.) (1980) *Caring for Separated Children—Plans, Procedures and Priorities* (London: Macmillan)

Parkinson, L. (1986) *Conciliation in Separation and Divorce* (London: Croom Helm)

Parsloe, P. (1978) *Juvenile Justice in Britain and the United States—The Balance of Needs and Rights* (London: Routledge)

Pettitt, P.H. (1957) "Parental Control and Guardianship" in Graveson, R.H. and Crane, F.R. *A Century of Family Law* (London: Sweet and Maxwell)

Pollock, S. and Sutton, J. (1985) "Father's Rights, Women's Losses" (1985) 8 *Women's Studies International Forum* 593

Pratt, J. and Grimshaw, R. (1985) "An Aspect of 'Welfare Justice': Truancy and the Juvenile Court" [1985] *Journal of Social Welfare Law* 257

Priest, J. and Whybrow, J. (1986) *Custody Law in Practice in the Divorce and Domestic Courts* Supplement to Law Commission W.P. No. 96 (London: H.M.S.O.)

Priestley, P., Fears, D. and Fuller, R. (1977) *Justice for Juveniles—The 1969 Children and Young Persons Act: A Case for Reform?* (London: Routledge)

Raynor, L. (1980) *The Adopted Child Comes of Age* (London: George Allen and Unwin)

R.C.C.L. (1985) *Review of Child Care Law: Report to Ministers of an Interdepartmental Working Party* (London: H.M.S.O.)

Richards, M. (1982) "Post Divorce Arrangements for Children: A Psychological Perspective" [1982] *Journal of Social Welfare Law* 133

Richards, M. (1986) "Behind the Best Interests of the Child: An Examination of the Arguments of Goldstein, Freud and Solnit Concerning Custody and Access at Divorce" [1986] *Journal of Social Welfare Law* 77

Richards, M. (1987) "Parents and kids: the new thinking" *New Society*, 27 March 1987

Richards, M. and Dyson, M. (1982) *Separation, Divorce and the Development of Children: A Review* (Cambridge: Child Care and Development Group)

Richards, M. and Light. P. (eds.) (1986) *Children of Social Worlds* (Oxford: Polity Press)

Rights of Women (1985) *Lesbian Mothers on Trial. A report on lesbian mothers and child custody (London: Rights of Women)*

Rowe, J. and Lambert, L. (1973) *Children who wait* (London: Association of British Adoption Agencies)

Roman, M. and Haddad, W. (1978) *The Disposable Parent: The Case for Joint Custody* (New York: Penguin)

Rowe, J., Cain, H., Hundleby, M. and Keane, A. (1984) *Long-term fostering and the Children Act—a study of foster parents who went on to adopt* (London: British Agencies for Adoption and Fostering)

Rowe, J., Cain, H., Hundleby, M., and Keane, A. (1984) *Long-Term Fostering Care* (London: Batsford)

Russell, Lord Justice (1966) *Report of the Committee on the Law of Sucession in relation to Illegitimate Persons* Cmnd. 3051 (London: H.M.S.O.)

Rutter, M. (1971) "Parent-Child Separation: Psychological Effects on the Children" (1971) 12 *Journal of Child Psychology and Psychiatry* 233

Rutter, M. (1972 and 1981) *Maternal Deprivation Reassessed* 2nd edn. with Postscript (Harmondsworth: Penguin)

Rutter, M. and Giller, H. (1983) *Juvenile Delinquency: Trends and Perspectives* (Harmondsworth: Penguin)

Scottish Law Commission (1984) *Report on Illegitimacy* Scot. Law Com. No. 82 (Edinburgh: H.M.S.O.)

Seglow, J., Kellmer Pringle, M.L., and Wedge, P. (1972) *Growing Up Adopted* (Windsor: National Foundation for Educational Research)

Shaw, M. (1984) "Growing up adopted" in Bean, P. (ed.), *op. cit.*

Sinclair, R. (1984) *Decision Making in Statutory Reviews on Children in Care* (Aldershot: Gower)

Slomnicka, B.I. (1982) *Law of Child Care* (London: Macdonald and Evans)

Smart, C. (1976) *Women, Crime and Criminology* (London: Routledge)

Snowden, R. and Mitchell, G. D. (1981) *The Artificial Family—A Consideration of Artificial Insemination by Donor* (London: George Allen and Unwin)

Social Work Services Group, Scottish Education Department (1982) *Violence in the Family—Theory and Practice in Social Work* (Edinburgh: H.M.S.O.)

Stockdale, Judge F.A. (1972) *Report of the Departmental Committee on the Adoption of Children* (Chairman: Sir William Houghton, later Judge F.A. Stockdale) Cmnd. 5107 (London: H.M.S.O.)

Taylor, R., Lacey, R. and Bracken, D. (1979) *In Whose Best Interests? The Unjust Treatment of Children in Courts and Institutions* (London: Cobden Trust/MIND)

Terry, J. (1979) "Childminding: Time for Reform?" [1978–79] *Journal of Social Welfare Law* 389

Thoburn, J., Murdoch, A., and O'Brien, A. (1986) *Permanence in Child Care* (Oxford: Blackwell)

Thorpe, D., Grey, C. and Smith, D. (1983) *Punishment and Welfare: case studies of the workings of the 1969 Children and Young Persons Act* (Lancaster: University of Lancaster Centre of Youth Crime and Community)

Tizard, B. (1977) *Adoption: A Second Chance* (London: Open Books)

Triseliotis, J. (1973) *In Search of Origins: The Experiences of Adopted People* (London: Routledge)

Triseliotis, J. (ed.) (1980) *New Developments in Foster Care and Adoption* (London: Routledge)

Triseliotis, J. (1983) "Identity and Security in Adoption and Long-Term Fostering" (1983) 7(1) *Adoption and Fostering* 22

Triseliotis, J. (1984) "Obtaining birth certificates" in Bean, P. (ed.) *op. cit.*

Tutt, N. and Giller, H. (1987) "Manifesto for Management: the Elimination of Custody" (1987) 151 *Justice of the Peace* 200

Vernon, J. and Fruin, D. (1986) *In Care—A Study of Social Work Decision-Making* (London: National Children's Bureau)

Wadsworth, M.E.J. (1985) "Parenting skills and their transmission through generations" (1985) 9(1) *Adoption and Fostering* 28

Walczak, Y. with Burns, S. (1984) *Divorce: the Child's Point of View* (London: Harper and Row)

Wallerstein, J.S. and Kelly, J.B. (1980) *Surviving the Break-Up—How Children and Parents Cope with Divorce* (London: Grant McIntyre)

Warnock, Dame Mary (1984) *Report of the Committee of Inquiry into Human Fertilisation and Embryology* (Chairman: Dame Mary Warnock DBE) Cmnd. 9314 (London: H.M.S.O.)

Webb, D. (1986) "The Use of Blood Grouping and DNA 'Fingerprinting' Tests in Immigration Proceedings" (1986) 1 *Immigration and Nationality Law and Practice* 53

Wolstenholme, G.E.W. and Fitzsimmon, D.W. (eds.) (1973) *Law and Ethics of A.I.D. and Embryo Transfer* Ciba Foundation Synposium No. 17 (Amsterdam: Associated Scientific Publishers)

INDEX

LIVERPOOL UNIVERSITY LIBRARY